The History of Nations

Russia

Derek C. Maus, *Book Editor*

Daniel Leone, *President*
Bonnie Szumski, *Publisher*
Scott Barbour, *Managing Editor*

GREENHAVEN
PRESS®

THOMSON
——✳——™
GALE

San Diego • Detroit • New York • San Francisco • Cleveland
New Haven, Conn. • Waterville, Maine • London • Munich

LIBRARY OF CONGRESS CATALOGING-IN-PUBLICATION DATA

Russia / Derek C. Maus, book editor.
   p. cm. — (History of nations)
   Includes bibliographical references and index.
   ISBN 0-7377-1199-X (pbk. : alk. paper) —
   ISBN 0-7377-1200-7 (lib. bdg. : alk. paper)
    1. Russia—History. 2. Soviet Union—History. 3. Russia (Federation)—History—
1991– . I. Maus, Derek C. II. History of nations (Greenhaven Press)
   DK40 .R847 2003
   947—dc21
                                                   2002034721

CONTENTS

demanded sole political authority to the point that he became a despot. Ivan the Terrible, as he came to be known, turned Russia into a police state under his *oprichnina* system in 1565.

Chapter 3: Revolutionary Times

ary groups formed the Provisional Government to replace the deposed Romanov dynasty, but over the course of the next eight months, the Bolsheviks, led by Lenin, undermined the power of the Provisional Government and eventually assumed control on October 25.

extensive military might of the Soviet Union helped repel the Nazis, the Soviet leadership's extensive and diverse use of propaganda during the "Great Patriotic War" to control public perception greatly assisted the cause as well.

political and economic system that had been devastated by corruption. The choices that Putin makes to correct these problems will help determine the direction Russia takes in the twenty-first century.

2. The Orthodox Church in Post-Soviet Russia
Traditionally one of the central elements of Russian culture, the Russian Orthodox Church's role was extremely limited during the Soviet period. Its reemergence in the post-Soviet period has been hampered by depleted resources, outdated theology, and competition for the attention of ordinary Russians.

3. Russia's Economic and Political Future: Three Scenarios
Although the economic and political situation in Russia has improved somewhat since the difficult years of the mid-1990s, the immediate future of the country is still somewhat uncertain. It may move more quickly toward democratization, settle into a familiar pattern of relatively comfortable authoritarianism, or descend into renewed turmoil.

4. The Changing Nature of U.S.-Russian Relations
While substantial disagreements still exist between the former superpowers of the Cold War, the relationship between the United States and Russia at the outset of the twenty-first century is one based more on collaboration and cooperation than rivalry.

FOREWORD

I n 1841, the journalist Charles MacKay remarked, "In reading the history of nations, we find that, like individuals, they have their whims and peculiarities, their seasons of excitement and recklessness." At the time of MacKay's observation, many of the nations explored in the Greenhaven Press History of Nations series did not yet exist in their current form. Nonetheless, whether it is old or young, every nation is similar to an individual, with its own distinct characteristics and unique story.

The History of Nations series is dedicated to exploring these stories. Each anthology traces the development of one of the world's nations from its earliest days, when it was perhaps no more than a promise on a piece of paper or an idea in the mind of some revolutionary, through to its status in the world today. Topics discussed include the pivotal political events and power struggles that shaped the country as well as important social and cultural movements. Often, certain dramatic themes and events recur, such as the rise and fall of empires, the flowering and decay of cultures, or the heroism and treachery of leaders. As well, in the history of most countries war, oppression, revolution, and deep social change feature prominently. Nonetheless, the details of such events vary greatly, as does their impact on the nation concerned. For example, England's "Glorious Revolution" of 1688 was a peaceful transfer of power that set the stage for the emergence of democratic institutions in that nation. On the other hand, in China, the overthrow of dynastic rule in 1912 led to years of chaos, civil war, and the eventual emergence of a Communist regime that used violence as a tool to root out opposition and quell popular protest. Readers of the Greenhaven Press History of Nations series will learn about the common challenges nations face and the different paths they take in response to such crises. However a nation's story may have developed, the series strives to present a clear and unbiased view of the country at hand.

The structure of each volume in the series is designed to help students deepen their understanding of the events, movements, and persons that define nations. First, a thematic introduction provides critical background material and helps orient the reader. The chapters themselves are designed to provide an accessible and engaging approach to the study of the history of that nation involved and are arranged either thematically or chronologically, as appropriate. The selections include both primary documents, which convey something of the flavor of the time and place concerned, and secondary material, which includes the wisdom of hindsight and scholarship. Finally, each book closes with a detailed chronology, a comprehensive bibliography of suggestions for further research, and a thorough index.

The countries explored within the series are as old as China and as young as Canada, as distinct in character as Spain and India, as large as Russia, and as compact as Japan. Some are based on ethnic nationalism, the belief in an ethnic group as a distinct people sharing a common destiny, whereas others emphasize civic nationalism, in which what defines citizenship is not ethnicity but commitment to a shared constitution and its values. As human societies become increasingly globalized, knowledge of other nations and of the diversity of their cultures, characteristics, and histories becomes ever more important. This series responds to the challenge by furnishing students with a solid and engaging introduction to the history of the world's nations.

INTRODUCTION

Almost immediately after the fall of the Soviet Union in late 1991, commentators worldwide began debating the prospects for Russia's recovery from the social and economic chaos that had plagued the nation since the onset of Communist rule in 1917. Dominant topics were the vast challenges Russia faced in establishing a democratic government and a free-market economy. The guiding assumption behind most discussions of these topics was that post-Soviet Russia would want to conform to the dominant ideologies of the United States and its Western European allies. Such a line of reasoning argued that the outcome of the Cold War had unquestionably proven that those ideologies were superior to the Soviet Union's authoritarian government and rigidly state-controlled economy.

There is an important flaw within this view, though—one that has been common among Western observers of Russian politics and culture for centuries. Russia's relation to the nations of Europe (and later to the United States) has been ambivalent for more than a thousand years; the assumption that this legacy would either be forgotten or easily overcome in the wake of the Cold War has proven to be premature. The lengthy tradition of Russian autocracy that preceded the Soviet Union still exerts a strong (and, for many Russians, welcome) pull on both the policies and the institutions of post-Soviet Russian government. Moreover, a combination of widespread corruption and skepticism over the advantages of Russia's integration into the global market has limited expansion of the Russian economy beyond its old Soviet boundaries (as of 2000 the majority of Russia's international trade was conducted with other former Soviet republics). Analysts seem to have overestimated the extent to which both ordinary Russians and their leaders *want* to become like their Western counterparts. An overview of Russian history suggests that this is not the first occasion on which such a mistaken assessment has been made.

Russia: European, Asian, Neither, or Both?

As should perhaps be expected of a gigantic nation that spans two continents and more than 17 million square kilometers (nearly twice the size of the United States, including Alaska and Hawaii), Russian society is simultaneously a part of and separate from Western cultural and political traditions. The vast majority of Russians live in the European portion of the country—generally defined as the area west of the Ural Mountains—which makes up less than one quarter of Russia's total area. Likewise, the Slavic culture of Russia is generally associated with Europe because of its close cultural cousins (such as Ukraine, Belarus, Poland, Bulgaria, Serbia, and Slovakia) in the eastern portions of that continent. Nevertheless, the influence of various Asiatic cultures on Russia, while generally less pronounced than that of Europe, has been a consistent factor for thousands of years. The inherent tension caused by these dual influences has constantly affected the development of the country. As a result Russia's culture has emerged as distinct from both its Asian neighbors to the south and east and its European relations to the west. Although establishing closer ties with Europe was the stated goal of several of Imperial Russia's most illustrious pre-Soviet rulers—including Peter the Great (who ruled from 1689–1725), Catherine the Great (1762– 1796), and Alexander II (1855–1881)—that goal was not necessarily accepted by the population as a whole. The notion that being Russian is a unique condition, distinct from (and perhaps superior to) being European or Asian, has persisted in Russian culture for centuries.

From the earliest recorded history of the region, there has been conflict between competing cultures. By the ninth century A.D. the lands of Kievan Russia—the Russian state centered around the city of Kiev and bound by the Black Sea and the Caucasus Mountains on the south, the Carpathian Mountains on the west, and the Caspian Sea and Ural Mountains to the east—lay directly at the crossroads between Europe and Asia. The frequent, if not always amicable, intermingling of a wide range of European and Asian peoples there laid a complex cultural foundation on which Russian civilization would be built.

The exact geographical origin of the Slavs is somewhat unclear, but they (along with another group called the Cimmerians) appear to have lived in scattered settlements in the area around the three principal rivers of Russia (the Dnieper, the

Don, and the Volga) as early as 1000 B.C. Though remaining among the most populous groups in that area, the Slavs were ruled by a long succession of outsiders. Between 600 B.C. and A.D. 200 two nomadic Central Asian groups, the Scythians and Sarmatians, conquered and ruled vast portions of this territory. At the same time, however, there was a substantial Greek and, later, Roman presence around the edge of the Black Sea that injected doses of the cultural traditions of those two great European civilizations into the region as well. The Sarmatians were displaced as the dominant power in the region by Goth invaders who swept in from the Baltic seacoast around A.D. 200 and were, in turn, supplanted by three successive groups of Asiatic nomads—the Huns, the Avars, and the Khazars—over the course of the next five hundred years. Finally, a Scandinavian people, the Varangians or Rus, entered the region in massive numbers, led by their semimythical warrior-king Riurik, and established a strong centralized government in the fortified city of Kiev.

The Establishment of Kievan Russia

The Kievan state that was created by the Varangians quickly expanded and began actively trading with major Byzantine cities such as Kherson and Constantinople by the middle of the tenth century. Along with goods and materials the Kievans also imported two other things from the Byzantine world (the vast empire whose capital was Constantinople, known in ancient times as Byzantium) that would dramatically alter the future of Russia: the Cyrillic alphabet and Orthodox Christianity. The Cyrillic alphabet (a modified version of which is still used today in Russia) was brought to the region in the ninth century by a Byzantine monk named St. Cyril. It was a combination of Greek, Roman, and other characters that allowed the religious writings of the Orthodox Church to be translated from Greek into Old Russian, thereby greatly facilitating the spread of Christianity among the predominantly Slavic populace of the Kievan state. This was a daunting task given the complex religious environment in Russia at the time.

Prior to Grand Prince Vladimir's conversion to Christianity in the year 988, the religious life of the Kievan Rus had been a patchwork affair, as historian Janet Martin describes: "Christianity, Judaism, and Islam had long been known in these lands. . . . When Vladimir assumed the throne [in 980], however, he set idols of Norse, Slav, Finn, and Iranian gods, worshipped by the disparate elements of his society, on a hilltop in Kiev in an attempt to create a single pantheon for his people."[1] Once Vladimir converted, though, he tried to bring the whole Kievan people with him. Priests brought from Constantinople immediately baptized all the inhabitants of Kiev in the Dnieper River. As a result the Orthodox Church became inextricably linked with the political power structure, although the actual beliefs of the people were much slower to change, as Martin notes:

> When Prince Vladimir dispatched his sons to their portions of his realm, each was accompanied by clergymen and charged with establishing and defending Christianity as well as the dynasty's own authority. In some regions the introduction of the new religion and its clergy met overt resistance. When representatives of the new Church threw the idol of the [Slavic] god Perun into the Volkhov River in Novgorod, for example, their action provoked a popular uprising. Elsewhere, resistance was passive; the populace simply continued to

honor their traditional gods and practice their rituals in
relatively private settings.[2]

Thus, although the Orthodox Church unmistakably assumed a
position of power, its actual effect on the life of everyday Russians was limited for centuries after 988.

Dvoeverie as a Way of Life

The reality of religious practice in the Kievan state is best
summed up by the Russian word *dvoeverie* (literally, "two beliefs"), which takes into consideration the people's adherence to
Vladimir's new state religion on the surface, but also their continued maintenance of older, often contrary, traditions. Furthermore, the concept of *dvoeverie* serves as a useful metaphor for explaining the ways in which Russian society has dealt with some
of its most divisive conflicts—such as the debate over the country's direction after the Cold War—in the thousand-plus years
since Vladimir attempted to unify Russia's faith in a single stroke.
Russian culture has always demonstrated the ability to accommodate competing or even contradictory viewpoints. This has
rarely, however, been accomplished by giving equal validity to
both options; rather, as in the case of the original *dvoeverie*, it results from the superficial appearance of acceptance of one idea,
while the other remains concealed beneath the surface.

Although this practice has frequently served as a practical survival strategy for a society that has endured colossal hardships—
both internally and externally initiated—since its beginning, it
has also led to a distorted view of national history. As literary historian David Bethea notes: "Russia has tended to define itself by
radically breaking, or at least *by seeing itself* as radically breaking,
with an earlier period. This break is never, to be sure, as clean and
final as the principals might imagine for the very reason that the
earlier period which is supposedly overcome is preserved willy-nilly in the cultural memory as a necessary opposition."[3] The case
of Vladimir's attempted conversion of the Russian people is only
one of many instances in which perceived clean breaks with an
earlier period turn out to be more a matter of changing a superficial form rather than altering the actual substance.

The Mongol Yoke

For example, both the arrival (from 1237–1240) and the departure (finalized in 1480) of the Mongols represented periods in which the outward form of Russian life seemed to have changed radically, but the reality beneath the surface was somewhat less dramatic. The invading armies of the Golden Horde (the western portion of the larger Mongol Empire) ruthlessly sacked several southern and eastern Russian city-states, most notably Vladimir and Kiev, on their way west from the Central Asian steppes. Though they did not reach Novgorod, that city's beloved prince, Alexander Nevsky, eventually submitted to the authority of the Mongol khan (the title given to Mongol leaders) Batu, recognizing the futility of opposing the Horde's overwhelming might. In doing so he became a favorite of the khan, and Novgorod, which had by that time begun to supplant Kiev as the center of Russian culture, continued to flourish even as other major Russian cities burned. Novgorod had gained its independence from the Kievan Rus in 1136 and had been expanding its influence ever since. In many ways the Mongol invasion only cemented a process of transition that had begun almost a hundred years earlier. Both Novgorod and the relatively new city of Muscovy (Moscow) rose to prominence during the time of the so-called Mongol Yoke. Moreover, although the princes of the Riurikid dynasty (now scattered among several smaller principalities) were forced to pay both symbolic and monetary tribute to the khan for over two hundred years, there was little direct interference by the Mongols in the governing of Russia after the initial invasion.

The actual impact of the end of Mongol influence in Russia was questionable. The authority of the Golden Horde had been declining and the power of the Muscovite branch of the Riurikid princes had been ascending since 1380, when Dmitrii Donskoi, grand prince of Vladimir (the title given to the most powerful of the Muscovite princes), had defeated a Mongol army at the Battle of Kulikovo. Martin describes the decreasing power of the Mongols as follows:

> The battle of Kulikovo did not terminate the Muscovite princes' subordination to the Mongol khans, but it did reduce their dependence upon them for legitimacy. The battle demonstrated Moscow's pre-eminence among the principalities of north-eastern Rus; no other branch of Riurikids ever again challenged the authority of the Muscovite line and its claim to the position of grand prince of Vladimir. Although the

princes of Moscow formally recognized the suzerainty [authority] of the khan of the Golden Horde, their practice, begun by Dmitrii Donskoi, of naming their own heirs implicitly minimized the significance of the khan's right to bestow the patent to rule.[4]

Essentially, Donskoi's victory set up a hundred-year *dvoeverie* among the grand princes of Vladimir in regard to the Mongol khan; they publicly professed their subservience, but they increasingly ignored his orders in practice. Thus, when the "yoke" was permanently removed by Ivan III at the bloodless Battle of Ugra in 1480, the change was more symbolic than actual.

Nevertheless, the general Russian historical view of the Mongols is that they were, at worst, a punishment sent to the Russian people by God or, at best, a foreign presence that froze Russia's cultural development in place for over two hundred years and deprived Russia of direct participation in the great intellectual awakening of the Renaissance. The Mongols undoubtedly altered the course of Russian history, but much of what they have been solely blamed for (or credited with) causing in Russia was already well underway prior to their arrival. Similarly, though the final ousting of the Mongols was widely interpreted as a renewed sign of divine favor shining upon the Russians and their Muscovite leader Ivan III, it rather punctuated a lengthy process of transition that was already all-but complete.

Old Versus New and East Versus West

The two centuries between the end of the Mongol Yoke and the ascension of czar (the title, derived from the Latin *caesar*, adopted by Russian rulers from Ivan III onward) Peter II witnessed the beginning of an internal conflict that has troubled Russia in varying forms and to varying degrees ever since. The divide between those who desired closer cultural ties with the outside world (especially Europe) and those who wanted to maintain a "pure" Russian culture free from any foreign influence grew increasingly larger during the sixteenth and seventeenth centuries. Almost all of the most divisive periods of Russian history since 1500 can be traced back to some form of this deep split between innovators and traditionalists. The two sides have tended to define themselves according to their positions in a series of old versus new and East versus West (East here representing Russia in opposition to the European West) arguments within Russian culture. Traditionalists have rejected technological advancements and political reforms, which they view as coming from the West, while innovators have embraced Western ideas and rejected their conservative counterparts as obstacles to progress. The irreconcilable differences between these competing perspectives made compromise almost impossible as the Muscovite czars sought to reform and to modernize Russia in the aftermath of the Mongol occupation.

A further complication to agreement was the intermingling of the Russian autocracy with the Russian Orthodox Church dating back to the time of Vladimir. This meant that plans to change any aspect of government, ranging from law codes and taxation to military service and land ownership, contained not only political but also religious implications. Proposals to change the status quo in Russian society in the sixteenth century met with a great deal of opposition from the fervently religious segment of the population that completely equated being Russian with Orthodox Christianity and vice versa. This group believed that the Mongols were defeated and that Moscow was allowed to flourish only because the nation found renewed favor with God by rededicating itself to true Orthodoxy. Any perceived departure from this was viewed as courting renewed divine disfavor and, thus, disaster.

The *raskol* (schism) between reformers and the *starovery* (Old Believers) in the seventeenth century serves as a good example of how sharply both the old/new and East/West distinctions could split Russian society. Upon becoming czar in 1645 Alexis I began refashioning his royal court along more Westernized models: He introduced theatrical performances and ballets to Russia and took an active role in larger social matters, much as monarchs like England's Queen Elizabeth I (1558–1603) had done. Alexis I tried to extend this Western-style reform to the Russian Orthodox Church claiming that its rituals had been distorted since Constantinople, the previous center of the Orthodox Church, had fallen to Muslim invaders in 1453. The Old Believers, who also became known somewhat mockingly as the Zealots of Piety for their unyieldingly traditionalist stance, offered vigorous and outspoken protest—which threatened at times to become all-out insurrection. The religious practices that the Old Believers were upholding were actually not as old as the Greek Orthodox rituals to which Alexis wanted to return. Nev-

ertheless, the Old Believers perceived them as being uniquely
Russian, as opposed to Hellenic (Greek), and thus needing protection against any non-Russian influence. The historical reality
here again is not as important as the national memory, as historian Nicholas V. Riasanovsky points out: "The Old Believers
were, characteristically, Great Russians, that is, Muscovite Russians and not, for example, Ukrainians. To them, the perfectly correct form and the untainted tradition in religion could not be
compromised. This, and their arrogant but sincere belief in the
superiority of the Muscovite Church and its practices, go far to
explain the rebellion."[5] Thus, the same strongly nationalist views
that had served to aggrandize the victory of the Christian Russians over the heathen Mongols eventually caused problems for
later Muscovite leaders.

Peter the Great's "Conversion" to Westernization

Although several Russian leaders since Ivan III had tried to reform Russian society in ways that would help the country recover
from the stagnation ostensibly caused by the Mongol Yoke, none
did so with the vigor of Peter I (Peter the Great). Peter's commitment to Westernizing Russia had its roots in his father Alexis
I's early attempts at reform, but also in his formative experiences
as czar. Young Peter was given a Western-style education and fur-
thered this training during the years (1682–1689) that his half-
sister Sofia served as his regent. In 1689, at the age of seventeen,
Peter I assumed the throne and soon began moving the country
grudgingly toward Europe in its societal forms. During 1697 and
1698 Peter and an enormous entourage made a trip to Europe
that came to be known as the Grand Embassy. Although this trip
largely failed in its stated goal of making new military allies
among the European powers, historian John T. Alexander notes
that it succeeded wildly at another goal:

> As regards recruitment of skilled manpower, intellectual
> and cultural broadening, the entire experience reaped
> manifold rewards and left vivid impressions. The host
> governments strove to impress the tirelessly inquisitive
> and shyly charming tsar. . . . Peter's learned advisors, Ja-
> cob Bruce and Peter Postnikov, visited educational,
> medical, and scientific institutions, bought many books,

medicaments, and instruments, and hired several hundred specialists including some sixty military surgeons.[6]

The Grand Embassy also directly exposed large numbers of the Russian ruling class for the first time to Western models of government and social organization. Similarly, the active recruitment of foreign scholars and military leaders brought widespread infusions of European ideas into Russia.

Upon his return to Russia after the Grand Embassy, Peter I spent the remainder of his reign engaged in expanding the power of the Russian Empire internationally and in forcefully reforming Russia to incorporate the distinctly European ideas of the Renaissance, the Reformation, and the Scientific Revolution into the culture. He built a new capital city in St. Petersburg that was modeled not on old Russian fortress-cities like Moscow or Kiev, but on modern European capitals like London and Paris. By 1713 he had transferred his court and many of the bureaucratic functions of Russian government away from Moscow to St. Petersburg, a symbolic break with the old Muscovite traditions of Russia.

Another largely symbolic, but extremely important, reform that Peter I introduced was in the matter of appearance. He decreed that Russian nobles and other state servants should abandon traditional Russian dress and appearance in favor of more modern European styles. According to Riasanovsky perhaps the most contentious reform in this area was his edict that civil servants should shave their beards, the wearing of which was a longstanding Muscovite tradition:

> While the government demanded it "for the glory and comeliness of the state and military profession" . . . the traditionalists objected on the grounds that shaving impaired the image of God in men and made the Russians look like such objectionable beings as Lutherans, Poles, Kalmyks [a Turkic ethnic group], Tartars [i.e., Mongols], cats, dogs, and monkeys. . . . Yet by the end of Peter's reign members of the civil service, army, and navy, of the upper classes and to some extent even of the middle classes, particularly in the two leading cities [Moscow and St. Petersburg], were shaven and wearing foreign dress.[7]

As his campaigns to remake Russian society proceeded successfully, Peter I became even more convinced of the correctness of his actions. In 1721 he adopted the grandiose title "Emperor of All the Russias and the Great, Most Wise Father of the Fatherland" above and beyond that of simply czar, a move that separated him from his predecessors in both name and symbolic importance. The adoption of the title gave official sanction to the idea that Peter the Great had single-handedly transformed Russia from simply another country into a great empire through both his forcible internal reforms and his numerous military victories against hostile rivals such as the Ottoman Empire and Sweden.

However, much as Vladimir's conversion had forced the remainder of Russia to outwardly adopt the new ways, Peter the Great's campaign of Westernization imposed new practices on the Russian people, and his often violent treatment of dissenters assured a high level of apparent conformity with his wishes. Nevertheless, many of the same people who dressed the part of Westernized Russians still sympathized in their hearts and minds with the traditionalists, as was demonstrated by the moderate backlash against reform that took place following Peter the Great's death in 1725. *Dvoeverie* proved to be alive and well, although it was no longer practiced in a solely religious context as it had been in 988.

Westernizers Versus Slavophiles

The debate between supporters and detractors of Peter the Great's reforms would continue for most of the next two centuries, dividing Russian society into two broad categories that came to be known as Westernizers and Slavophiles. The former group wholeheartedly supported Peter's policies as the first acts of reform that would help pull Russia out of the ignorance that first the Mongols and then despotic leaders such as Ivan the Terrible had brought to Russia. The Slavophiles steadfastly opposed this view, rejecting any imported cultural values as pollution of the authentic Russian ideals. These ideals invariably included a powerful Russian Orthodox Church, a strong autocratic czar, and the unchallenged predominance of the distinctly Slavic aspects of Russian heritage. Novelist Andrei Sinyavsky argues that this Slavophile sensibility is reinforced by the Russian language itself:

> Notions such as *svoy* (one's own) and *chuzhoy* (alien), *nashi* (ours) and *ne nashi* (not ours), are profoundly ingrained in the Russian psychology. . . . "Ours" can mean only Russians. Whereas the German spirit is alien, inhuman. The Russian word for Germans (*nemtsy*) has

the same root as the word dumb (*nemy*): the Germans are those who can't speak Russian, "nonpersons," sometimes evil spirits. "Tatars" [another name for the Mongols] are those who come from Tartar, from Hell [Tartarus was a name for the underworld in ancient Greek mythology]. But we Russians, we are bright, we are good, we are Orthodox, we are Slavs.[8]

Peter the Great's actions entrenched this "us" versus "them" outlook in the more nationalistic segments of Russian society. As a result, during the eighteenth and nineteenth centuries issues such as serfdom, autocratic government, and public education became entangled in a larger conflict that pitted old, Russian values against new, Western innovations. Riasanovsky argues that Peter the Great's reforms came to be seen in the popular memory as either a new beginning for a better Russian future or the introduction of a foreign illness:

> Peter the Great was revered and eulogized by the liberals, who envisaged him as a champion of light against the darkness, and also by the imperial government and its ideologists, for after all, that government was the first emperor's creature. Those who hated the reformer and his work included, in addition to the Old Believers and some other members of the inarticulate masses, such quixotic romantic intellectuals as the Slavophiles, who fancied that they had discovered in pre-Petrine Russia the true principles and way of life of their people and who regarded the emperor as a supreme perverter and destroyer.[9]

The various successors to Peter the Great between 1725 and 1917 all had to contend with a country whose people were divided along these lines.

Catherine the Great

Catherine II (Catherine the Great) tried to resolve the division by another variation of political *dvoeverie*, namely becoming an "enlightened despot" along the lines of Louis XIV of France or Joseph II of Austria. To accomplish this she intended to blend French and German philosophical ideas, in which she was educated as a member of the Prussian nobility, with the strong traditions of power granted to the Russian autocrat. As a foreigner herself—she was born Princess Sophie of Anhalt-Zerbst, a small German principality, and had married into the ruling Romanov family—Catherine II already had credibility issues with the hard-line Slavophiles, who saw her as the undesirable product of Peter the Great's efforts to blend Russian and European cultures. Her ascension in 1762, after a coup against her husband, the widely disliked and inept czar Peter III, did not help matters with her detractors, since she could now be seen both as an unwelcome foreigner *and* a usurper of the Russian throne. The substantial opposition to her ascension among the aristocracy and the gentry (the landowning class) required that she rule with both considerable cunning and occasional brutality. Nevertheless, during the first five years of her reign she built roads and hospitals, engaged in several ambitious campaigns to secularize and improve education, and introduced a number of sweeping proposals to dramatically transform Russian society according to the principles of the philosophical movement known as the Enlightenment that had taken hold throughout Western Europe earlier in the century.

The Legislative Commission that Catherine II assembled in 1767 to create a new, reason-oriented, secular law code for the country was only one example of her attempts at driving Russia even further along the course that Peter the Great had charted (although it ultimately failed to implement the sweeping changes that Catherine II had proposed). The Statute on Provincial Adminstration of 1775 and the Charter to the Nobility of 1785 brought the gentry into an unprecedented position of influence in Russia. This was accomplished by further reducing the power of the hereditary boyar nobility, many of whom traced their lineage back to Kievan Russia and therefore tended to oppose the kinds of reforms that the two "Great" rulers—Peter I and Catherine II—had advocated. The lowest classes of Russians also paid for the rise of the gentry as Catherine the Great's policies strengthened the already widespread practice of serfdom. By the end of her reign nearly half of all Russians had become serfs, meaning that they were legally bound to a life of serving their landlords. Many of Catherine the Great's social reforms were eventually watered down because of the resistance of the disempowered boyars and the peasants.

Under Catherine the Great, Russia's intelligentsia (the educated classes), grew in size and power, but at the cost of much of their innately Russian culture. By the start of the nineteenth century, the process of Westernization had accelerated to such a point that much of the Russian aristocracy and military leadership spoke better French and German than Russian (if they spoke Russian at all)—a fact that Slavophile writers such as Leo Tolstoy later satirized mercilessly. Westernization seemed to be inevitably advancing in Russia as the gentry and the intelligentsia, both of which owed their high positions in society to rulers closely allied with the ideas of Europe, became the dominant classes during the first quarter of the nineteenth century. However, the years between 1825 and 1917 turned out to be a prolonged battle between Westernizers and Slavophiles over the direction that Russia would take.

The Failure of Enlightened Despotism

The enlightened despotism that Catherine and several of her successors, most notably Alexander II (1855–1881), attempted to practice proved to be an unmanageable blend of irreconcilable forces. It ultimately failed to appease the groups (such as the gentry and the intelligentsia) that favored the "enlightened" portion of the equation; at the same time it alienated those groups (such as the boyar nobility and the Orthodox clergy) that it attempted to please by retaining the form of the traditional Russian autocracy. Having absorbed the democratic rhetoric of the French and American Revolutions, the proponents of liberalization in Russia during the nineteenth century frequently were dissatisfied with the extent to which autocracy, even enlightened autocracy, remained an unjust system for vast segments of the population, especially the serfs. This dissatisfaction resulted in several abortive uprisings, such as the Decembrist Revolt of 1825, and ultimately brought the Russian monarchy to an end. In 1917 the ruling Romanov dynasty (in power since 1613) was deposed by leftist revolutionaries, most of whom were members of the intelligentsia acting in the name of the peasants and the working class.

Alexander II's reign embodied the dilemma that faced the nineteenth-century Russian autocrat. His desire to end serfdom made him too liberal for the Slavophiles, while his insistence on maintaining the sole authority of the autocracy drew the scorn of reformers. In fact it was during Alexander II's reign that the various movements that would ultimately coalesce into the revolutionaries of 1905 and 1917 began to gain momentum. One such group, "Will of the People," was responsible for assassinating Alexander II in 1881, which brought on a long period of reactionary reprisal under his successors Alexander III and Nicholas II. The harshness with which these two rulers undermined the progressive policies undertaken by Alexander II only served to fortify the revolutionaries' complaints against the autocracy, and the years between 1881 and 1917 represent the unraveling of enlightened despotism in Russia.

A brief revolution in 1905 stopped short of overthrowing the monarchy but did succeed in forcing Nicholas II to form a legislature (the Duma) whose representatives would be elected by the Russian people as a whole. Although the power of this legislature was limited, it gave revolutionaries a taste of what was possible—without satisfying their appetite for change. Each time Nicholas II tried to reassert the dominance of the czar, the revolutionaries' complaints gained new listeners, and when Russia began suffering tremendous economic and military hardships as a result of World War I, the time was ripe for an end to the autocracy.

Dvoeverie, Soviet-Style

In retrospect the fall of the autocracy was another of those seemingly radical breaks with the past that turned out to change the surface more than the reality beneath. The difficult process of overthrowing the old social order spilled a substantial amount of blood between 1917 and 1921. As Riasanovsky notes: "In the years following the originally 'bloodless' October Revolution epidemics, starvation, fighting, executions, and the general breakdown of the economy and society had taken something like twenty million lives. Another two million had left Russia . . . rather than accept Communist rule."[10] Despite this turmoil the Soviet system of rule in many ways reproduced the autocratic structure that it claimed to be replacing. In principle the Soviet government was headed by a Communist Party committee (the Politburo) that expressed the will of the proletariat (the working class). In practice, though, a very small group of revolutionary leaders, such as Vladimir Lenin, Leon Trotsky, and Joseph Stalin, almost immediately began to dominate the policy-making decisions of the new regime. After Lenin's death in 1924 Stalin began consolidating power, in the process establishing a "cult of personality" that effectively made him the sole ruler of the Soviet Union by the early 1930s.

By the mid-1930s the Soviet government had taken on many

familiar characteristics of Russian autocracy, even though it continued to use rhetoric that proclaimed the rule of the proletariat
(as it would until its very end). In truth the Soviet Union quickly
produced an elite upper class of Communist Party officials to replace the czarist aristocracy that had been destroyed during the
revolution. The supposedly democratic institutions of the Soviet •
Union, such as the legislative body known as the Supreme Soviet,
remained largely ceremonial bodies that had no real decision-
making power. That was reserved largely for the Politburo and
especially its leader, the general secretary of the Communist
Party. The governing power of the general secretary from Stalin's
time forward was in many ways as thorough as that of the czar
in the old autocratic system.

Russian Orthodoxy, the former state religion, was officially
banned (along with all other religions) during the early years of
the Soviet regime. Numerous historians have pointed out that it
was essentially replaced as the unquestioned guiding principle of
the state by the communist theories of Marxism-Leninism (the
political principles derived from a combination of the ideas of
the nineteenth-century German philosopher Karl Marx with
those of Lenin, the foremost thinker among the revolutionaries).
This wholesale substitution of one ideology for another afforded
a new opportunity for *dvoeverie* among the Russian populace.
Though there were clearly a large number of genuinely devoted
communists throughout the Soviet Union from its earliest days,
the majority of Russians merely accepted communism more
than they embraced or even believed it.

Not being accustomed to government by representation—having only twelve years (1905–1917) of prerevolutionary experience with a legitimate legislature—the Russian people did not
necessarily feel its absence as keenly as Western observers assumed
they did. Moreover, following the brutally repressive years of
Stalin's reign (various purges, resettlement programs, and deportations are estimated to have cost millions of Russians their lives)
and the extreme hardships of World War II (in which more than
20 million Russian soldiers and civilians died) life outside the major cities returned to a form not so different from pre-Soviet Russia. For example, once the state-sponsored suppression of religion
eased in the 1940s, the Orthodox Church and the supposedly
atheistic regime entered into a mutually beneficial relationship, albeit a much less visible and pervasive one than had existed in

czarist Russia. Sinyavsky notes that it was a desire to utilize the inherent propaganda value of persistent traditional Russian values that caused the Soviets to abandon their talk of internationalism in favor of a modified form of Russian nationalism:

> In 1934, the heroic rescue of the *Chelyushkin* crew [a crew of sailors who became trapped in the arctic ice] prompted Stalin to solemnly reintroduce the forgotten word *Rodina* (Motherland). The word was a surprise since all official ideology until then had supposed that the actions and emotions of the Soviet man were determined by love for the revolution and for communism, by a feeling of fraternity and solidarity with the workers of the world, not by love for one's own country or national roots. Notions of the Motherland and patriotism smacked of the prerevolutionary past, of tsarist Russia.[11]

Stalin coupled this upswing in nationalism in the 1930s with a heightened emphasis on Russia, which at its peak was comprised of nearly two dozen ethnic and/or national groups with populations of at least half a million, as the dominant culture within the Soviet Union, Russian became the unquestioned state language, which forced millions of non–Russian speakers to learn it, thereby reinstating the predominance of Slavic culture in a country with a wide variety of non-Slavic citizens.

In sum, although the Soviet Union claimed its ideology to be the complete opposite of its czarist predecessor, the effect on the Russian people was not as dramatic: They were still ruled by an autocrat who was supported by a small but powerful elite class; they still had their deeply seated notions of national pride and distinction reinforced for them by leaders of the state; their Slavic cultural heritage, though changed in many ways, was still largely intact and in its traditionally privileged position within the country. Apart from the initial upheaval of the 1917–1922 revolution/civil war and Stalin's bloody and unpredictable campaign of repression against the Soviet people during the late 1930s—neither of which was an entirely unprecedented (except perhaps in terms of scale) event in Russian history—everyday life had not changed as dramatically as it might seem to an outside observer. After Stalin's death in 1953 the ordinary Soviet citizen needed only make a good show of accepting communism—much as his or her ancestors had accepted Christianity in 988, the authority of the Mongols in 1240, or Westernization in 1700—and life in the Soviet Union could be made tolerable, if not necessarily ideal. This particular *dvoeverie* was so complete that genuine support for maintaining Soviet power was hard to find among the people when the end of the regime finally loomed in the late 1980s. Though Mikhail Gorbachev's perestroika (economic restructuring) and glasnost (societal openness) policies attempted to liberalize the existing Soviet structure, these reforms failed to satisfy the desires of those forces clamoring for greater democracy. At the same time Gorbachev had alienated the old guard of the Communist Party who feared that his actions would cause them to lose their monopoly on power in the country. Much like the "enlightened despots" who came before him in the nineteenth century, Gorbachev found himself without significant allies in a time of crisis. When the unexpected wave of prodemocracy sentiment rippled through the Communist states of Eastern Europe in 1989 and 1990, opposition to Communist rule was emboldened and the Soviet Union began to crumble. As Nicholas II had done during the final years of the czarist autocracy, Gorbachev attempted to crack down on groups and individuals advocating greater freedom; but he found little support either among the liberalizers or the old guard. He was even briefly deposed in August 1991 during a coup led by a group of hard-line Communist leaders but managed to return to power after three days. His authority to rule had effectively been destroyed, however, and by the end of 1991 Gorbachev resigned, and the Soviet Union ceased to exist. The Russian Republic was declared on December 31, 1991, with Boris Yeltsin, a moderate former Communist like Gorbachev, as its leader.

Post-Soviet Russia

One should not conclude that the history of Russia is solely a tragic series of self-deceptions that have resulted in an ability to accept brutality and deprivation without protest. Few if any civilizations have had to endure the seemingly perpetual difficulties that the Russians have, yet their culture has managed to produce some of the most important artists, philosophers, statesmen and stateswomen, scientists, and religious leaders of the modern world. They have done so within a model of society that is profoundly different from the norm with which Westerners are familiar, and this is something readers should be aware of before they tackle the difficult task of trying to understand Russia. Many Westerners admit to being baffled as to why die-hard Russian nationalists and ex-Communists still command so much attention in a nation allegedly moving towards democracy or why many polls of the Russian citizenry show more support for either restoration of the monarchy or the Communists than for representative democracy. Yeltsin, his successor Vladimir Putin, and a substantial number of representatives in the Duma (the legislature of the Russian Republic) were devoted Communists for at least part of their political careers. They now claim, in the post-Soviet world, to be devoted democratizers and free-market advocates. But students seeking to understand modern Russia should not forget the central lesson of Russian history: Russians are a people skilled at *dvoeverie*. It has allowed them to survive, and occasionally thrive, while other nations have been destroyed, so there is no good reason to believe that they will abandon it. The Russian Orthodox Church and autocratic government structures have already begun to reemerge. The transition from Soviet Russia to post-Soviet Russia may indeed prove to be more important to the outside world than to Russia itself.

Notes

1. Janet Martin, "From Kiev to Muscovy: The Beginnings to 1450," in Gregory L. Freeze, ed., *Russia: A History*. Oxford: Oxford University Press, 1997, p. 5.

2. Martin, "From Kiev to Muscovy," p. 5.

3. David Bethea, *The Shape of Apocalypse in Modern Russian Fiction*. Princeton, NJ: Princeton University Press, 1989, p. 13.

4. Martin, "From Kiev to Muscovy," p. 21.

5. Nicholas V. Riasanovsky, *A History of Russia*, 5th ed. New York: Oxford University Press, 1993, p. 200.

6. John T. Alexander, "The Petrine Era and After," in Gregory Freeze, ed., *Russia: A History*. Oxford: Oxford University Press, 1997, pp. 93–94.

7. Riasanovsky, *A History of Russia*, pp. 237–38.

8. Andrei Sinyavsky, *Soviet Civilization: A Cultural History*. New York: Arcade, 1990, p. 260.

9. Riasanovsky, *A History of Russia*, p. 240.

10. Riasanovsky, *A History of Russia*, p. 488.

11. Sinyavsky, *Soviet Civilization*, p. 250.

THE HISTORY OF NATIONS
Chapter 1

Ancient Russia Through the Mongol Invasion

The Early Inhabitants of Russia

BY NICHOLAS V. RIASANOVSKY

The history of the settlement of the area that makes up contemporary Russia is a complex one involving Central Asian, Mediterranean, Scandinavian, and Slavic ethnic and tribal groups. Nicholas V. Riasanovsky, professor emeritus of history at the University of California at Berkeley, examines several of the most influential peoples that migrated to or conquered the regions of present-day Russia in the years between 1000 B.C. and A.D. 800. He also discusses the East Slavs, the most direct linguistic ancestors of modern Russians. Riasanovsky notes the ways in which the culture of the East Slavs combined with the traditions of the nomadic peoples who came through the region from the Middle East and Central Asia to form the earliest distinctively Russian culture around the beginning of the ninth century.

A number of ancient cultures developed in the huge territory that [was] enclosed within the boundaries of the U.S.S.R. Those that flourished in Transcaucasia and in Central Asia, however, exercised merely a peripheral influence on Russian history, the areas themselves becoming parts of the Russian state only in the nineteenth century. As an introduction to Russian history proper, we must turn to the northern shore of the Black Sea and to the steppe beyond. These wide expanses remained for centuries on the border of the ancient world of Greece, Rome, and Byzantium. In fact, through the Greek colonies which began to appear in southern Russia from the seventh century before Christ and through commercial and cultural contacts in general, the peoples of the southern Russian steppe

Nicholas V. Riasanovsky, *A History of Russia.* New York: Oxford University Press, 1993. Copyright © 1993 by Oxford University Press. Reproduced by permission.

participated in classical civilization. [The Greek historian] Herodotus himself, who lived in the fifth century B.C., spent some time in the Greek colony of Olbia at the mouth of the Bug river and left us a valuable description of the steppe area and its population. Herodotus' account and other scattered and scarce contemporary evidence have been greatly augmented by excavations pursued first in tsarist Russia and subsequently, on an increased scale, in the Soviet Union. At present we know, at least in broad outline, the historical development of southern Russia before the establishment of the Kievan state. And we have come to appreciate the importance of this background for Russian history.

The best-known neolithic [dating from roughly 10,000 to 5,000 years ago] culture in southern Russia evolved in the valleys of the Dnieper, the Bug, and the Dniester as early as the fourth millennium before Christ. Its remnants testify to the fact that agriculture was then already entrenched in that area, and also to a struggle between the sedentary tillers of the soil and the invading nomads, a recurrent motif in southern Russian, and later Russian, history. This neolithic people also used domestic animals, engaged in weaving, and had a developed religion. The "pottery of spirals and meander" links it not only to the southern part of Central Europe, but also and especially, as [Russian historian Mikhail] Rostovtzeff insisted, to Asia Minor, although a precise connection is difficult to establish. At about the same time a culture utilizing metal developed in the Kuban valley north of the Caucasian range, contemporaneously with similar cultures in Egypt and Mesopotamia. Its artifacts of copper, gold, and silver, found in numerous burial mounds, testify to the skill and taste of its artisans. While the bronze age in southern Russia is relatively little known and poorly represented, that of iron coincided with, and apparently resulted from, new waves of invasion and the establishment of the first historic peoples in the southern Russian steppe.

The First Outside Invaders

The Cimmerians, about whom our information is very meager, are usually considered to be the earliest such people, again in large part thanks to Herodotus. They belonged to the Thracian subdivision of the Indo-European language family and ruled southern Russia from roughly 1000 B.C. to 700 B.C. At one time their dominion extended deep into the Caucasus. Recent historians have generally assumed that the Cimmerians represented the upper crust in southern Russia, while the bulk of the population consisted of indigenous elements who continued the steady development of culture on the northern shore of the Black Sea. The ruling group was to change several times during the subsequent centuries without destroying this fundamental cultural continuity.

The Scythians followed the Cimmerians, defeating them and destroying their state. The new invaders, who came from Central Asia, spoke an Iranian tongue and belonged thus to the Indo-European language family, although they apparently also included Mongol elements. They ruled southern Russia from the seventh to the end of the third century B.C. The Scythian sway extended, according to a contemporary, Herodotus, from the Danube to the Don and from the northern shore of the Black Sea inland for a distance traveled in the course of a twenty-day journey. At its greatest extent, the Scythian state stretched south of the Danube on its western flank and across the Caucasus and into Asia Minor on its eastern.

The Scythians were typical nomads: they lived in tentlike carriages dragged by oxen and counted their riches by the number of horses, which also served them as food. In war they formed excellent light cavalry, utilizing the saddle and fighting with bows and arrows and short swords. Their military tactics based on mobility and evasion proved so successful that even their great Iranian rivals, the mighty Persians, could not defeat them in their home territory. The Scythians established a strong military state in southern Russia and for over three centuries gave a considerable degree of stability to that area. Indigenous culture continued to develop, enriched by new contacts and opportunities. In particular, in spite of the nomadic nature of the Scythians themselves, agriculture went on flourishing in the steppe north of the Black Sea. Herodotus who, in accordance with the general practice, referred to the entire population of the area as Scythian, distinguished, among other groups, not only "the royal Scythians," but also "the Scythian ploughmen."

The Scythians were finally defeated and replaced in southern Russia by the Sarmatians, another wave of Iranian-speaking nomads from Central Asia. The Sarmatian social organization and culture were akin to the Scythian, although some striking differences have been noted. Thus, while both peoples fought typically as cavalry, the Sarmatians used stirrups and armor, lances, and long swords in contrast to the light equipment of the Scythians. What is more important is that they apparently had little difficulty in adapting themselves to their new position as rulers of southern Russia and in fitting into the economy and the culture of the area. The famous Greek geographer Strabo, writing in the first century A.D., mentions this continuity and in particular observes that the great east-west trade route through the southern Russian steppe remained open under the Sarmatians. The Sarmatians were divided into several tribes of which the Alans, it would seem, led in numbers and power. The Ossetians of today, a people living in the central Caucasus, are direct descendants of the Alans. The Sarmatian rule in southern Russia lasted from the end of the third century B.C. to the beginning of the third century A.D.

The Influx of Greek and Iranian Culture

It was during the Scytho-Sarmatian period that the Graeco-Iranian culture developed on the northern shore of the Black Sea and in the Russian steppe. The Iranian element was represented in the first place by the Scythians and the Sarmatians themselves. They established large and lasting military states which provided the basic pattern of political organization for the area. They brought with them their languages, their customs, their religion emphasizing war, an original style in decorative art known as the Scythian animal style, and generally vigorous and varied art and craftsmanship, especially in metalwork. The enormously rich Greek civilization came to the area primarily through Greek colonies. These colonies began as fishing enterprises and grew into major commercial centers and flourishing communities. They included the already mentioned Olbia, founded as early as the middle of the seventh century B.C., Chersonesus in the Crimea near present-day Sevastopol, Tanais at the mouth of the Don, and Panticapaeum and Phanagoria on either side of the Strait of Kerch, which links the Sea of Azov to the Black Sea and separates the Crimea and the Caucasus. The Greeks engaged in varied trade, but especially significant was their importation of southern Russian grain into the Hellenic world. The settlements near the Strait of Kerch, enjoying a particularly favorable position for trade and defense, formed the nucleus of the Bosporan kingdom which was to have a long and dramatic history. That kingdom as well as other Greek centers in southern Russia fell in the first century before Christ under the sway of Mithridates the Great of Pontus and, after his ultimate defeat by the Romans, of Rome. Even after a retrenchment of the Roman Empire and its eventual collapse, some former Greek colonies on the northern shore of the Black Sea, such as Chersonesus, had another revival as outposts of the Byzantine Empire.

Thus for many centuries the Iranians and the Greeks lived and worked side by side. It has been noted that the Scythians and the Sarmatians made no sustained effort to destroy Greek colonies in southern Russia, choosing instead to maintain vigorous trade relations and other contacts with them. Intermarriage, Hellenization of Iranians, and Iranization of Greeks proceeded apace. The resulting cultural and at times political synthesis was such that the two elements became inextricably intertwined. As Rostovtzeff explains in regard to the Bosporan kingdom, a prize example of this symbiosis: "It is a matter of great interest to trace the development of the new community. A loosely knit confederation of cities and tribes in its beginning, it became gradually a political body of dual nature. The ruler of this body was for the Greeks an elected magistrate, for the natives a king ruling by divine right." Today one can readily appreciate some of the sweep and the glory of the ancient Graeco-Iranian culture in southern Russia after visiting the appropriate rooms of the Hermitage [in St. Petersburg] or of the historical museum in Moscow.

Later Germanic and Asiatic Invaders

The Sarmatian rule in the steppe north of the Black Sea was shattered by the Goths. These Germanic invaders came from the north, originally from the Baltic area, reaching out in a southeasterly direction. In southern Russia they split into the Visigoths and the Ostrogoths, and the latter eventually established under Hermanric a great state stretching from the Black Sea to the Baltic. But the Gothic period in Russia, dated usually from A.D. 200 to A.D. 370, ended abruptly with the appearance of new intruders from Asia, the Huns. Furthermore, while the Goths proved themselves to be fine soldiers and sailors, their general cultural level lagged considerably behind the culture of southern Russia, to which they had little to contribute.

The Huns, who descended upon the Goths around A.D. 370, came in a mass migration by the classic steppe road from Central Asia to southern Russia. A remarkably mixed group when they appeared in European history, the Huns were, on best evidence, a Turkic-speaking people supported by large Mongol and Ugrian contingents. Later, as they swept into central and even western Europe, they also brought with them different Germanic and Iranian elements which they had overwhelmed and picked up on the way. Although one of the most primitive peoples to come to southern Russia, the Huns had sufficient drive and military prowess to conquer that area and, indeed, to play a key role in the so-called period of great migrations in Europe. Even after their defeat in the battle of Châlons, deep in France, in 451, they invaded Italy and, according to tradition, spared Rome only because of the influence of Pope Leo I on their leader, Attila. But with the sudden death of Attila in 453 the poorly organized Hunnic state crumbled. Its successors included the large horde of the Bulgars and the smaller ones of the Utigurs and the Kutrigurs.

The next human wave to break into southern Russia consisted again of an Asiatic, Mongol- and Turkic-speaking, and relatively primitive people, the Avars. Their invasion is dated A.D. 558, and their state lasted for about a century in Russia and for over two and a half centuries altogether, at the end of which time it dissolved rapidly and virtually without trace, a common fate of fluid, politically rudimentary, and culturally weak nomadic empires. At the height of their power, the Avars ruled the entire area from eastern Russia to the Danubian plain, where they had their capital and where they remained after they had lost control in Russia. Avar armies threatened Byzantium, and they also waged major, although unsuccessful, wars against Charlemagne and his empire.

In the seventh century A.D. a new force emerged in southern Russia, to be more exact, on the lower Volga, in the northern Caucasus, and the southeastern Russian steppe in general: the Khazar state. The impact of the Khazars split the Bulgars sharply in two: one group definitely settled in the Balkans to dissolve in the Slavic mass and give its name to present-day Bulgaria; the other retreated to the northeast, eventually establishing a state at the confluence of the Volga and the Kama, with the town of Great Bulgar as its capital. The Utigurs and the Kutrigurs retrenched to the lands along the Sea of Azov and the mouth of the Don.

Although the Khazars were still another Turkic-speaking people from Asia, their historical role proved to be quite different from that of the Huns or of the Avars. To begin with, they fought bitter wars against the Arabs and served as a bulwark against the spread of Islam into Europe. When their own state assumed form in southeastern European Russia, it became notable for its commerce, its international connections, and the tolerance and enlightenment of its laws. Although a semi-nomadic people themselves, the Khazars promoted the building of towns, such as their capital of Itil—not far from the mouth of the Volga—Samandar, Sarkil, and certain others. The location at the crossroads of two continents proved to be of fundamental importance for the Khazar economy. In the words of a recent historian of the Khazars, [Douglas] Dunlop: "The prosperity of Khazaria evidently depended less on the resources of the country than on its favorable position across important trade-routes." The Khazar revenue, consequently, came especially from commercial imposts as well as from the tribute which increased as the Khazar rule expanded westward on the Russian plain. Pagans, Moslems, Christians, and Jews mingled in Khazaria, where all enjoyed considerable freedom and autonomy to live under their own laws. In the eighth and ninth centuries the Khazars themselves embraced Judaism, or at least their ruler, who bore the title of khakan, and the upper class did, thus adding another exceptional chapter to their unusual history. The Khazars have also been cited as one of the first peoples to institute a permanent paid armed force. The development of Khazaria, with its close links to the Arabic and Byzantine worlds, as well as to some other civilizations, its far-flung trade connections, and its general cosmopolitanism, well represents one line of political, economic, and cultural evolution on the great Russian plain at the time of the emergence of the Kievan state. It may be added that, while the Khazars were outstanding in commercial development, varied commercial intercourse on a large scale also grew further north, in the country of the Volga Bulgars.

The East Slavs

Cultures on the northern shore of the Black Sea and in the southern Russian steppe, from the neolithic period to the time of the Khazars, form an essential part of the background of Kievan Russia. Yet it is true too that the people of the Kievan state who came to be known as Russians were not Scythians, Greeks, or Khazars, much as they might have been influenced in one way or another by these and other predecessors and neighbors; they were East Slavs. Therefore, East Slavs also demand our attention. The term itself is linguistic, as our better classifications of ancient peoples usually are. It refers to a group speaking the Eastern variety of Slavic. With time, three distinct East Slavic languages developed: Great Russian, often called simply Russian, Ukrainian, and White Russian or Belorussian. Other branches of the Slavic languages are the West Slavic, including Polish and Czech, and the South Slavic, represented, for instance, by Serbo-Croatian and Bulgarian. The Slavic languages, in turn, form a subdivision of the Indo-European language family which includes most of the tongues spoken today in Europe and some used in Asia. To be more precise, in addition to the Slavic this family contains the Teutonic, Romance, Hellenic, Baltic, Celtic, Iranian, Indic, Armenian, and Thraco-Illyrian subfamilies of languages. The Cimmerians, it might be recalled, belonged apparently to the Thraco-Illyrian subfamily, the Scythians and the Sarmatians to the Iranian, and the Goths to the Teutonic or Germanic, while the Greeks are, of course, the great representatives of the Hellenic. Early Russian history was also influenced by other Indo-European peoples, such as the Baltic Lithuanians, as well as by some non-Indo-Europeans, notably by different Turkic tribes—some of which have already been mentioned—the Mongols, and Finno-Ugrian elements. . . .

The first extant written references to the Slavs belong to the classical writers early in our era, including Pliny the Elder and Tacitus. Important later accounts include those of the sixth century produced by the Byzantine historian Procopius and the Gothic Jordanes. The terms most frequently used to designate the Slavs were "Venedi" and "Antes," with the latter coming to mean the East Slavs—although "Antes" has also been given other interpretations, such as pre-Slavic Iranian inhabitants of southern Russia or Goths. Soviet archaeologists insist that Slavic settlements in parts of Russia, notably in the Don area, date at least from the middle of the first millennium B.C. It is now assumed by some historians that the Slavs composed a significant part, perhaps the bulk, of the population of southern and central Russia from the time of the Scythians. For instance, they may be hidden under various designations used by Herodotus, such as "Scythian ploughmen." It is known that the East Slavs fought against the Goths, were swept westward with the Huns, and were conquered by the Avars; certain East Slavic tribes were paying tribute to the

Khazars at the dawn of Kievan history. At that time, according to our main written source, the Kievan *Primary Chronicle* of the early twelfth century, the East Slavs were divided into twelve tribes located on the broad expanses of the Russian plain, from the Black Sea, the Danube, and the Carpathian mountains, across the Ukraine, and beyond, northward to the Novgorod territory and eastward toward the Volga. Their neighbors included, in addition to some of the peoples already mentioned, Finnic elements scattered throughout northern and eastern Russia and Lithuanian tribes to the west.

By the ninth century A.D. East Slavic economy, society, and culture had already experienced a considerable development. Agriculture was well and widely established among the East Slavs. Other important occupations included fishing, hunting, apiculture, cattle-raising, weaving, and pottery-making, as well as other arts and crafts, such as carpentry. The East Slavs had known the use of iron for centuries. They had also been engaging in varied and far-flung commerce. They possessed a remarkable number of towns; even [historian Mikhail] Tikhomirov's count of them, some 238, is not complete. Certain of these towns, such as Novgorod, Smolensk, and Kiev, a town belonging to the tribe of the Poliane, were to have long and important histories. Very little is known about the political organization of the East Slavs. There exist, however, a few scattered references to the rulers of the Antes and of some of the component tribes: for example, Jordanes's mention of Bozh, a prince of the Antes at the time of the Gothic wars; and the statement of Masudi, an Arabian writer, concerning Madzhak, apparently a prince of the East Slavic tribe of the Duleby in the Avar period.

Kiev as the Center of Medieval Russian Culture

By Richard Pipes

The first major city in Russia was Kiev, which is located in the modern nation of Ukraine. Richard Pipes, professor emeritus of Russian history at Harvard University, examines the founding and development of the city of Kiev, as well as the medieval state whose capital it eventually became. Pipes begins by discussing the settlement of Russia in the ninth century by the Normans, a Scandinavian people, focusing especially on their interest in trade routes that led through the area where Kiev is located. Pipes describes the manner by which the Normans governed the territories they controlled in Russia, how the trade they fostered allowed for cultural influences from outside the region to enter in, and the somewhat unusual nature of the fortified cities that the Normans built. Finally, he relates how the dominant Norman culture in Russia gradually merged with that of the East Slavs by the eleventh century, thereby bringing a distinctly Russian state—known as the Kievan Rus—into existence.

I n the ninth century, the Volga trade plied by the Khazars [an Asiatic tribe that inhabited what is now Ukraine as early as the seventh century] attracted the attention of the Normans. The ninth century was for the Normans a period of extraordinary expansion. Scattering far and wide from Scandinavia, they roamed with impunity in central and western Europe, conquering in the process, Ireland (820), Iceland (874), and Normandy (911). During this initial phase of their expansion, some of the Normans turned east and founded settlements on territory of what later became Russia. The first Norse colony on Russian soil was Aldeigjuborg, a fortress on the shores of Lake Ladoga. This

Richard Pipes, *Russia Under the Old Regime*. New York: Charles Scribner's Sons, 1974. Copyright © 1974 by Richard Pipes. Reproduced by permission.

was an excellent base from which to launch exploration of the water routes leading south, towards the great centres of Levantine [the area of the Middle East from Greece to Egypt] wealth and civilization. Routes connecting northern Europe with the Near East by way of Russia acquired special value at this particular time, because Muslim conquests of the eighth century had closed the Mediterranean to Christian trade. From Aldeigjuborg and other fortresses built near by and to the south, the Normans explored in their flat, capacious boats the rivers leading to the Near East. They soon discovered what medieval Russian sources call 'the Saracen route', the network of rivers and portages connecting the Baltic Sea with the Caspian by way of the Volga, and entered into commercial relations with the Khazars. Hoards of Arabic coins dating from the ninth and tenth centuries discovered throughout Russia and Sweden attest to the wide reach and intensity of these commercial activities of the Normans. The Arab traveller Ibn Fadlan left a vivid description of a ship burial of a Norman ('Russian') chieftain which he had witnessed on the Volga early in the tenth century.

In the long run, however, the 'Saracen route' proved to the Normans of lesser importance than the 'Greek route' leading down the Dnieper to the Black Sea and Constantinople. Utilizing this road, they carried out several raids against the capital of the Byzantine Empire, compelling the Byzantines to grant them commercial privileges. The texts of the treaties in which these privileges are enumerated, recorded complete in the Primary Chronicle, are the oldest documents bearing on Norman rule in Russia. In the ninth and tenth centuries, regular commercial relations developed between the Russian forest and Byzantium, the management of which was in the hands of Norman merchant-soldiers.

Russia Under Norman Rule

In most of Europe under their control, the Normans settled down and assumed the role of territorial sovereigns. In Russia they behaved differently. . . . They had little inducement to bother with agriculture and territorial claims, preferring to concentrate on foreign trade. They gradually gained control of all the principal riverways leading to the Black Sea, along which they built fortresses. From these bases they extracted as tribute from the Slavs, Finns and Lithuanians commodities most in demand in

Byzantium and the Arab world: slaves, furs and wax. It is precisely in the ninth century that there began to appear in Russia populated centres of a new type; no longer the tiny earthern or wooden stockades of the Slavic settlers, but regular fortress-cities. These served as habitations for the Norman chieftains, their families and retainers. Around them there often grew up suburbs populated by native artisans and shopkeepers. Each of these fortress-cities had near by its burial grounds. Normans and Slavs were often buried in the same mounds, but the tombs of the two were quite different, the Norman ones containing weapons, jewels and home implements of a distinctly Scandinavian type, and on occasion entire boats. Judging by archaeological evidence, the Normans maintained in Russia four major settlement areas: one along the Gulf of Riga; a second around Lake Ladoga and the Volkhov river; a third to the east of Smolensk; and a fourth in the mesopotamia between the upper Volga and the Oka. In addition, they had isolated settlements, of which Könugard (Kiev) was by far the largest. All four of the major Norman settlement areas lay along the trade routes connecting the Baltic with the Caspian and Black seas. In their sagas, the Normans called Russia 'Gardariki', 'the country of strongholds'.

Since only a part of the tribute levied on the native population was required for support of the garrisons, and its most valuable portion was intended for export to distant markets reached by a route full of hazards, the Norman fortress-cities had to organize. This process, begun around 800 CE when the first Norse settlements were formed around Lake Ladoga, was completed around 882 when Prince Helgi (Oleg) united under his authority the two terminal points of the 'Greek Route', Holmgard (Novgorod) and Kiev. Kiev became the headquarters of the central trade organization. The choice of Kiev was dictated by the fact that the Normans experienced no difficulty shipping the goods collected as tribute all over Russia and destined for Constantinople as far south as that city, being in full control of western Russia to that point. It was the next leg of the journey, from Kiev to the Black Sea, that presented the greatest problems, because here the merchandise had to traverse a steppe infested with nomad freebooters [pirates]. Every spring, as soon as the ice on the rivers had broken, the tribute was floated from its scattered collection points to Kiev. May was devoted to the task of outfitting the great annual flotilla. In June, the ships laden with slaves and produce sailed under heavy guard from Kiev down the Dnieper. The most dangerous segment of the journey was a stretch of granite rapids twenty-five to sixty-five miles south of Kiev. As Emperor Constantine VII Porphyrogenitus describes it, the Normans learned how to navigate the first three of the cataracts [waterfalls], but upon reaching the fourth they had to unload the merchandise and proceed on foot. The boats were partly dragged, partly carried. Some of the Normans helped bear the merchandise, others guarded the slaves, others yet were on the look-out for the enemy and, if attacked, beat him off. The flotilla was reasonably safe only after it had passed the last cataract, and the personnel with the goods could be reloaded on the boats. The importance of Kiev and the reason why it was chosen as the capital of the Norman trade organization in Russia thus becomes apparent. Kiev functioned in a double capacity: as the main depot of the tribute collected in all parts of Russia, and as the port from where it was transhipped under guard to its ultimate destination.

Riurik and the Kievan Rus'

It is in this manner, almost as a by-product of international trade between two alien peoples, Normans and Greeks, that the first East Slav state came into being. Sovereign power over the fortress-cities and the territories adjoining them was assumed by a dynasty claiming descent from the semi-legendary Norse prince Hroerekr or Roderick (the Riurik of Russian chronicles). The head of the dynasty, the Great Prince, officiated in Kiev, while his sons, relatives, and leading retainers manned the provincial towns. Lest, however, the name 'Kiev state' evoke the image of a territorial entity familiar from Norman history of France, England or Sicily, it must be stressed that it was nothing of the kind. The Norman state in Russia rather resembled the great merchant enterprises of seventeenth- and eighteenth-century Europe, such as the East India or Hudson's Bay companies, founded to make money but compelled by the absence of any administration in the area of their operations to assume quasi-governmental responsibilities. The Great Prince was a merchant *par excellence,* and his realm was essentially a commercial enterprise, composed of loosely affiliated towns whose garrisons collected the tribute and maintained, in a rough sort of way, public order. The princes were quite independent of one another. Together with their retainers (*druzhiny*) the Norman rulers of Russia formed a distinct caste. They lived apart from the rest of the population, they judged their own members by special laws, and preferred to have their remains buried in separate tombs. Norman administration was carried out in a most casual fashion. During the winter months, the princes accompanied by their druzhiny travelled in the countryside arranging for the delivery of the tribute and dispensing justice. It is only in the eleventh century, when the Kievan state already showed symptoms of decline, that in the larger cities there appeared popular assemblies called *veche*. Composed of all the adult males, these assemblies gave the prince advice on important policy questions. In Novgorod and Pskov, the veche even succeeded in arrogating to itself legislative authority and forcing the princes to execute its will. But these two cases apart, the prince-veche relationship tended to be informal and unstructured. Certainly one cannot speak of the populace of Kievan Russia exerting any institutional pressure on the ruling élite, least of all in the ninth and tenth centuries, when the veche did not as yet even exist. In the heyday of Kievan statehood, authority was exercised on the model of a pre-modern commercial enterprise, subject to restraint neither by law nor popular will.

Nothing reflects better the relationship of the Normans towards their Russian realm than their failure to work out an orderly system of princely succession. In the ninth and tenth centuries the problem seems to have been solved by force: on the death of the Kievan ruler, prince fell upon prince, and all semblance of national unity vanished until the victor made good his claim to the Kievan throne. Later various attempts were made—none of them successful—to assure a regular procedure of succession. Before his death in 1054, Great Prince Iaroslav apportioned the main cities among his five sons, urging them 'to heed' the eldest, to whom he entrusted Kiev. This device did not work, however, and conflicts persisted. Subsequently, Kievan princes held conferences at which they discussed and sometimes settled their disagreements, including conflicts over cities. . . .

However, no matter which system the Russian Normans and their successors may have adopted in theory, they adhered to none in practice, with the result that the Kievan state was constantly shaken by internal conflicts of a kind which later were to destroy the empire of Genghis Khan. As [anthropologist] Henry Maine has shown, the absence of primogeniture [pattern of sucession in which power passes to the first-born son] is a characteristic quality of authority and ownership in the pre-individualistic and pre-public phase of society's development. The fact that the Normans considered Russia their common dynastic property, rather than that of a single member or branch of the family, howsoever they thought proper to apportion it, suggests that they lacked any clear notion of political authority and viewed their power not so much in public as in private terms.

The Transformation of the Normans into Russians

The Normans nowhere displayed much resistance to assimilation, and at least in this one respect their Russian branch was no exception. A nation of crude freebooters, originating in a backward region on the periphery of the civilized world, they tended everywhere to succumb to the culture of the people whom they subjugated by force of arms. The Kievan Normans were Slavicized by the middle of the eleventh century, which is about the same time that the Normans in France became Gallic. An important factor in their assimilation was conversion to Orthodox Christianity. One of the consequences of this act was the adoption of Church Slavonic, a literary language devised by Byzantine missionaries. The use of this language in all written documents, lay and clerical, undoubtedly contributed greatly to the loss by the Norman élite of their ethnic identity. Another factor promoting assimilation was intermarriage with Slavic women and the gradual infiltration of indigenous warriors into the ranks of the once solidly Scandinavian druzhiny. In the treaty concluded between Kievan princes and Byzantium in 912, all the Kievan signatories bore Scandinavian names (e.g. Ingjald, Farulf, Vermund, Gunnar). Subsequently, these names were either Slavicized or replaced by Slavic names, and in the chronicle narratives (the earliest complete text of which dates from 1116), the Norman names appear already in their Slavic form; thus Helgi becomes Oleg, Helga turns into Olga, Ingwarr into Igor, and Waldemar into Vladimir.

By a related linguistic process, the ethnic name which the Normans of eastern Europe had originally applied to themselves was transferred on to the Eastern Slavs and their land. In Byzantine, western and Arabic sources of the ninth and tenth centuries, *Rus'*—the root of '*Rossiia*' and 'Russia'—always referred to people of Scandinavian ancestry. Thus, Constantine Porphyrogenitus in *De Administrando Imperio* provides two parallel sets of names for the Dnieper cataracts, one of which, that labelled 'Russian', turns out to be Scandinavian, while the other is Slavic. According to the Bertinian Annals, a Byzantine delegation which came in 839 to the court of Emperor Louis the Pious at Ingelheim brought along a body of men called 'Rhos'; on being questioned about their nationality, they identified themselves as Swedes. *'Quos alios nos nomine Nordmannos appellamus'* ('whom by another name we call Northmen') is how the tenth-century historian, Liutprand of Cremona, defines 'Rusios'. We have mentioned already the description of the burial of a 'Russian' prince by Ibn Fadlan, which fully conforms to what is known of Norse practices, the contents of tombs, and the signatures of Kievans on treaties with Byzantium. All these facts require emphasis because in the past two hundred years hyper-patriotic Russian historians have often thought it incumbent on them to deny what to third parties seems incontrovertible, namely that the founders of the Kievan state and the first bearers of the name 'Russians' were men of Scandinavian origin. The source of the name Rus' is by no means certain, however. One possibility is Roslagen, the Swedish coast north of Stockholm, whose inhabitants to this day are known as Rospiggar (pronounced Ruspiggar). Another is the Nordic 'Ropsmenn' or 'Ropskarlar', meaning 'men of the rudder'. The Finns, with whom the Norman settlers at Ladoga first came in contact, called them Ruōtsi—a name which survives in the modern Finnish for Sweden. (The Finnish word for Russia is Venäjä.) Following the standard linguistic rule by which the Slavs assimilate Finnic ethnic names, Ruōtsi became Rus'. Originally, Rus' designated the Normans and their country. Ibn Rusta, an Arab geographer writing around the year 900, spoke of Rus' (which he distinguished from Slavs) as living in a country of lakes and forests, probably meaning the region Ladoga-Novgorod. But as the Normans assimilated and the ranks of their retainers filled with Slavs, Rus' lost its ethnic connotation and came to designate all the people manning the fortress-cities and involved in the annual expeditions to Constantinople. From such usage, it required only a minor shift for 'Rus'' to be extended to the country where these people lived, and, finally, to all of this country's inhabitants, regardless of ancestry and occupation. Examples of such name transfers from conqueror to the conquered are not uncommon, the case of France, a name adopted for Gaul from the invading

German Franks, being the one that most readily comes to mind.

The Normans gave the Eastern Slavs several elements essential to forging out of their disparate tribes and tribal associations a national entity: a rudimentary state organization headed by one dynasty, a common religion and an ethnic name. How much national unity the East Slavs actually perceived during the tenth and eleventh centuries no one knows, because the only indigenous documents bearing on this period, the chronicles, are of a later provenance.

Factors That Led to the Decline of Rus'

One more legacy bequeathed by the Normans to the Eastern Slavs deserves mention. . . . The Kievan state which they had founded and which their Slavicized and Slavic descendants had inherited did not emerge out of the society over which it ruled. Neither the princes nor their retainers, the raw material of a future nobility, issued from the Slavic communities. The same, of course, holds true of England after the Norman Conquest. But in England, where land is fertile and valuable, the Norman élite promptly divided it among themselves and turned into a landowning aristocracy. In Russia, the Norman élite retained all along a semi-colonial character: its principal interest lay not in exploiting land but in extracting tribute. Its local roots were extremely shallow. We have here a type of political formation characterized by an unusually sharp gulf between rulers and ruled. The Kievan state and Kievan society lacked a common interest capable of binding them: state and society coexisted, retaining their separate identities and barely conscious of a sense of commitment to one another.

The Kievan state distintegrated in the twelfth century. Its collapse can be explained by the combined action of internal and external factors.

The internal factor was the inability of the ruling dynasty to resolve the issue of succession. Because there existed no orderly system by which Kiev and the provincial cities with their adjoining tributary territories, the *volosti,* passed from hand to hand upon the death of their rulers, the princes tended to develop a proprietary interest in whatever areas happened to have come under their control. Thus, what had been intended as a temporary and conditional right to exploit a given city and region transformed itself into outright ownership. The princely custom of bequeathing their sons cities and volosti in perpetuity must have been well established by 1097 when a conference of Kievan princes held at Liubech [a city in modern Germany] acknowledged the right of each prince to retain as property territories inherited from his father. This principle implied that princes were also at liberty to bequeath cities and volosti to their sons. The common dynastic ownership of Russia, though never formally abjured, thus ceased to be observed in practice.

The centrifugal force inherent in this process was aggravated by a concurrent external development, namely the decline of Russia's trade with Byzantium. In 966–7 the impetuous Prince Sviatoslav, in an argument over control of the only remaining Slavic group still paying tribute to the Khazars, attacked and destroyed the capital of the Khazar kaganate. By this foolhardy act he helped open the flood-gates through which at once poured into the Black Sea steppe belligerent Turkic tribes, until then kept in check by the Khazars. First came the Pechenegs. They were followed in the eleventh century by the Cumans (Polovtsy), an exceptionally aggressive nation who carried out such vicious attacks on the flotillas sailing from Kiev to Constantinople as eventually to bring this traffic to a standstill. Expeditions to dislodge the Cumans had little success; one such disastrous campaign, launched in 1185, is commemorated in the Song of the Host of Igor, the medieval Russian epic. In the middle of the twelfth century, Russian princes ceased to mint coins, which suggests they were in serious financial difficulty and that the economic unity of the country was distintegrating. To compound Kiev's calamities, in 1204 the Fourth Crusade captured and sacked Constantinople, at the same time opening up the eastern Mediterranean to Christian navigation. In other words, around 1200 there disappeared those particular circumstances which in the preceding four centuries had brought the territories inhabited by Eastern Slavs under a single authority.

Vladimir and the Christianization of Russia

FROM THE *PRIMARY CHRONICLE*

The Primary Chronicle *is the most important historical document from the Kievan period of Russian history. Compiled by Orthodox monks in the eleventh and twelfth centuries, this work retrospectively recounts the history of the Kievan state back two centuries to the time of Riurik, a Norman prince to whom all the rulers of Russia claimed kinship until 1598. This passage from the* Primary Chronicle *relates the story of how Prince Vladimir of Kiev converted from paganism to Eastern Orthodox Christianity in the year 988 (the year is also given in the text as 6496, which was the biblically calculated number of years since the creation). Because of Vladimir's insistence that all his subjects also be converted to this new religion, the date became known as the year that Russia was, in theory, Christianized, although pagan beliefs remained common in the country for decades afterward. Given that the monks composed this history more than a century after Orthodoxy had become the official religion of the state, the details of the story are less important for their factual accuracy than for communicating the sense of wisdom and divine will that guided Vladimir's decision to become a Christian. This passage is one of the most important in Russian history, since it established the link between the ruling class and the Orthodox Church that remained in place until the Bolshevik revolution in 1917.*

6 495 (987). Vladimir summoned together his boyars [members of the nobility] and the city-elders, and said to them, "Behold, the Bulgars came before me urging me to accept their religion [Islam]. Then came the Germans and praised their own faith [Catholicism]; and after them came the Jews. Finally

Samuel Hazzard Cross and Olgerd P. Sherbowitz-Wetzor, eds. and trans., *The Russian Primary Chronicle: Laurentian Text.* Cambridge, MA: The Medieval Academy of America, 1974. Copyright © 1953 by The Medieval Academy of America. Reproduced by permission.

the Greeks appeared, criticizing all other faiths but commending their own [Orthodox Christianity], and they spoke at length, telling the history of the whole world from its beginning. Their words were artful, and it was wondrous to listen and pleasant to hear them. They preach the existence of another world. 'Whoever adopts our religion and then dies shall arise and live forever. But whosoever embraces another faith, shall be consumed with fire in the next world.' What is your opinion on this subject, and what do you answer?" The boyars and the elders replied, "You know, oh Prince, that no man condemns his own possessions, but praises them instead. If you desire to make certain, you have servants at your disposal. Send them to inquire about the ritual of each and how he worships God."

Their counsel pleased the prince and all the people, so that they chose good and wise men to the number of ten, and directed them to go first among the Bulgars and inspect their faith. The emissaries went their way, and when they arrived at their destination they beheld the disgraceful actions of the Bulgars and their worship in the mosque; then they returned to their country. Vladimir then instructed them to go likewise among the Germans, and examine their faith, and finally to visit the Greeks. They thus went into Germany, and after viewing the German ceremonial, they proceeded to Tsar'grad, where they appeared before the Emperor. He inquired on what mission they had come, and they reported to him all that had occurred. When the Emperor heard their words, he rejoiced, and did them great honor on that very day.

On the morrow, the Emperor sent a message to the Patriarch [the head of the Orthodox Church] to inform him that a Russian delegation had arrived to examine the Greek faith, and directed him to prepare the church and the clergy, and to array himself in his sacerdotal robes, so that the Russes might behold the glory of the God of the Greeks. When the Patriarch received these commands, he bade the clergy assemble, and they performed the customary rites. They burned incense, and the choirs sang hymns. The Emperor accompanied the Russes to the church, and placed them in a wide space, calling their attention to the beauty of the edifice, the chanting, and the pontifical services and the ministry of the deacons, while he explained to them the worship of his God. The Russes were astonished, and in their wonder praised the Greek ceremonial. Then the [Byzantine] Emperors Basil and Constantine invited the envoys to their presence, and said, "Go hence to your native country," and dismissed them with valuable presents and great honor.

Thus they returned to their own country, and the Prince called together his boyars and the elders. Vladimir then announced the return of the envoys who had been sent out, and suggested that their report be heard. He thus commanded them to speak out before his retinue. The envoys reported, "When we journeyed among the Bulgars, we beheld how they worship in their temple, called a mosque, while they stand ungirt. The Bulgar bows, sits down, looks hither and thither like one possessed, and there is no happiness among them, but instead only sorrow and a dreadful stench. Their religion is not good. Then we went among the Germans, and saw them performing many ceremonies in their temples; but we beheld no glory there. Then we went to Greece, and the Greeks led us to the edifices where they worship their God, and we knew not whether we were in heaven or on earth. For on earth there is no such splendor or such beauty, and we are at a loss how to describe it. We only know that God dwells there among men, and their service is fairer than the ceremonies of other nations. For we cannot forget that beauty. Every man, after tasting something sweet, is afterward unwilling to accept that which is bitter, and therefore we cannot dwell longer here." Then the boyars spoke and said, "If the Greek faith were evil, it would not have been adopted by your grandmother Olga who was wiser than all other men." Vladimir then inquired where they should all accept baptism, and they replied that the decision rested with him.

The Role of Kherson in Vladimir's Conversion

After a year had passed, in 6496 (988), Vladimir proceeded with an armed force against Kherson, a Greek city, and the people of Kherson barricaded themselves therein. Vladimir halted at the farther side of the city beside the harbor, a bowshot from the town, and the inhabitants resisted energetically while Vladimir besieged the town. Eventually, however, they became exhausted, and Vladimir warned them that if they did not surrender, he would remain on the spot for three years. When they failed to heed this threat, Vladimir marshalled his troops and ordered the construction of an earthwork in the direction of the city. While this work was under construction, the inhabitants dug a tunnel under the city-wall, stole the heaped-up earth, and carried it into the city, where they piled it up in the center of the town. But the soldiers kept on building, and Vladimir persisted. Then a man of Kherson, Anastasius by name, shot into the Russ camp an arrow on which he had written, "There are springs behind you to the east, from which water flows in pipes. Dig down and cut them off." When Vladimir received this information, he raised his eyes to heaven and vowed that if this hope was realized, he would be baptized. He gave orders straightway to dig down above the pipes, and the water-supply was thus cut off. The inhabitants were accordingly overcome by thirst, and surrendered.

Vladimir and his retinue entered the city, and he sent messages to the Emperors Basil and Constantine, saying, "Behold, I have captured your glorious city. I have also heard that you have an un-wedded sister. Unless you give her to me to wife, I shall deal with your own city as I have with Kherson." When the Emperors heard this message they were troubled, and replied, "It is not meet for Christians to give in marriage to pagans. If you are baptized, you shall have her to wife, inherit the kingdom of God, and be our companion in the faith. Unless you do so, however, we cannot give you our sister in marriage." When Vladimir learned their response, he directed the envoys of the Emperors to report to the

Vladimir converted from paganism to Christianity in 988 and established the Russian Orthodox Church in Kievan Russia.

latter that he was willing to accept baptism, having already given some study to their religion, and that the Greek faith and ritual, as described by the emissaries sent to examine it, had pleased him well. When the Emperors heard this report, they rejoiced, and persuaded their sister Anna to consent to the match. They then requested Vladimir to submit to baptism before they should send their sister to him, but Vladimir desired that the Princess should herself bring priests to baptize him. The Emperors complied with his request, and sent forth their sister, accompanied by some dignitaries and priests. Anna, however, departed with reluctance. "It is as if I were setting out into captivity," she lamented; "better were it for me to die at home." But her brothers protested, "Through your agency God turns the land of Rus' to repentance, and you will relieve Greece from the danger of grievous war. Do you not see how much harm the Russes have already brought upon the Greeks? If you do not set out, they may bring on us the same misfortunes." It was thus that they overcame her hesitation only with great difficulty. The Princess embarked upon a ship, and after tearfully embracing her kinfolk, she set forth across the sea and arrived at Kherson. The natives came forth to greet her, and conducted her into the city, where they settled her in the palace.

By divine agency, Vladimir was suffering at that moment from a disease of the eyes, and could see nothing, being in great distress. The Princess declared to him that if he desired to be relieved of this disease, he should be baptized with all speed, otherwise it could not be cured. When Vladimir heard her message, he said, "If this proves true, then of a surety is the God of the Christians great," and gave order that he should be baptized. The Bishop of Kherson, together with the Princess's priests, after announcing the tidings, baptized Vladimir, and as the Bishop laid his hand upon him, he straightway received his sight. Upon experiencing this miraculous cure, Vladimir glorified God, saying, "I have now perceived the one true God." When his followers beheld this miracle, many of them were also baptized.

Vladimir was baptized in the Church of St. Basil, which stands at Kherson upon a square in the center of the city, where the Khersonians trade. The palace of Vladimir stands beside this church to this day, and the palace of the Princess is behind the altar. After his baptism, Vladimir took the Princess in marriage. Those who do not know the truth say he was baptized in Kiev, while others assert this event took place in Vasil'ev, while still others mention other places. . . .

Vladimir Christianizes the Kievans

Hereupon Vladimir took the Princess and Anastasius and the priests of Kherson, together with the relics of St. Clement and of Phoebus his disciple, and selected also sacred vessels and images for the service. In Kherson he thus founded a church on the mound which had been heaped up in the midst of the city with the earth removed from his embankment; this church is standing at the present day. Vladimir also found and appropriated two bronze statues and four bronze horses, which now stand behind the Church of the Holy Virgin, and which the ignorant think are made of marble. As a wedding present for the Princess, he gave Kherson over to the Greeks again, and then departed for Kiev.

When the Prince arrived at his capital, he directed that the idols should be overthrown, and that some should be cut to pieces and others burned with fire. He thus ordered that Perun [the pagan god of thunder] should be bound to a horse's tail and dragged down Borichev [another pagan deity] to the stream. He appointed twelve men to beat the idol with sticks, not because he thought the wood was sensitive, but to affront the demon who had deceived man in this guise, that he might receive chastisement at the hands of men. Great art thou, oh Lord, and marvelous are thy works! Yesterday he was honored of men, but today held in derision. While the idol was being dragged along the stream to the Dnieper, the unbelievers wept over it, for they had not yet received holy baptism. After they had thus dragged the idol along, they cast it into the Dnieper. But Vladimir had given this injunction "If it halts anywhere, then push it out from the bank, until it goes over the falls. Then let it loose." His command was duly obeyed. When the men let the idol go, and it passed through the rapids, the wind cast it out on the bank, which since that time has been called Perun's sandbank, a name that it bears to this very day.

Thereafter Vladimir sent heralds throughout the whole city to proclaim that if any inhabitants, rich or poor, did not betake himself to the river, he would risk the Prince's displeasure. When the people heard these words, they wept for joy, and exclaimed in their enthusiasm, "If this were not good, the Prince and his boyars would not have accepted it." On the morrow, the Prince went forth to the Dnieper with the priests of the Princess and those from Kherson, and a countless multitude assembled. They all went into the water: some stood up to their necks, others to their breasts, and the younger near the bank, some of them holding children in their arms, while the adults waded farther out. The priests stood by and offered prayers. There was joy in heaven and upon earth to behold so many souls saved. But the devil groaned, lamenting, "Woe is me! how am I driven out hence! For I thought to have my dwelling-place here, since the apostolic teachings do not abide in this land. Nor did this people know God, but I rejoiced in the service they rendered unto me. But now I am vanquished by the ignorant, not by apostles and martyrs, and my reign in these regions is at an end."

When the people were baptized, they returned each to his own abode. Vladimir, rejoicing that he and his subjects now knew God himself, looked up to heaven and said, "Oh God, who has created heaven and earth, look down, I beseech thee, on this thy new people, and grant them, oh Lord, to know thee as the true God, even as the other Christian nations have known thee. Confirm in them the true and inalterable faith, and aid me, oh Lord, against the hostile adversary, so that, hoping in thee and in thy might, I may overcome his malice." Having spoken thus, he ordained that wooden churches should be built and established where pagan idols had previously stood. He thus founded the Church of St. Basil on the hill where the idol of Perun and the other images had been set, and where the Prince and the people had offered their sacrifices. He began to found churches and to assign priests throughout the cities, and to invite the people to accept baptism in all the cities and towns.

The Influence of the Medieval Russian Church

By George Vernadsky

Within a century of Prince Vladimir's conversion to Orthodoxy in 988, the church had come to occupy a prominent role in almost all walks of life within Kievan Russian society. George Vernadsky, professor of Russian history at Yale University until his death in 1974, details the influence that the early church had on Kievan culture. He begins by explaining how the blending of old pagan beliefs with the new Orthodox religion created a Russian Orthodox Church with significant differences from its Greek cousin. He goes on to discuss the religious literature produced during the first few centuries of the church's existence. Vernadsky analyzes several noteworthy hymns and hagiographies (a semibiographical genre in which the lives of holy men and women are likened to spiritual models such as Jesus or St. Augustine) to see how they reflect the religious values that the church was trying to instill in the Russian people during the eleventh and twelfth centuries, as the Kievan state was coming into its full maturity.

While the pagan cult was forbidden from the close of the tenth century, pagan beliefs could not be so easily eradicated. At first only the city people took Christianity more or less seriously; in remote rural districts paganism held its ground for a long time under the thin veneer of Christian rites. The result was the so-called "double-faith," *dvoeverie*. People may have worn crosses and attended church services but they did not abandon the celebration of the pagan festivals, too.

Gradually the two rituals merged, with victory on the Christian side, at least in outward appearance. Christian saints replaced

the old deities in the people's mind. Elija the prophet was identified with Thunder, substituting for Perun; the old God Veles
was transformed into St. Vlas (Blasius); St. Trifon, through a series of iconographic accidents, became associated with falconry,
and so on. Similarly, old pagan festivals were adapted to Christian holy days; thus the traditional *Semik* (summer equinox rites)
merged with *Troitsa* ("Pentecost").

At first the adaptation was somewhat mechanical. Gradually,
however, the old beliefs waned and the new struck firmer roots.
As a matter of fact, paganism had no chance of withstanding
Christianity, not only because the latter was the higher religion
but also because it represented a higher civilization in general. Being accepted by the elite of Russian society as early as the eleventh
century, it produced a number of truly enlightened leaders.

It is the "cult"—that is, the totality of church services and
prayers—that best reveals the core of Greek Orthodoxy and it is
the celebration of the Mass that constitutes the core of the Orthodox cult. Indeed, historically speaking it was mainly through
the Mass—or, perhaps better, through the church ritual in general—that people were trained to become Christians in Kievan
Russia. To be sure, the symbolism of the church ritual could at
first be appreciated by only a few. There were, however, many elements in the church service which to a greater or lesser degree
appealed to the bulk of the congregations. Such were, for example: readings from both the New and the Old Testament, which
were a regular part of the services; hymns arranged in the so-
called "canon," devoted to the glorification of Christ and the
Virgin Mary and to prayer to them for intercession and protection; collect-hymns of a special kind (known as *kondak*), the object of which was to explain the meaning of the church holy
days, and so on. All this was offered not in Latin or Greek but in
Slavonic [a precursor to modern Slavic languages like Russian]
and was thus accessible to the audience. Icons and murals representing biblical scenes were meant to illustrate the contents of the
readings and the hymns and were undoubtedly of great help to
the congregation. Finally, further explanation was offered in sermons. The latter, especially when delivered by outstanding church
leaders, were usually written down and circulated in many copies
for the literate, the number of whom had increased considerably
by the end of the eleventh century. Besides the sermons, excerpts
from the works of the Byzantine church fathers and lives of saints

were also at the disposal of readers, helping them to master the new faith.

Early Effects of Christianization

What was the cumulative effect of the Orthodox "cult" and didactic literature on the minds of the first generations of churchgoers in Russia? Perhaps the most important result was the new sense of moral responsibility of every man or woman for his or her deeds, and even thoughts, to which the idea of the future life and the Last Judgment supplied a sanction. While the notion of a future life was known to Slavic paganism, there was hardly any connotation attached to it of responsibility for life on earth. Far as the Russian neophyte may have been from the Christian ideal in his actual living, that ideal became an important factor in his mind. If he sinned, he also repented, and a new element of inner struggle for perfection enriched his spiritual life and religious experience. Thus an important psychological change came about for the Russian people.

The change affected not only the individual but likewise the society as a whole. The new attitude made it possible for the legislator to abolish altogether the old custom of class feud and bloody revenge. Broadly speaking, the notion of social responsibility accompanied that of individual responsibility. Church leaders were expected to show the way to the nation and some of them duly contributed their share; among other things, by objecting to the institution of slavery. Monasteries became so many centers of what may be called social work, by organizing hospitals and homes for the aged as well as promoting charities. Some of the princes followed suit. Education was likewise sponsored by both the church and the princes and it was also the church which first assumed the task of recording the history of the nation.

In the old Russian historical annals the basic idea of the responsibility of both rulers and people for their deeds was emphasized and misfortunes such as famines and wars were explained as so many cases of God's visitation to punish men for their sins.

Let us now examine some of the literary documents of the Kievan period—hymns, prayers, lives of saints, and so on—which may illuminate for us the religious mentality of Russians in that age. It is significant that, not content with the traditional hymns received from Byzantium, a number of educated Russians tried their own hand at writing new hymns and prayers. Bishop Kirill of Turov is the author of a penitence canon (not preserved) and several hymns and prayers, all permeated with the notion peculiar to him of a stern Godhead and helpless mankind. The metropolitan Ilarion wrote a "prayer for Russia" which is another sample of his forceful literary style and greatness of mind.

THE MURDER OF BORIS, RUSSIA'S FIRST MARTYR

Two of Vladimir's sons, Boris and Gleb, became the first sainted martyrs of the Russian Orthodox Church. In this passage from Boris's hagiography, written by a Kievan monk named Nestor as part of what would become the Primary Chronicle, *the murder of Boris by his brother Sviatopolk is recounted (Sviatopolk would later have Gleb killed as well). As is normal in hagiography, the episode is told with numerous allusions to biblical precedents—for example, Sviatopolk's treachery is compared to that of Cain and Boris's piety in death is compared to that of Jesus. The canonization of native saints such as Boris and Gleb indicated the growing stability of the church in the century after Vladimir's conversion.*

Sviatopolk settled in Kiev after [Vladimir's] death, and after calling together all the inhabitants of Kiev, he began to distribute largess [money, presumably as a bribe to ensure loyalty] among them. They accepted it, but their hearts were not with him, because their brethren were with Boris. When Boris returned with the army. . .he received the news that his father [Vladimir] was dead. He mourned deeply for him, for he was beloved of his father before all the rest.

When he came to the Alta [River], he halted. His father's retainers then urged him to take his place in Kiev on his father's throne, since he had at his disposal the latter's retainers and troops. But Boris protested: "Be it not for me to raise my hand against my elder brother. Now that my father has passed away, let him take the place of my father in my heart." When

A prayer attributed to a layman, Prince Vladimir Monomach, in a sense continues Ilarion's tradition but is more personal in its scope. It is addressed to Christ and the Virgin Mary. As a ruler Vladimir implores the Holy Virgin to preserve the city over which he reigns as her city. As a man he is concerned with his own soul: "Incline, O my soul, and consider my deeds that thou

---

the soldiery heard these words, they departed from him, and Boris remained with his servants.

But Sviatopolk was filled with lawlessness. Adopting the device of Cain, he sent messages to Boris that he desired to live at peace with him, and would increase the territory he had received from his father. But he plotted against him how he might kill him. So Sviatopolk came by night to Vyshegorod. After secretly summoning to his presence Putsha and the *boyars* [nobles] of the town, he inquired of them whether they were wholeheartedly devoted to him. Putsha and the men of Vyshegorod replied, "We are ready to lay down our lives for you." He then commanded them to say nothing to any man, but to go and kill his brother Boris. They straightway promised to execute his order. . . .

These emissaries came to the Alta, and when they approached, they heard the sainted Boris singing vespers. . . . After finishing vespers, he prayed, gazing upon the icon, the image of the Lord. . . . After offering [his] prayer, he lay down upon his couch. Then they fell upon him like wild beasts about the tent, and overcame him by piercing him with lances. . . .

The desperadoes, after attacking Boris, wrapped him in a canvas, loaded him upon a wagon, and dragged him off, though he was still alive. When the impious Sviatopolk saw that he was still breathing, he sent two Varangians to finish him. When they came and saw that he was still alive, one of them drew his sword and plunged it into his heart. Thus died the blessed Boris.

Samuel Hazzard Cross and Olgerd P. Sherbowitz-Wetzor, eds. and trans., *The Russian Primary Chronicle: Laurentian Text.* Cambridge, MA: The Medieval Academy of America, 1974.

has done; bring them before thine eyes, shed tears from mine eyes and confess openly all thine actions and thoughts to Christ, and be purified."

The First Russian Saints

From the ecclesiastical point of view, the appearance of saints is a barometer of the level of religion in a nation and the newly converted Russia needed saints to convince herself as well as the outside Christian world of her religious maturity. While most of the Byzantine saints are bishops and monks, Russia's first two canonized saints were, characteristically enough, laymen and not members of the clergy: they were the princes Boris and Gleb, both sons of Vladimir "the Saint," who was himself canonized much later. The third Russian saint was Feodosi, abbot of the Monastery of the Caves. In all, in the Kievan period, eleven Russians were canonized.

Canonization calls for the writing of lives of the saints, and hagiography constituted an important branch of Byzantine literature. Among the innumerable Byzantine vitae [Latin for "lives"] some are purely legendary while others are based upon real biographical traits; which, however, were often shaded by the later editors and compilers. Gradually a conventional standard was established for writing a *"life."* In spite of the fact that authors of the early Russian vitae tried to follow the Byzantine pattern, their work is less conventional and closer to life than that of their masters.

The life of Feodosi was written by Nestor, a learned monk of the Monastery of the Caves. His object was to collect materials essential for the canonization of the late abbot, which the elders of the monastery were then striving to have officially approved. In spite of this, Nestor's work is not an official panegyric [a speech of praise] but an honest biographical record, although adapted to the rules of Byzantine hagiography. The monk had not known Feodosi personally, for he entered the monastery shortly after the great abbot's death, but he lived in the atmosphere of fresh memories of the departed leader and had ample opportunity of conversing with Feodosi's disciples. Thus, for Nestor, Feodosi is in a sense a living man and not a mere ideal, which makes his work personal rather than abstract. On Ss. Boris and Gleb two works exist: their "Life," written by the same Nestor, and the anonymous "Tale" (*Skazanie*). Both were written at the close of the eleventh or in the initial years of the twelfth century.

Saints Boris and Gleb ... were murdered in 1015 immediately after the death of their father Vladimir by order of their brother Sviatopolk I, who wanted to eliminate any potential rivals for the Kievan throne.

The assassination of the two brothers was a shock to the Russian people at large. While not exactly martyrs for the faith, they were considered innocent "sufferers" who sacrificed themselves for the ideal of brotherly love. It is noteworthy that the first Czech saint, Václav, was also a murdered prince; and incidentally Nestor was acquainted with his "Life."

Boris' attitude is that of nonresistance to evil, the result of a literal acceptance of Christ's words. It was for their innocent suffering that Boris and Gleb were considered saints by the larger masses of the Russian people.

Sympathy for suffering was one of the basic expressions of Christian feeling in old Russia—one may say, indeed, one of the pillars of popular religion as opposed to official theology, especially as interpreted by monks of the type of Kirill of Turov. Were a man even a criminal or a heretic, from the point of view of the popular religion suffering purified him. . . .

Other Religions and Denominations

Of other religions and denominations, Roman Catholicism and Judaism had a number of followers in Kievan Russia. . . .

As to Roman Catholicism, its adherents were chiefly German merchants staying in Russia. There was a Roman Catholic church in Smolensk and two in Novgorod. A Dominican monastery in Kiev is mentioned in western sources. In spite of the fact that the break between the Greek and the Roman churches was made final in 1054, the attitude of the Russians toward Roman Catholicism was not belligerent in this period and individual Russians did not shun contact with Roman Catholics; in any case, certainly neither the princes nor the merchants.

It is significant that all the anti-Catholic polemic treatises which circulated in Russia in the Kievan period were either translations from the Greek or written by Greeks in Russia.

The Arrival of the Mongols

FROM THE *NOVGORODIAN CHRONICLE*

The city of Novgorod in northern Russia became increasingly prominent in the late twelfth and early thirteenth century as the influence of Kiev began to fade. Just as the Primary Chronicle *had done in Kiev, the* Novgorodian Chronicle *recounted the history of how Novgorod had risen to prominence and thereafter recorded the noteworthy happenings in the city. Unquestionably, the arrival of the Mongol invaders in the year 1238 (or year 6746 since the creation of the world) was such an event. This passage from the* Novgorodian Chronicle *describes the efforts of Novgorod's leaders to repel the Mongols (also called Tatars, or Tartars) during that year. Although they were successful in holding off the Mongols, most of the remainder of Russia was eventually brought under control of the so-called Golden Horde and remained that way until the middle of the fifteenth century. The final paragraph of this excerpt shows that the Novgorodians believed the invasion to be a punishment sent to the Russian people by God, and Novgorod's relative escape from that punishment—which also helped it become a prominent part of Muscovy after the end of the Mongol occupation—was seen by many as evidence of the city's superior virtue.*

A.D. 1238. A.M. 6746.

That same year foreigners called Tartars came in countless numbers, like locusts, into the land of Ryazan, and on first coming they halted at the river Nukhla, and took it, and halted in camp there. And thence they sent their emissaries to the *Knyazes* [princes] of Ryazan, a sorceress and two men with her, demanding from them one-tenth of everything: of men and *Knyazes* and horses—of everything one-tenth. And the *Knyazes* of Ryazan, Gyurgi, Ingvor's brother, Oleg, Roman Ingvorevich, and those of Murom and Pronsk, without letting them into their

Robert Michell and Nevill Forbes, trans., *The Chronicle of Novgorod, 1016–1471.* New York: AMS Press, 1970.

towns, went out to meet them to Voronazh. And the *Knyazes* said to them: "Only when none of us remain then all will be yours." And thence they let them go to Yuri in Volodimir, and thence they let the Tartars at Voronazh go back to the Nukhla. And the *Knyazes* of Ryazan sent to Yuri of Volodimir asking for help, or himself to come. But Yuri neither went himself nor listened to the request of the *Knyazes* of Ryazan, but he himself wished to make war separately. But it was too late to oppose the wrath of God, as was said of old by God, to Joshua the son of Nun, when leading them to the promised land, then he said: "I shall before you send upon them perplexity, and thunder, and fear, and trembling." Thus also did God before these men take from us our strength and put into us perplexity and thunder and dread and trembling for our sins. And then the pagan foreigners surrounded Ryazan and fenced it in with a stockade. And *Knyaz* Yuri of Ryazan, shut himself in the town with his people, but *Knyaz* Roman Ingorovich began to fight against them with his own men. Then *Knyaz* Yuri of Volodimir sent Yeremei as *Voyevoda* [military governor] with a patrol and joined Roman; and the Tartars surrounded them at Kolomno, and they fought hard and drove them to the ramparts. And there they killed Roman and Yeremei and many fell here with the *Knyaz* and with Yeremei. And the men of Moscow ran away having seen nothing. And the Tartars took the town on December 21, and they had advanced against it on the 16th of the same month. They likewise killed the *Knyaz* and *Knyaginya* [princess], and men, women, and children, monks, nuns and priests, some by fire, some by the sword, and violated nuns, priests' wives, good women and girls in the presence of their mothers and sisters. But God saved the Bishop, for he had departed the same moment when the troops invested the town. And who, brethren, would not lament over this, among those of us left alive when they suffered this bitter and violent death? And we, indeed, having seen it, were terrified and wept with sighing day and night over our sins, while we sigh every day and night, taking thought for our possessions and for the hatred of brothers.

The Mongols Advance Deeper into Russia

But let us return to what lies before us. The pagan and godless Tartars, then, having taken Ryazan, went to Volodimir, a host of shedders of Christian blood. And *Knyaz* Yuri went out from Volodimir and fled to Yaroslavl, while his son Vsevolod with his mother and the *Vladyka* [a high-ranking cleric] and the whole of the province shut themselves in Volodimir. And the lawless Ismaelites approached the town and surrounded the town in force, and fenced it all round with a fence. And it was in the morning *Knyaz* Vsevolod and *Vladyka* Mitrofan saw that the town must be taken, and entered the Church of the Holy Mother of God and were all shorn into the monastic order and into the *schema,* the *Knyaz* and the *Knyaginya,* their daughter and daughter-in-law, and good men and women, by *Vladyka* Mitrofan. And when the lawless ones had already come near and set up battering rams, and took the town and fired it on Friday before Sexagesima Sunday, the *Knyaz* and *Knyaginya* and *Vladyka,* seeing that the town was on fire and that the people were already perishing, some by fire and others by the sword, took refuge in the Church of the Holy Mother of God and shut themselves in the Sacristy. The pagans breaking down the doors, piled up wood and set fire to the sacred church; and slew all, thus they perished, giving up their souls to God. Others went in pursuit of *Knyaz* Yuri to Yaroslavl. And *Knyaz* Yuri sent out Dorozh to scout with 3,000 men; and Dorozh came running, and said: "They have already surrounded us, *Knyaz.*" And the *Knyaz* began to muster his forces about him, and behold, the Tartars came up suddenly, and the *Knyaz,* without having been able to do anything, fled. And it happened when he reached the river Sit they overtook him and there he ended his life. And God knows how he died; for some say much about him. And Rostov and Suzhdal went each its own way. And the accursed ones having come thence took Moscow, Pereyaslavl, Yurev, Dmitrov, *Volok,* and Tver; there also they killed the son of Yaroslav. And thence the lawless ones came and invested Torzhok on the festival of the first Sunday in Lent. They fenced it all round with a fence as they had taken other towns, and here the accursed ones fought with battering rams for two weeks. And the people in the town were exhausted and from Novgorod there was no help for them; but already every man began to be in perplexity and terror. And so the pagans took the town, and slew all from the male sex even to the female, all the priests and the monks, and all stripped and reviled gave up their souls to the Lord in a bitter and a wretched death, on March 5, the day of the commemoration of the holy Martyr Nikon, on Wednesday in

Easter week. And there, too, were killed Ivanko the *Posadnik* [po-
litical office roughly equivalent to mayor] of Novi-torg, Yakim
Vlunkovich, Gleb Borisovich, and Mikhailo Moisievich. And the
accursed godless ones then pushed on from Torzhok by the road
of Seregeri right up to Ignati's cross, cutting down everybody like
grass, to within 100 *versts* [roughly 66 miles] of Novgorod. God,
however, and the great and sacred apostolic cathedral Church of
St. Sophia, and St. Kyuril, and the prayers of the holy and orthodox *Vladyka,* of the faithful *Knyazes,* and of the very reverend
monks of the hierarchical *Veche,* protected Novgorod. And who,
brothers, fathers, and children, seeing this, God's infliction on the
whole Russian Land, does not lament? God let the pagans on us
for our sins. God brings foreigners on to the land in his wrath,
and thus crushed by them they will be reminded of God. And
internecine war comes from the prompting of the devil: for God
does not wish evil amongst men, but good; but the devil rejoices
at wicked murder and bloodshed. And any land which has sinned
God punishes with death or famine, or with infliction of pagans,
or with drought, or with heavy rain, or with other punishment,
to see whether we will repent and live as God bids; for He tells
us by the prophet: "Turn to me with your whole heart, with fast-
ing and weeping." And if we do so we shall be forgiven of all our
sins. But we always turn to evil, like swine ever wallowing in the
filth of sin, and thus we remain; and for this we receive every
kind of punishment from God; and the invasion of armed men,
too, we accept at God's command; as punishment for our sins.

Russia Under the "Mongol Yoke"

BY LEO DE HARTOG

Although the lengthy domination of Russia by the Mongols (1238–1480) is not one that is generally remembered fondly by Russians, the so-called "Mongol Yoke" (alternately, the "Tatar Yoke") contributed greatly to the development of some important aspects of Muscovite Russia in the fourteenth and fifteenth centuries. Leo de Hartog, a Dutch scholar who has written extensively on the Mongols and their leader, Genghis Khan, argues that the lasting effect of the Mongols' control of Russian lands was more ambiguous than many Russian historians have made it out to be. Although the Mongols did exact a heavy toll in monetary tribute and slave laborers, they also brought more advanced systems of military organization, governmental structure, and communication that indirectly helped to strengthen the numerous Russian principalities that were under their control. As a result, the Russian czarist state that emerged late in the fifteenth century centered around Moscow was considerably more efficient in governing than its Kievan predecessor had been before the "Yoke."

Before the coming of the Mongols, the principality of Kiev was relatively prosperous. Its cities conducted an extensive trade, with both the west and the east. Various trades and professions were practised in the cities, and farming communities were able to provide ample food for them. Because many cities were damaged and their population partly killed and partly carried off, for the first decades after being overrun by the Mongols in their campaigns of 1237–40, Kiev's economy suffered heavily. Destroyed cities that were no longer favourably located with respect to trade routes, were often left in ruins or only partly rebuilt. Russia suffered more under Mongol ravages than did, for instance, Persia, because the Russian economy had neither the re-

Leo de Hartog, *Russia and the Mongol Yoke: The History of Russian Principalities and the Golden Horde, 1221–1502.* London: British Academic Press, 1996. Copyright © 1996 by Leo de Hartog. Reproduced by permission.

silence nor the wealth of the Persian economy. The ravages caused by the invasion of 1237–40 were heaviest in southern and south-west Russia, but those in the north-east were more serious than the devastation caused by the Mongols in Hungary in 1241–2 and certainly worse than that in Poland. Later Mongol attacks also devastated much of Russia. However, it must be noted that in these last campaigns the Russian princes, to promote their own interests, all too often gave the Mongols a helping hand.

Over the course of the years, tens of thousands of people suffered the sad fate of being sold as slaves far from Russia. In addition, the invaders from Central Asia regularly carried off skilled artisans and trained craftsmen to ply their trades for the benefit of the khan and his foremost associates. The result was a permanent decline of a number of traditional crafts, which was undoubtedly the most destructive effect the Mongols had on urban life in Russia. Some crafts were so severely affected that the old skills were entirely forgotten. The most important were the arts of cloisonné enamelling and filigree work. It was not until the sixteenth century that these crafts returned to Russia and even then they never attained the level they had reached in the pre-Mongol period.

Nomads needed an economic base with sufficient pasturage for their herds and, in particular, for the horses of their cavalry. These regions had to lie close enough to the sedentary population they wished to control and exploit. In the Pontic and Caspian steppes, the Mongols had such pastures in abundance and were also reasonably close to the Russian forest zones. For provisioning its armies, the Golden Horde did not need any Russian territory, so, unlike in China and Persia, the Mongol domination of Russia could be indirect. As a consequence of the geographic separation of Mongol and Russian territories, the principalities took on only a few Mongol customs or institutions. The Golden Horde was not politically influenced by Russia; the difference in religion undoubtedly also played a major role. In contrast to Persia, where the Mongols were partly assimilated into the population, because of their separation the Mongols did not enter into Russian society. In contradiction, however, the Mongols, to the extent that they came to the west with Batu, were entirely submerged into the Turkish population that lived in the Pontic steppes.

The Influence of the Golden Horde

The Mongols were no strangers to the Russian princes. The Russians, who had to go to the steppes in order to arrange their political affairs, learnt to know their rulers well there. In order to get a full picture of the Mongols' influence on Russian history, one must take into consideration not only what the Mongols did to the Russians, but also how the Russians perceived the Mongols and the ways in which they encountered them off the battlefield. There is little record of this in the chronicles, but it must be assumed that on a broad scale the Russian élite did gain some insight into the society of the Golden Horde and the individuals who led it.

The autocracy and despotism that are characteristic of the grand-principality of Moscow after the fifteenth century are only in part an inheritance from the Mongols. In this area, the influence of Byzantium is at least as great as that of the Golden Horde. Although autocracy in Muscovy can hardly be explained as a successor to the Golden Horde, the despotism that manifested itself ever more clearly in this grand-principality must be seen as following in the Mongols' footsteps. The particular form of autocracy in Moscow can, in certain respects, be traced back to Byzantine attitudes. The grand-princes helped themselves to this concept, to the extent that it was useful in reaching their objectives.

The Mongols contributed a great deal to the growth of the grand-principality of Moscow. This did not happen out of their goodwill for Ivan Kalita and his successors. More precisely, the outcome of some events was sometimes the opposite of that which the rulers of the Golden Horde had intended. In the conflict between Moscow and Tver for supremacy in Russia, the Mongols probably did not foresee that by supporting the former they were losing their opportunity to use a divide-and-rule policy to continue to dominate Russia. Granting Moscow the right to collect tribute was one of the actions whose consequences the Mongols did not foresee. This privilege provided the grand-prince with enormous power. Even when the tribute was regularly paid to the Golden Horde, it must be assumed that the sum which remained behind in the treasury at Moscow was considerable.

Among the most important institutions that the Russians took over from the Mongols were the tax system, the war levy, the military draft and the mounted courier service, which in the Mongol empire was called the *yam*. In the time of Genghis Khan the *yam* had grown into one of the most important institutions in the extensive empire. Resting places were set up along a number of routes which the couriers of this information service used. The couriers could not only get new horses at these stations, but also had the opportunity to eat and rest. The smooth functioning of the *yam* was closely connected with the strong discipline maintained throughout the Mongol empire which, for its part, brought with it a large measure of security. To the degree that the Mongol power spread, the *yam* increased in both extent and importance. When the occasion arose, every inhabitant of the empire had to put the interests of the *yam* above his own. Towards the end of Genghis Khan's life, the *yam* had grown into an impressive organization. The stations developed stables with great numbers of horses. Foreign embassies also made use of its services. The *yam*, one of the pillars on which the Mongol empire rested, is still acknowledged as an exceptional example of organizational skill.

It was also true for Moscow that the smooth functioning of the state was dependent on good connecting roads. The first mention of the *yam* in Muscovite documents dates from the beginning of the fifteenth century. In the second quarter of that century, during the reign of Vasili II, the mounted courier service is increasingly mentioned as a separate responsibility. The disintegration of the Golden Horde meant that the *yam* practically ceased to exist. In order to maintain a system of courier services, Moscow had to institute its own postal system, modelled on the Mongol example. The reputation of the *yam* was such that it was logical for the Russians gradually to take over its organization, which served Moscow as effectively as it had the Mongols.

At the end of the fifteenth century, *yam* was the name for the network of stations, exchange points for horses and postal stops that came into existence in the time of Ivan III at various distances along the most important roads in Muscovy. The hundreds of horses that were necessary for the service were imported from the steppes. Ivan III and his successors not only maintained the *yam*, but perfected it as an instrument for maintaining governmental control. This meant that the *yam* developed into the safest and most comfortable travel routes in Europe at the time. Where it ended, a journey could be continued by boat on the rivers. Although the concept of the *yam* came from the Mongols, the

Russian service can be considered an organization that came into existence independently.

We have today a valuable report of a journey in Muscovy at the beginning of the sixteenth century. The observations of Sigismund von Herbertstein, the ambassador from the Habsburg emperor, indicate that post routes existed in all parts of the grand-principality of Moscow. Along every route there were well-appointed stations, says Herbertstein, each with a great number of horses that were kept ready for travellers' use. Moreover, during a trip from Novgorod to Moscow a greater distance could be covered in a day than was then possible anywhere else in Europe.

Mongol Influence on the Military, Foreign Policy, and the Economy

There can be no doubt about the fact that the Russians, who first encountered the Mongols as enemies and thereafter were subordinate to them for a long time, were thoroughly acquainted with the Mongols' military organization and their ways of conducting war. A number of Russian princes, together with their troops, took part in Mongol campaigns, and the efficiency of the Mongol army would undoubtedly have made a lasting impression on them.

Rule by the Golden Horde did not imply that the Mongols made attempts to break off ties between the principalities and the rest of Europe. The khans had no objection to maintaining trade and cultural contacts with the West. Taking into account the great distances and the means of transport at that time, the principality of Kiev and its princes maintained regular contacts with the West. Neither the Mongols nor the antipathy of the Orthodox Church towards the Latin West formed any barrier to such contacts. Indeed, the Mongols themselves would have been disadvantaged by any attempt to complicate contacts with the West, because this would have seriously harmed trade. The foreign policy of the Golden Horde encompassed eastern Europe, the Middle East and Central Asia. Armenian and Georgian princes, merchants and ambassassdors from Italy and Khwarazm [a Central Asian nation that was located in what is now Uzbekistan] all regularly came to Sarai [the Mongol capital]. It is therefore difficult to see how and why during the thirteenth and fourteenth centuries the Mongol rulers could have exercised an isolationist influence on Russia.

There is no denying that at first the Mongol conquest had a disastrous effect on Russia's economy. Mongol domination meant not only raids, campaigns, mass deportations and looting, but also heavy taxes and exploitation. However, this is only one aspect of the economic consequences of the Mongol presence in Russia. In the perspective of history, after establishing their state the Central Asian nomads made increasingly large contributions to international trade among their sedentary neighbours. In this respect, the Mongol empire was no exception. Mongol patronage encouraged the expansion and development of international trade via the caravan routes that ran from eastern Asia to the Mediterranean.

After the Mongols had conquered the Russian principalities and the Bulgarian territory on the Volga and Kama rivers, the Golden Horde formed a link in the chain of trade and a connection with the rest of the Mongol empire. It was therefore possible to bring products like, for instance, silk from China via South-West Asia to the lower Volga. From there these commodities found their way into European markets via the Black Sea. The Mongols, who themselves took no part in this activity, certainly profited from the taxes they levied on the trade. Although the northern region of Russia initially played no meaningful role in trade with Central and eastern Asia, within a century after the first Mongol invasion north-south trade had developed; it included fur and other products from the north. Under compulsion from the Mongols, in the course of years, these wares moved down the Volga to Sarai and the Golden Horde began to function as a distribution point for fur.

The Rise of Muscovy

By Alexander E. Presniakov

Although Kiev was the dominant city from the ninth century through the onset of the Mongol invasion in the early thirteenth century, a number of powerful cities such as Rostov-Suzdal, Vladimir, Novgorod, and, later, Moscow arose in the northeastern Russian lands. Alexander E. Presniakov, a prominent Russian medieval historian until his death in 1929, analyzes the increasing interrelation of these powerful and prosperous city-states from their rise to prominence in the twelfth century, through the Mongol invasion, to their eventual organization into the Russian state centered around the city of Moscow and the principality of Muscovy. Presniakov discusses how Ivan Kalita, or "Ivan Moneybags," used the economic and strategic importance of his princedom of Moscow to organize a new centralized "Great Russian" state (related to, yet distinct from the Ukrainian, or "Little Russian," and Belarussian cultures to the southeast and east, respectively). From the mid-fourteenth century onward, Moscow became the center of Russian culture, thereby making the northeastern, or "Great Russian," variant of culture dominant throughout the nation.

The Muscovite state, from its very inception, was the political focus of Great Russia. The nucleus which made the formation of this political organization easier was the Rostov-Suzdal region, limned geographically on the map of Eastern Europe by a broad belt of forests. It occupied approximately the area between the Volga and Oka rivers, the basin of the Kliazma and Northern Volga rivers from the mouth of the Tvertsa to the mouth of the Oka. The area was surrounded to the east by the Vetluga forest, to the north by the forests along the watershed between the Volga and Northern Dvina basins, to the west by the Oka forest and the forests and marshes between

Alexander E. Presniakov, *The Tsardom of Muscovy*, edited and translated by Robert F. Price. Gulf Breeze, FL: Academic International Press, 1986. Copyright © 1986 by Academic International Press. Reproduced by permission.

the Mologa and the Sheksina rivers, and on the south by the forested expanses that connect the Bryn and Murom forests. From the south the territories of Riazan and Chernigov Seversk adjoined it, from the west the lands of Smolensk and Novgorod. On the north was the territory of Novgorod the Great, and the eastern lands were inhabited by Finnish tribes.

An indigenous political life sprang forth there in the Rostov-Suzdal realm, "downstream" from Novgorod the Great and called "beyond the forest" by the Kievans from the moment Vladimir Monomakh had sent his son Yury, called Dolgoruky or the "Long Arm," to reign in the Rostov principality. Only from the time of that event in the 1120s do Russian chroniclers present any information whatsoever about the Russian lands of the Northeast. This state of knowledge about the most ancient ages in Great Russian life has fostered the illusion that the lands of Rostov in the twelfth century were more foreign than Russian, and that they were colonized anew during the era of Yury Dolgoruky and his son Andrei [Bogoliubsky], thanks to the leadership and initiative of princely authority. Actually, it is not difficult to observe, through a more careful analysis of northern chronicles, features in North Russian life under Yury Dolgoruky and Andrei Bogoliubsky which witness a considerable complexity in society in Rostov in the twelfth century.

Influential and prosperous boyars [hereditary nobles] stood beside the princes. The town centers, even those of secondary importance, were embellished with gleaming stone churches, whose architectural forms and sculptured decorations provide one of the most significant pages in the history of ancient Russian art. Both the value of the building materials, which had to be brought from the Kama river via the Volga, and the execution of the unique artistic style, indicate a level of local physical and cultural development which would be unimaginable had the conditions been those of a newly-colonized, barbaric land. The powerful local landowning boyars provoked Andrei Bogoliubsky to join a cruel struggle in which he perished. After his death the rule of the boyars materialized in the form of internecine wars seeking to usurp princely authority, features of the same social and economic order then experienced in southern Russia. Throughout Russia the eleventh century was a time of growing land ownership by the boyar class, accompanied by increasing boyar influence and privileges. In the Great Russian North the foundations of a social order were then emerging which would characterize it throughout the following centuries.

By the twelfth century events in the Russian Northeast posed a threat sufficient to demand the special attention of the prince. The first princes to arrive found no place as leaders of peaceful colonization; rather, they encountered the unsettled conditions of an international travel route. Great Russia had spread out along the ancient commercial artery of the Volga river. Its early princes evolved a unique set of outside interests, which largely remained the same for several centuries, centering in the urge to control the East-West routes between the Baltic Sea and the Volga region. Crucial to this control was the hegemony of these downriver princes over Novgorod the Great, and the maintenance of free commercial and colonization routes to the southeast and east, down the Volga and towards non-Russian lands as far as the Urals, whose natural riches beckoned.

The Rise of Novgorod and Vladimir

Over the course of two generations the political silhouette of Great Russia assumed a definite, although still elementary and weakly-sketched form. Russia now consisted of two mighty political systems—Novgorod and Rostov-Suzdal. During the age of Yury Dolgoruky the territory of Rostov underwent an experience typical of the early history of Great Russia. The center of power shifted from the city of Rostov to the city of Suzdal, just as under Andrei Bogoliubsky it again shifted, this time to Vladimir. The princes entered into the conquest of the southern borderlands, including the Oka river basin and territories belonging to Riazan and Chernigov. Under Vsevolod III called the "Big Nest," the Great Russian principality gained further definition, its center at Vladimir on the Kliazma river. At this moment the meaning of the title "grand prince" found its true significance as a political title and the confines of his realm were drawn, becoming the limits of the Great Russia of that time. Vsevolod III succeeded in subjugating entirely the Riazan princes, and at one interval his appointed governors ruled all the lands of Riazan. He enjoyed the same success with the princes of Murom. Novgorod itself fell under the sway of the grand prince, who sent his sons and nephews there to reign. The Russians of that era now grew aware of a unified political entity, which they called "the grand principality of Vladimir and Novgorod the Great."

Indeed, these two polities were connected by strong political and economic bonds. The commercial routes of Suzdal were essential arteries for Novgorod's trade; to Novgorod goods flowed from the Kama river region, from the Riazan lands, and from Suzdal itself. In turn, commodities came from the west and south; without grain from the trans-Volga regions Novgorod could not have survived. Unrestrained trade with Great Russia at large was the prerequisite of Novgorod's well-being and provided a powerful lever to the "downriver" princes in supporting Novgorod's independence from the center at Vladimir. For their part, the grand princes at Vladimir took on the responsibility of defending the western regions. The commercial centers of Novgorod and Pskov could not survive through their own strength alone. They depended upon the support of the grand prince and his military leaders in the struggle against the advancing Swedes and the Germans of Livonia [a region on the Baltic coast]. The same held true to the south. Battles against the nomads of the steppes and eastern Finnish tribes placed constant pressure on the forces of Riazan and Murom, and the support of the rest of Great Russia was just as essential for those principalities as it was for Novgorod. At this early stage in Great Russian history it was economic interest and the need for security from outside enemies that created the first and still immature forms of unity under a single political leadership. . . .

Foreign Relations in Muscovy

For proper understanding of these features it is essential to keep in mind that they developed under the strong pressure of, and in constant subjection to, foreign relations in Great Russian national life. For example, the raids of Khan Batu [leader of the Golden Horde] dealt a convulsive blow to the grand principality of Vladimir. The main victims of the massacre were the localities with large populations in the eastern part of the Vladimir realm. These areas still had not recovered as late as the end of the thirteenth century because of harassment by their Tatar neighbors, the terrible suppression of popular unrest, and the burdens imposed by Batu's tributes and taxes. At the end of the fourteenth century the population wandered to the west, spawning the "young" cities Tver and Moscow, towns which brought significant territories under their control. Vassalage to the Golden Horde greatly hindered Great Russia's eastern march and halted for many years military advances and colonization to the southeast. Commerce beyond the Volga did not revive until after mid-century, and then slowly and painfully. This revival brought with it new claims to the eastern Finnish lands and aggressive struggle with foreign neighbors. Great Russia's relations with southern Russia also faded. To the west, independent Novgorod the Great became stronger; its free people pursued their economic interests without restriction in their northern districts. At least temporarily, they were exempt from taxation of their commercial income by the Great Russian government.

That government had been weakened greatly. Its scope of operations was sharply attenuated and the authority of Vladimir as a ruling center had fallen. Its last bright flash of energy had been the activities of Alexander Nevsky [ruler of Novgorod from 1252 to 1263], who had battled to defend the western regions from the Swedes and Livonian Germans. Even this success was made possible by political restraint and cautious submissiveness to the Tatars. Under Alexander Nevsky the "Tatar yoke" was organized and the attendant tribute rendered by the vassal Russian realm; the Tatar khan held supreme authority over the Russian princes. Russo-Tatar relations fell into a definite pattern. Recognition of the khan's suzerainty [sovereignty] over Russia earned the confirmation of the princes' authority, and thereby allowed the princes to become intermediaries between the Horde and Russia. The Russian princes undertook to collect the taxes and pay the Tatars their tribute. The positive effect of their intercession was to eliminate direct Tatar involvement in governing the Russian lands. In these new circumstances Russian political activities gradually expanded, rekindling the thought of a geographic center which might unify Russia's strengths and interests. Vladimir had not recovered from the general catastrophe it had suffered. Even the leadership of Great Russia's international affairs, including relations with the Golden Horde and border defense, slipped away from the grand princes of Vladimir. Individual local officials began to establish their own arrangements directly with the Horde. Conflicts with belligerent neighbors lay as a heavy burden on the border areas of Great Russia, which began to organize themselves as independent military forces and political entities.

In northeastern Russia the pressures of self-defense brought increasing importance to the larger principalities of Tver, Riazan, and Nizhny Novgorod. The foreign relations of Great Russia literally were divided among these strong principalities. Local interest encouraged Tver to take responsibility for the struggle against Lithuania, protection of Novgorod the Great, and support of commercial and cultural ties with the West. Riazan defended its territory from restless neighbors in the steppes, preserving the southern borders of the forest zone in the upper Don basin for Russian settlements. Only toward the middle of the fourteenth century did the eastern part of Great Russia recover from profound decay. The center of its renaissance was Nizhny Novgorod, which drew into its sphere the remains of the former Suzdal principality. This larger entity then vied with the restive border peoples and trans-Volga Tatars for trade and colonization routes. Yet in their isolation all these border groups were unable to cope with the tasks that fell to them. Compelling military demands forced them to seek allies in central Great Russia.

Unifying the City-States Under Muscovite Rule

The traditions of unity in a single large principality enjoyed a bright new vitality thanks to the popular recollections of Grand Prince Vsevolod III and Alexander Nevsky. At the very beginning of the fourteenth century Prince Michael Yaroslavich of Tver made a fitful attempt to revitalize that unity. He cultivated ties with the leading groups in society, the metropolitanate [the Orthodox bishops] of the Russian Orthodox Church, now in Vladimir, and the boyar class of Vladimir. Michael received the title of "grand prince of all Russia" and sought to take control of the chief cities in the realm, Novgorod the Great, Nizhny Novgorod, Vladimir, Pereiaslavl, and Kostroma. His attempt was foiled by the opposition of Moscow and Novgorod the Great. Riazan was too weak for such endeavors, but it pressed north toward the Oka river, whose shoreline was to serve for a long time as the chief Great Russian line of defense against dangers from the south. Riazan attempted to maintain fortified outposts beyond the Oka as well. Soon, however, it lost Kolomna and other districts to the merciless expansion of Moscow. Nizhny Novgorod's grand princes, like those of Tver, sought to deepen and expand their might by usurping the grand princedom. Complete failure awaited them. Tver and Riazan along with Nizhny Novgorod remained merely foreposts of Great Russia. The prince of

Moscow, who from the time of Ivan Kalita [who ruled from 1328 to 1341] held the title of grand prince of all Russia, assumed the leadership of the burgeoning realm. Moscow princes tied anew the scattered threads of Great Russian foreign relations into a singular pattern.

Moscow's historical role was determined primarily by its politically strategic importance. Lasting warfare on three fronts fueled the drive to centralize authority in Great Russia and compelled the unification of Great Russia around Moscow. The character of Russia's political organization found its basis in the subordination of the entire social fabric and all resources of the country to the powerful and unlimited central government of the grand prince. Naturally, this form of rule was the product of a long and persistent struggle, which found in strong and durable Moscow a new focus and rallying point. The Moscow princes had cause to consider this struggle to be a battle for preservation of the tradition of the grand principality, and for the satisfaction of the ancient claims of the senior prince to primacy among the fraternal princes of Russia, to patriarchal authority, and to "the seat of the father." The scribes and chroniclers were right when they extolled Alexander Nevsky or Vsevolod III, and in a more distant time, Vladimir Monomakh, as the precursors of this urge toward a strong central authority under the grand prince.

It was not until the fourteenth century that conditions developed in the Great Russian ethnic region of Northern Russia that were essential to foster political unity. There the populace grew unified thanks to the hostility of neighboring tribes with organized military forces. No longer might this population migrate, for it had lost its freedom to resettle, a factor in the colonization of the Eastern European plain responsible for the extreme instability of the historical underlay of Ancient Russia. The people were constrained to seek their own territorial and political security and to wage protracted warfare for clearly defined borders. In the west they faced Swedish assaults on the Novgorod districts, the advances of the Livonian Germans toward Pskov, and most threatening, the thrusts of the Lithuanian Russian state from the west. Meanwhile, on the southern and eastern flanks, combat continued with the Tatars and eastern Finnish tribes. These peoples maintained unrelenting pressure on the Russian forces and gradually compelled them to rally for self-defense and pursuit of greater freedom of trade, commerce and colonization. All of these factors were crucial for the safeguarding of the foundations of national economic life.

Following the initial flareup during the thirteenth century, the era of Ivan Kalita's son, Grand Prince Semën Ivanovich, witnessed the onset of the conflict between Russia and Lithuania. While Dmitry Donskoy reigned [1359–89] the battles against the Tatar states grew in number, and the perennial defense of Novgorod and Pskov from "Germans," as the Swedish and Lithuanian forces were called, required the might of the grand princes of Great Russia. The alternative was to lose the trade cities that nourished the further economic and cultural interests of Great Russia. In addition, the methodical, progressive advances of Russian colonization into the Finnish Northeast offered trade benefits worthy of active organizational support.

This foreign affairs agenda confronting the central Great Russian state originated in its geographic and intertribal situation, and foreign affairs in turn determined that state's militant and authoritarian character. Under the pressure of these circumstances the entire process of the social and political organization of the Great Russian people took place.

The End of Mongol Rule in Russia

FROM THE *NIKONIAN CHRONICLE*

Ivan III was the first prince of Moscow to use the title of czar, *a word derived from the old Roman imperial title of* caesar. *He earned this title largely for his aggressive expansion of the Muscovite state's influence and power, the most symbolic act of which was expelling the Mongols (Tatars) from Russian lands. By 1480, the Mongols' power over Russia had diminished significantly after nearly 250 years of indirect rule. The once mighty Golden Horde had splintered into several smaller factions, many of which spent as much time fighting with each other as attending to their administrative duties. As a result, Ivan III's expulsion of the remnant of the Horde that still threatened Moscow was not the military feat it might have been a century earlier. Nevertheless, as this excerpt from the* Nikonian Chronicle—*a sixteenth-century work that covers the history of Russia from the ninth century through the year 1520—shows, Ivan's removal of the so-called "Mongol Yoke" was heralded as a great victory for Russia and for the Orthodox faith against the Horde and their alleged Polish (and, therefore, Catholic) allies.*

I n the year [1480] the Grand Prince [Ivan III] received news that Khan Akhmat was advancing with the entire Horde, with his sons and feudal lords and princes, in accordance with an agreement reached with King Casimir [of Poland], whereby the King incited him against the Grand Prince in order to destroy [Orthodox] Christianity. The Grand Prince went to Kolomna, where he remained, and sent his son, Grand Prince Ivan, to Serpukhov, while Prince Andrei Vasilevich Menshoi [brother of Ivan III] was in Tarusa; the remaining princes and *vo-*

Basil Dmytryshyn, ed., *Medieval Russia: A Source Book, 850–1700.* Fort Worth, TX: Harcourt Brace Jovanovich College Publishers, 1991. Copyright © 1991 by Holt, Rinehart and Winston, Inc. All rights reserved. Reproduced by permission.

evodas [military governors] were in other places on the Oka River. Khan Akhmat, upon learning that the Grand Prince was along the [Oka] river with all his forces, advanced toward Lithuania, around the Oka River, where he expected the arrival of the King [Casimir] and his armies, but his guides led him to the ford on the Ugra River. The Grand Prince dispatched his son and his brother and *voevodas* with all of their forces to the Ugra River. Upon reaching the Ugra, their destination, they occupied the ford and ferries. The Grand Prince himself left Kolomna for Moscow to attend a council and get advice from his [spiritual] father, Metropolitan Gerontii, his mother, Grand Princess Maria, his uncle, Prince Michael Andreevich [of Mozhaisk], and his [spiritual] father, Archbishop Vassian Rostovskii, and all of his *boyars* [nobles], inasmuch as they were all in Moscow preparing for a siege. And they pleaded with the Grand Prince to remain firm against Islam on behalf of Orthodox Christianity. The Grand Prince took note of these pleas, received a blessing, and went to the Ugra, where he encamped himself at Kremnets with a small group of people, sending others to Ugra. Back in Moscow, the mother of the Grand Prince, Metropolitan Gerontii, Archbishop Vassian, and the Abbot of the Troitsk Monastery, Paisii, pleaded that the Grand Prince request the help of his brothers [Andrei the Elder, and Boris, with whom Ivan III was not on speaking terms]. The Grand Prince consented to their pleas and allowed his mother to send for them, promising to reward them. The Grand Princess sent after them, instructing them to go immediately to the aid of the Grand Prince.

Khan Akhmat went to Lithuania near Mtsensk and Liubutsk and Odoev with his Tatars, and camped at Vorotinsk, where he expected the royal aid. The King [of Poland], however, did not come to his aid; neither did he send any army, because he was engaged in another war [with the Crimean Tatars]. At that time Khan Mengligirei of the Crimean Tatars pillaged the royal lands of Podolie, thereby helping the Grand Prince.

The Fighting Begins

Akhmat arrived at the Ugra with all of his forces, with the intent of crossing the river. When the Tatars came they began to shoot at our [forces], and our [forces] shot at them. Some Tatars advanced against Prince Andrei; others against the Grand Prince; while still others unexpectedly advanced against the *voevodas*. Our forces, using arrows and harquebusses, killed many Tatars; their arrows were falling among our forces but did not hurt anyone. They pushed the Tatars away from the river, though they tried to advance for many days; as they could not cross the river they stopped and waited until it should freeze.

The brothers Prince Andrei and Prince Boris came to Kremenets to the Grand Prince, who greeted them cordially. When the river froze, the Grand Prince, afraid of Tatar invasion, ordered his son, Grand Prince Ivan, and his brother Andrei, and his *voevodas* to join him at Kremenets with all of their forces in order to unite their forces in the struggle with the enemy. In Moscow itself everyone was afraid. When our forces left the bank of the river, then the Tatars were frightened and fled, thinking that the Russians were letting them across the river in order to fight them, while our forces thought that the Tatars had crossed the river and were pursuing them, and so they came to Kremenets.

The Grand Prince with his son and brothers and with all his *voevodas* went to Borovsk, saying that he would fight them there.

Khan [Akhmat] fled to the Horde, and Khan Ivak of the Nogai Tatars advanced against him, killed him, and took the Horde; one of the Tatar Khans wanted to occupy some frontier lands beyond the Oka River, but the Grand Prince sent his two brothers against him, and when the Tatars heard about it they fled.

O, brave and courageous Russian sons, try to defend your country, Russian land, from the Tatars! Make all necessary sacrifices in order to put an end to the burning and pillaging of your homes, the killing of your children, the abusing of your wives and your daughters—things that other great lands are now suffering from the Turks, such as Bulgaria, Serbia, Greece, Trapezund, Peloponnesus, Albania, Croatia, Bosnia, Mankup, Kafa, and many other lands. They did not defend themselves courageously and were defeated, and lost the countries, lands, and states, and now they move through foreign lands poor and homeless, . . . because they were not courageous enough. Those who fled to foreign lands with wealth and gold, wives and children, have lost their soul and body and think that those who died during the initial conquest are better off than they who wander homeless through foreign lands.

The History of Nations
Chapter 2

Czarist Russia

Ivan the Terrible and His *Oprichnina*

By Jules Koslow

*The lengthy reign of Czar Ivan IV (1547–1584) witnessed an un-
paralleled growth in the power, size, and influence of the Muscovite state.
Ivan IV consolidated the power of the state to himself to a degree never
before seen in Russia and, in doing so, earned himself the name by which
he is more commonly known: Ivan the Terrible. Jules Koslow, a scholar
with diverse interests ranging from Russian history to the Irish play-
wright Sean O'Casey, discusses the infamous* oprichnina *system that
Terrible implemented from 1565 to 1572. The* oprichnina *system created a police state within Russia and unleashed nearly a decade of repression upon the Russian people that remained unparalleled until the
Stalinist terrors of the 1930s. Koslow examines the paranoid reasoning
behind Ivan IV's creation of the* oprichnina, *which designated both a
separate political entity within greater Russia and a separate aristocracy
selected especially by the czar himself. Koslow enumerates the effects that
the* oprichnina *had on Russia and argues that it ultimately failed to
subdue the nobility to the extent Ivan IV had hoped. Instead, it helped
ferment the violent instability that marred Russia for nearly thirty years
after Ivan's death.*

As Ivan saw it, conditions in Russia [in early 1565] had
reached such a critical point that he, as the supreme
leader, had to take the most extreme measures to save the
throne and the country. He believed the boyars [nobles] were ru-
ining Russia by insisting on their entrenched privileges and
rights, and that they would go to any lengths to maintain them.
And now that he had pledged Russia to a fight to the death to
conquer the western lands to assure Russia her place in the sun,
when everything had to be done for the winning of the war, the
boyars, because of their resistance and intransigence, were particularly dangerous.

Jules Koslow, *Ivan the Terrible*. London: W.H. Allen and Company, 1961.

Still, this political reasoning, valid to an extent, was not the whole truth—and Ivan knew it. Ivan was neither a fool nor a charlatan. He was brilliant, dedicated, and—above all—ambitious. He was a master at deceiving others; but he constantly searched within himself for the truth. And in this situation the truth was that he was using this political reasoning to justify his personal ambition for unlimited power.

Ivan's ideas and plans for a police state had not come to him on the spur of the moment or without the influence and instruction of prior events. In a sense, the very history of Russia itself until his time was a gradual building-up process for his action. The two hundred-odd years of Tatar subjection, in which the authoritarian khans had acted with proverbial Oriental despotism, had had its influence, penetrating in a subtle way into the very fabric of Russian governmental life and into the very relation of the Russian princes and their subjects. With only a few exceptions, such as in Novgorod, there was no democratic tradition, no body of literature, philosophy, or law that concerned itself with the rights of men. The very early paternalistic relation of ruler and ruled, exemplified by such rulers as the pre-Tatar Prince Vladimir Monomakh, had been destroyed by centuries of Tatar domination and Russian royal subservience as vassals to their Eastern masters. And after the Tatar domination had ended, the ruling grand dukes in many ways acted more despotic than their former masters.

Another factor, specific in plan and intent, that possibly influenced Ivan was the presentation of a petition by a government official named [Ivan] Peresvetov to Ivan some time before the capture of Kazan. In this petition, the knowledgeable Russian-Lithuanian Peresvetov, who had been in the service of various foreign governments—Hungarian, Polish, Walachian—proposed that the power of the Czar should be increased, to coincide with an increase in the power and prestige of the army. The central point of this reorganization was to deny the nobles the right to have their own private military retinues, and that the army should be completely under the control and jurisdiction of the Czar. He urged that the state should be reorganized on the basis of strict military discipline. In this military state, administration should be strict, and justice should be stern and quick. Many of his specific proposals, by design or coincidence, were used subsequently by Ivan.

That Ivan lost no time in putting into practice the unlimited power guaranteed to him by his successful coup d'etat was demonstrated the day after the Council had bowed to his will; he placed all so-called traitors under a court ban, and gave orders that various adherents of Prince [Andrei] Kurbsky should be seized. Without a trial or formalities of any kind, Ivan had six 'traitors' beheaded; the seventh was impaled.

The dictatorship had begun.

And so had the terror. But terror was not enough. What Ivan foresaw was an operational area that was completely under his domination, and in which no other force but his own could operate. It was to be a separate private state within the Russian state complex in which there was no other authority—political, administrative, or judicial—except the Czar's.

The Oprichnina was the answer.

The Establishment of the Oprichnina

The term 'Oprichnina' itself was not new; it had been used in ancient appanage days [the earlier period of Russian history in which rulers would divide their lands among all their heirs in their wills, thus creating countless small principalities] to mean certain districts separated from others, especially those districts given in perpetuity to princes' widows. Ivan merely borrowed the term for his separatist state.

As Ivan conceived it, the Oprichnina was both a territory and an institution. As a territory, it embraced—eventually—half the land area of Russia, though its various sections were not contiguous. As an institution, it was a separate organization. The court entourage was no longer based upon inherited position, but was selected by Ivan, and consisted of some boyars, retainers, guards, government personnel; in other words, the usual functionaries of a court.

He began setting up this state within a state, or state alongside another state, by hand-picking a thousand men and assigning them to certain streets and wards in the quarter of Moscow known as the White City. The inhabitants of this quarter were evicted from their homes and resettled in other parts of the city.

In order to support this new court, he took for himself some twenty cities and town-districts, together with other districts, and assigned them to the members of his new organization—the Oprichniki, or as Ivan called them, 'court people'. As in Moscow, the inhabitants of these cities, towns, and districts were resettled in non-Oprichnina areas.

Frightful hardships were endured by the dispossessed inhabitants. At one time, more than twelve thousand heads of families together with their wives and children were forced out of their homes, and, carrying whatever few possessions they could manage to salvage, had to walk hundreds of miles through the snow in the middle of winter to other areas assigned them. In many cases, these new areas were completely undeveloped, consisting of nothing more than virgin forest.

The Oprichnina area, as already mentioned, was not a contiguous province or state, but, as the organization grew, a collection of cities, towns, and districts scattered over the country, though primarily in the northern and central parts of Russia.

The areas not assigned to the Oprichnina were made over to various boyars known as *zemskie boyaré,* or provincial boyars, who had the responsibility of administering them. This section of Russia was known as the Zemschina, or provincial section. In effect, what now existed was a country that was divided into two parts—the Oprichnina and the Zemschina.

Ivan's Rationale for Creating the Oprichnina

Among other purposes in setting up such a complicated and elaborate structure was Ivan's plan that by doing this he would break the influence and power of the old boyar groups by dispossessing them of their lands, and thus impoverishing them. He refused to admit many of them to his new 'court', and when he annexed their lands he regarded them as conquered territory. The now-landless boyars who were forced to go to frontier areas or other undeveloped sections of Russia where there was no appanage tradition found themselves helpless and powerless. He filled their positions with his Oprichniki, who were completely loyal to and dependent upon the Czar.

For years Ivan continued this mass shifting around of the population from one area to another. Ivan euphemistically referred to it 'as sorting out folks', but his victims called it expropriation of their lands and holdings for the personal benefit and gain of the Czar. Their resentment towards their expropriator knew no bounds. And when Ivan compounded his action of expropriation by systematic extermination of the more stubborn boyars through sudden raids by his Oprichniki, the resentment of those who managed to survive turned to hatred.

Ivan gave as the justification for his actions the fact that the boyars had ruined Russia by possessing for themselves the peasants, land, and property of the state, and thus deprived the government of its means of existence. Ivan's actions, which introduced a form of anarchy to the country and rocked it to its very foundations, were further justified by Ivan's insistence that such extreme measures were necessary to stamp out 'treason', which he saw everywhere. And in the name of stamping out treason, his Oprichniki bullyboys were given a free hand to terrorize, torture, and execute.

By setting up his own private state, Ivan now had what he considered to be a secure political sanctuary where his rebellious boyars could not penetrate. In addition, he had a personal sanctuary, where he was safe from their murderous swords. The fear that he might be assassinated became an obsession with him, dominating his thoughts and actions till the day he died. In 1572, he had drawn up a will in which he pictured himself as a persecuted man, the target of evil-doers, who had forced him to become an exile in his own country and a wanderer in the wilderness. 'Through the multitude of my sins hath the wrath of God descended upon me,' he wrote, 'so that the boyars, of their conceit, have driven me from my possessions, and I wander through all the lands.' It was this never-ending fear that was to underlie the episode in which he later became involved with Elizabeth I of England.

The Oprichniki became, in effect, his personal bodyguard, in addition to a security police, who scoured the country stamping out traitors and malcontents. And when in time the hand-picked one thousand Oprichniki increased to over six thousand, Ivan had a corps of unswervingly loyal, tough, and ruthless men whose power was unchallenged and whose members were feared and hated.

The formation of the Oprichnina, complex as it was in conception and odious as it was in its ruthless operation, was the result of a cold, calculated plan to strengthen the state militarily, strategically, administratively, and financially. By expropriating the land of the boyars—and land, together with the peasants on it, was the main wealth of the country—Ivan strengthened the central state apparatus. By waging what can well be termed a 'class war' against the boyars, Ivan had a propaganda weapon that endeared him to the mass of the Russian people, who hated the selfish, greedy, merciless boyars. By establishing a security police that in many ways was more powerful than the army itself, he put the autocracy in a strategic position that was almost unassailable. And by creating a new group he was assuring the state of administrators whose only loyalty was to the autocracy and not, as in the case of the boyars, loyalty to their class, their sections of the country, their traditions.

The Effects of the Oprichnina

The Oprichnina, as it developed, was more than just a state within a state or an organization to further Ivan's plans. It developed a character, a ritual, an esprit typical of an fanatical political party or brotherhood. Its members were more devoted to 'the cause' than to their own families, friends, or, for that matter, their own personal advancement. They were constantly involved in a war against enemies, traitors, conspirators, and malcontents. Every means justified the ends, although they were hard put to explain exactly what the ends were, except to mouth slogans about stamping out treason, killing the greedy boyars, and protecting the safety and well-being of their beloved Czar. Terror was justified because it produced results beneficial to the state and Czar, and so was torture, expropriation, mass exile, murder of individuals, extermination of entire families, and eventually even the extermination of the population of an entire city. There were no laws of restraint that were applicable to them. There were no limits that were set for them. All that mattered was the achievement of individual tasks that in the aggregate advanced the general objectives. It mattered not at all that vile methods were used in completing the tasks that would—and this they were blindly convinced of—achieve the bright new day of complete autocratic rule. And this, of course, led to outrages and crimes against the human being that were almost beyond belief. These were days, in truth, in which monsters in the shape of men walked that piece of earth known as Mother Russia, and no amount of rationalizing about advancing historical, political, or territorial ambitions can wipe out the crimes committed in her name.

The Oprichnik was proud of his organization and of being a member of it. Upon his initiation, he kissed the cross and took an oath in which he renounced, in a fashion, the material things of the world in order to advance the welfare of the Czar, and swore to put the Czar and state above any consideration of self, friends, or family relations. He ostentatiously wore a special uniform that was entirely black, and rode on a black horse that had black trappings. On the Oprichnik's saddlebow there was a dog's head and a broom; the dog's head to signify that the Oprichnik devoured his enemies, and the broom to signify that it was his function to sweep treason from the land. . . .

DISCIPLINE UNDER IVAN THE TERRIBLE

The Domostroi, whose title is often translated into English as the "Book of Household Management," was composed in the early years of Ivan the Terrible's reign by one of his most trusted advisers, an Orthodox monk named Sylvester. Issued in 1550, this work helped form a moral basis for society to go along with the legal reforms that Ivan enacted. The strict household discipline demanded by the Domostroi echoes the attitude that Ivan himself would later take toward Russia as a whole. Tellingly, Sylvester himself fell out of Ivan's favor and was exiled in 1559.

How to Teach Children and Save Them Through Fear
Punish your son in his youth, and he will give you a quiet old age, and restfulness to your soul. Weaken not beating the boy, for he will not die from your striking him with the rod, but will be in better health: for while you strike his body, you save his soul from death. If you love your son, punish him frequently, that you may rejoice later. Chide your son in his childhood and you will be glad in his manhood, and you will boast among evil persons and your enemies will be envious. Bring up your child with much prohibition and you will have peace and blessing from him. Do not smile at him, or play with him, for though that will diminish your grief while he is a child, it will increase it when he is older, and you will cause much bitterness to your soul. Give him no power in his youth, but crush his ribs while he is growing and does not in his willfulness obey you, lest there be an ag-

Though Ivan found a great deal of pleasure and satisfaction in being among the virile, reckless, brutal Oprichniki, he had little satisfaction from the results of his grand scheme. The elaborate plan failed to crush the boyars; it merely scattered them. And by the thousands they licked their wounds in faraway places, waiting for the day when they could move back again to Moscow and other centres and regain their positions of power and prestige. 'Crushing the boyars' became more of a slogan than a real-

gravation and suffering to your soul, a loss to your house, destruction to your property, scorn from your neighbors and ridicule from your enemies, and cost and worriment from the authorities. . . .

How to Instruct Servants

Enjoin your servants not to talk about other people. If they have been among strangers, and have noticed anything bad there, let them not repeat it at home; nor should they spread rumors about what is going on at home. A servant must remember what he has been sent for, and he must not know, nor answer any other questions that are put to him. The moment he has carried out his commission, he should return home and report to his master in regard to the matter he has been sent for; let him not gossip of things he has not been ordered to report, lest he cause quarrel and coldness between the masters.

If you send your servant, or son, to tell, or do something, or buy a thing, ask him twice: "What have I ordered you to do? What are you to say, or do, or buy?" If he repeats to you as you have ordered him, all is well. . . . if you send anywhere some eatables or liquids, send full measures, so that they cannot lie about them. Send your wares after having measured or weighed them, and count the money, before you send it out. Best of all, dispatch under seal. Carefully instruct the servant whether he is to leave the things at the house, if the master should be absent, or if he is to bring them back home.

Leo Wiener, ed., *Anthology of Russian Literature: From the Earliest Period to the Present Time,* vol. 1. New York: Benjamin Blom, 1967, pp. 125–128.

ity, even though hundreds were literally crushed.

Besides the boyar class, there was no other group in Russia at the time that was capable of carrying on the administration of the state. The mass of the people were illiterate and backward. The clergy could have been called upon, but a state administered by churchmen was anathema to Ivan. He had had enough of Sylvesters [a priest who had been an adviser to Ivan early in his reign] and their moralizing. Moreover, the Church had its function to perform, and to divert it from its spiritual tasks would have been to secularize it, and this Ivan refused to consider. The dilemma that Ivan faced, and which he never was able to solve, was how to dispense with the boyars' power on the one hand and use their administrative ability on the other. What the establishment of the Oprichnina accomplished, therefore, was merely the separation of the country, with the two parts existing side by side, though not jointly. How long or how well this confusing situation could last was a question that constantly plagued Ivan, and for which he had no answer.

To really crush the boyars Ivan would have had to alter radically the social structure of Russian society by lifting out of the mire the overwhelming majority of the people, who were leading bestial, degrading lives in poverty, filth, disease, and ignorance. This called for a social reformer, and Ivan hadn't the faintest desire to be one. The miserable lot of the Russian masses was no concern of his. Since the Russian mass was a supine, listless, completely beaten group who made no powerful demands, he had no pressure upon him to do anything for them. The few faint grumblings of the masses were completely overshadowed by their devotion and respect for the Czar figure.

Thus what developed was a situation in which the Oprichnina became a check against the boyars, not its destroyer. It functioned as a security police, not as a revolutionary group. Its energies were directed against people, not a system. As such it became the bulwark of autocracy, and in the long run changed little in the basic system of government that had existed for hundreds of years in Russia—and was to exist for three hundred and fifty years more.

The political ideas and practices surrounding the Oprichnina, however, [were] only one side of its story; the other side was the human misery and suffering it caused. And it was this aspect of the Oprichnina that made the reign of Ivan so horrible and gave him the name 'the Terrible'.

Rumours, stories, and accounts of the Oprichnina terror began to overflow the borders of Russia to the outside world. When Russian ambassadors in European countries were questioned about the Oprichnina and its reign of terror, in many cases they were unable to explain its complicated origin and purpose. In other cases they were unwilling to do so. The Russian ambassador to Warsaw, for instance, was asked by King Sigismund, 'What is the Oprichnina?' Stonefacedly, he replied, 'There is no such thing'.

A very few foreigners, however, did understand to an extent what was going on in Russia at the time. One such person was Giles Fletcher, who arrived in Russia a few years after Ivan's death. He wrote:

> This tyrannical practice of making a general schism and public division among the subjects of his whole realm proceeded (as should seem) from an extreme doubt and desperate fear which he had conceived of most of his nobility and gentlemen of his realm, in his wars with the Polonian and Chrim [Crimean] Tatar. What time he grew into a vehement suspicion (conceived of the ill success of his affairs), that they practised treason with the Polonian and Chrim. Whereupon he executed some, and devised his way to be rid of the rest.
>
> And this wicked policy and tyrannous practice (though now it be ceased) has so troubled that country, and filled it so full of grudge and mortal hatred ever since, that it will not be quenched (as it seems now) till it burn again into a civil flame.

In Russia, however, a few enlightened and humane men raised their voices ever so quietly and secretively—to speak loudly or openly meant detection, with the result they would never speak again—against the Oprichnina terror. 'The Czar does continually stir up murderous strife,' one critic wrote, 'and does send the men of one town against the men of another town, and does many a time bid his own portion of the state ravish the other portion, and spoil its houses, and deliver it over unto death. Thus, the Czar has raised up against himself sore anger and lamentation in all the world, by reason of the many blood-sheddings and executions which he has commanded.'

Some critics, unable to understand the complex situation, believed the Oprichnina was a huge, cruel game, played by a wilful Czar. 'All the state has he sundered in twain, as it were with an axe, and thereby has he disturbed all men,' one observer wrote. 'He plays with God's people, and stakes against himself all such as do conspire.'

People lived in mortal terror at the sight of the black-uniformed Oprichniki on their black horses, and referred to them as 'the blackness of Hell', and 'as dark as the night'. As if out of nowhere they suddenly descended upon a house, seized its inhabitants, killed them on the spot, and then, after taking whatever valuables were there, burned it.

Henry Staden, a German adventurer who served in the Oprichnina, wrote of one such 'adventure' in which he participated.

Staden and his men made a raid upon a noble's house, and

> from the windows of the women's apartments stones came showering down upon us. Calling my servant Teshata I quickly ran up the stairs with an axe in my hand. At the top of the stairs I was met by the Princess who wanted to throw herself at my feet, but terrified by my frightful appearance she rushed back into her chamber. I struck her in the back with my axe and she dropped on the threshold. I stepped over her dead body and made familiar with her maidservants.

Russian nobles who had fled their country viewed with horror the excesses that were now taking place there. Although when they were in Russia they were brutal to their own serfs and completely callous to their sufferings and poverty, they now shed crocodile tears. In the courts of the Western kings where they had fled for refuge, and where they were now parading as defenders of right and justice, they condemned Ivan and his Oprichniki as barbarians and murderers. Kurbsky, for instance, from his Polish sanctuary, wrote that the Oprichniki were 'children of darkness', and that the 'bloodthirsty Oprichniki were hundreds and thousands of times worse than hangmen'.

For the most part, Ivan ignored the critics, except Kurbsky. In fact, it is doubtful that much of what they had to say ever reached him; Ivan had by now cut himself off almost completely from his former life in the Kremlin. His wife Maria was little more than a convenience, an ornament called Czaritsa. Since 1563, she had borne him no more heirs, and this displeased him. As time went on, he spent less and less time in the Kremlin, for it had become for him a distasteful place. The formal court life of the Kremlin, with its ceremonies and traditions, smacked too much of the very things he told himself he disliked. For weeks on end, he stayed at fortified lodges, which he had had built in the Oprichnina quarter of Moscow, and, in time, at the new palace at Alexandrov, which he had ordered to be built for him and his Oprichnina henchmen.

Eventually, Alexandrov became, in effect, the capital of Russia. And here Ivan and his Oprichniki led a strange, bewildering life in a fortified palace, which was a weird combination of governmental office, monastery, drinking hall, charnel house, and brothel.

The "Time of Troubles" and the Rise of the Romanovs

By Hans-Joachim Torke

After the tumultuous time of Ivan the Terrible, relative peace existed during the reign (1584–1598) of his son, Czar Fyodor I. After Fyodor died without leaving an heir—his son Dmitry having died under mysterious circumstances in 1591—a fifteen-year struggle for power ensued among a host of potential claimants to the throne. Hans-Joachim Torke, professor of Russian and East European history at the Free University of Berlin, details the whirlwind of political intrigues and social upheavals that accompanied this period, known as the "Time of Troubles." He begins by recalling how Boris Godunov, a trusted adviser to Fyodor I, was elected czar, and then moves through the lengthy series of pretenders to the throne—many of whom claimed to be Fyodor's dead son Dmitry— who succeeded him as rulers of Muscovy. Torke concludes with an account of Mikhail Romanov's ascension to the throne in 1613, which marked the beginning of a dynasty that would last until 1917.

The age of transformation began with acute crisis—the 'Time of Troubles' (*smutnoe vremia*). This protracted crisis inaugurated a new period in Russian history, marked by fundamental changes that would culminate in the passing of 'Old Russia' and the onset of new 'troubles' in the 1680s. Perhaps the best schema for the Time of Troubles, devised over a century ago by the historian Sergei Platonov, divides this period into successive 'dynastic', 'social', and 'national' phases that followed upon one another but, to a significant degree, had some overlap.

Hans-Joachim Torke, "From Moscovy Towards St. Petersburg, 1598–1689," *Russia: A History*, edited by Gregory L. Freeze. Oxford: Oxford University Press, 1997.

The period begins with the extinction of the Riurikid line [those rulers who claimed descent from Riurik] in 1598. The general crisis also had long-term social causes—in particular, the exhaustion of the land and its resources by the Livonian War and the *oprichnina* of Ivan the Terrible, which had devastated the boyars and triggered new restrictions on the peasants' freedom of movement. Without the trauma of 1598, however, the ensuing disorder would probably neither have been so intense nor have persisted for the entire seventeenth century, which contemporaries aptly called a 'rebellious age'. This first phase was portentous both because the only dynasty that had ever reigned in Russia suddenly vanished without issue, and because the ensuing events triggered the first assault on the autocracy. In the broadest sense, the old order lost a principal pillar—tradition (*starina*); nevertheless, there remained the spiritual support of the Orthodox Church (which held firm for several more decades) and the service nobility (which retained its resiliency until well into the eighteenth century). The year 1598 had one further consequence: a tradition-bound people could not believe that the dynasty had actually come to an end and therefore tended to support false pretenders claiming to be descendants of the Riurikids.

Muscovy responded to the extinction of its ruling dynasty by electing a new sovereign. Interestingly, no one as yet proposed to emulate other countries by electing someone from a foreign ruling house—a remarkable testament to the insularity of Muscovite society. Such a proposal, undoubtedly, faced an insuperable religious obstacle—obligatory conversion to Orthodoxy. In the end the choice fell on Boris Godunov—a Russian nobleman, though not from an élite family (i.e. descending from another Riurikid line or the Lithuanian grand princes). None the less, Boris had single-mindedly prepared his advancement under Tsars Ivan the Terrible (1533–84) and Fedor Ivanovich (1584–98): he himself married the daughter of a favourite in Ivan's court; his sister Irina married Ivan's successor, Fedor. Because the latter was personally incapable of exercising power, Godunov became regent and excluded all other competitors. After Fedor's death, on 17 February 1598 Boris was formally 'elected' as Tsar Boris by a council (*sobor*) of approximately 600 deputies drawn from the upper clergy, the boyar duma [a largely ceremonial legislative body of nobles], and representatives of the service nobility who had gathered in Moscow. Although transparently stage-managed by Boris, the council seemed to confirm that the realm had 'found' the candidate chosen by God Himself.

The Church, which Boris had earlier helped to establish its own Patriarchate, supported his election. The new tsar could also count on the sympathy of the lower nobility. But Boris also had to use coercion to eliminate rivals among the boyars—such as Fedor Nikitich Romanov, the head of a family with marital ties to the Riurikids, who was banished in late 1600 and forced to take monastic vows in 1601 (with the name Filaret). That tonsure [i.e., receiving the haircut of a monk, the tonsure] effectively eliminated him from contention for worldly offices.

Threats to Boris's Power

Nevertheless, Boris's position was anything but secure. Apart from the fact that his government was beset with enormous burdens and problems, Boris himself failed to evoke veneration from his subjects. In part, that was because he had married the daughter of Grigorii (Maliuta) Skuratov—the *oprichnik* blamed for murdering Metropolitan Filipp of Novgorod in 1569. Moreover, his blatant efforts to ascend the throne lent credence to rumours that he had arranged the murder of Tsarevich [presumed successor, as eldest son; like dauphin in French] Dmitrii, Ivan's last son, in 1591. Although an investigatory commission under Vasilii Shuiskii (a rival whom Boris had deftly appointed to lead the investigation) confirmed that the death was accidental, the death of the 9-year-old Tsarevich remains a mystery to this day. Indeed, it made no sense for Boris to kill the boy: at the time of Dmitrii's death, it was still conceivable that Fedor would father a son and avert the extinction of the Riurikid line. Nevertheless, Boris's adversaries exploited suspicions of regicide—a view which, because of Alexander Pushkin's play *Boris Godunov* (which Modest Mussorgsky later made into an opera), has persisted to the present.

Nor was Boris able to consolidate power after accession to the throne. His attempt to tighten control over administration failed—largely because of the traditional 'Muscovite procrastination' and corruption. His plan to reconstruct the towns also went awry, chiefly for want of a middle estate [i.e., a class of skilled administrators]. Nor was he able to train better state servants: when, for the first time, Muscovy dispatched a contingent (eighteen men) to study in England, France, and Germany, not a single one returned. He recruited large numbers of European specialists (military officers, doctors, and artisans), but met with remonstrations from the Orthodox Church. Clearly, Boris had an open mind about the West: he not only solicited the support of ruling houses in the West, but also sought to consolidate his dynastic claims through attempts to marry his daughter Ksenia to Swedish (later Danish) princes, although such plans ultimately came to nought.

Boris attempted to establish order in noble-peasant relations, but nature herself interceded. From the early 1590s, in an attempt to protect petty nobles and to promote economic recovery, the government established the 'forbidden years', which—for the first time—imposed a blanket prohibition on peasant movement during the stipulated year. In autumn 1601, however, Boris's government had to retreat and reaffirm the peasants' right to movement: a catastrophic crop failure in the preceding summer caused massive famine that claimed hundreds of thousands of lives. The following year the government again had to rescind the 'forbidden year', a step that virtually legalized massive peasant flight. Moreover the government welcomed movement towards the southern border area (appropriately called the *dikoe pole*, or 'wild field'), where they helped to reinforce the Cossacks and the fortified towns recently established as a buffer between Muscovy and the Crimean Tatars. But many peasants sought new landowners in central Muscovy, adding to the social unrest. In fact, in 1603 the government had to use troops to suppress rebellious peasants, bondsmen (*kholopy*), and even *déclassé* petty nobles [i.e., those who had fallen from the ranks of the nobility for whatever reason].

Social Unrest in the Early 1600s

That uprising signalled the onset of phase two—the social crisis. This stage, however, overlapped with the dynastic crisis: as the general sense of catastrophe mounted, rumours suddenly spread that Tsarevich Dmitrii had not died at Uglich, but had miraculously survived in Poland-Lithuania. In 1601 a pretender surfaced in Poland, winning the support of adventurous magnates (in particular, the voevoda [military governor] of Sandomierz, Jerzy Mniszech); he was actually a fugitive monk, Grigorii, who had fled from Chudov Monastery in Moscow and originally came from the petty nobility, bearing the name Iurii Otrepev before tonsure. That, at least, was the public claim of Boris Godunov, who himself had fallen ill and steadily lost the ability to rule. That declaration had no more effect than his representations to the Polish king, Zygmunt III, who remained officially uninvolved, but had secret assurances from the 'False Dmitrii' that Poland would receive Smolensk and other territories were he to succeed. When the Polish nobles launched their campaign from Lvov in August 1604, their forces numbered only 2,200 cavalrymen. When they reached Moscow in June 1605, however, this army had grown tenfold, for many others—especially Cossacks—had joined the triumphal march to Moscow. By the time they entered the Kremlin, Boris himself had already died (April 1605), and his 16-year-old son Fedor was promptly executed. Of Boris's reign, only the acquisition of western Siberia (with outposts as remote as the Enisei) and the expansion southward were achievements of enduring significance.

The pretender initially succeeded in persuading the populace that he was the real Dmitrii. The boyars were less credulous; several were judged guilty of a conspiracy under the leadership of Vasilii Shuiskii. But the pretender had the support of Boris's enemies (seeking personal advantage) and those who believed that the 'Pseudo-Dmitrii' (ostensibly a 'Riurikid') would restore the old order. Dmitrii, however, had secretly converted to Roman Catholicism, promised enormous territories to his Polish benefactors (especially Mniszech, whose daughter Maryna he had married), and even agreed to permit missionary activities by Catholic priests and to participate in a crusade against the Turks. Before fulfilling these commitments, he attempted to ensure the support of the petty nobility, for example, by issuing a decree in 1606 that re-established the five-year statute of limitations on the forcible return of fugitive peasants.

None the less, Dmitrii failed to consolidate his hold on power. Above all, the Polish presence exposed old Russian culture to massive Western influence and provoked a strong reaction, especially against the foreigners' behaviour—their clothing, customs, and contempt for Orthodox religious rites. Popular unrest reached its peak during the wedding ceremonies in May 1606 (intended to supplement Catholic rites conducted earlier in Cracow, though without formal marriage of the betrothed). Offended by the provocative behaviour of Polish aristocrats, Vasilii Shuiskii and fellow boyars organized a conspiracy that resulted in the overthrow and murder of the 'False Dmitrii'.

It is hardly surprising that Shuiskii himself mounted the throne—this time 'chosen' by fellow boyars, not a council of the realm. The scion of an old princely line and descendant of Alexander Nevsky [thirteenth-century prince of Novgorod], he represented the hope of aristocratic lines pushed into the background by Boris and Dmitrii. During the coronation ceremonies, Shuiskii openly paid homage to the boyars, not only promising to restore the right of the boyar duma to judge cases of capital punishment (denied by Ivan the Terrible), but also vowing neither to punish an entire family for the offence of a single member nor to subject their property to arbitrary confiscation. These concessions did not constitute an electoral capitulation for a limited monarchy, but were meant only to ensure a return to genuine autocracy.

Shuiskii immediately faced a serious challenge—the Bolotnikov rebellion, the first great peasant uprising in the history of Russia. To oppose the 'boyar tsar', Ivan Bolotnikov—himself a fugitive bondsman—mobilized a motley force of peasants and Cossacks from the south (who for several years had been fomenting disorder in the region), service nobles with military experience, and some well-born adversaries of Vasilii. The rebels did manage to encircle Moscow in October 1606, but their movement collapsed when petty nobles—alarmed by the insistent demand of peasants for freedom—abandoned Bolotnikov to join the other side. Bolotnikov, who had poor administrative skills, retreated to Tula; a year later, after months of siege by government troops, the town finally capitulated and turned Bolotnikov over for execution. In the interim, Vasilii cleverly attempted to win the nobility's allegiance by promulgating a peasant statute (9 March 1607) that extended the statute of limitations on the forcible recovery of fugitive peasants from five to fifteen years. The decree answered their primary demand: by tripling the period of the statute of limitations, his decree greatly increased the chances for finding and recovering fugitives. The statute also afforded some legal protection to the bondsmen: henceforth they might be held in bondage only on the basis of a written document (*kabala*).

Hardly had Vasilii eliminated the threat from peasants and Cossacks when he faced a new menace from the Poles: in late 1607 yet another pretender, likewise claiming to be Tsarevich Dmitrii, crossed the border with an army of Polish-Lithuanian warriors. The past of this second False Dmitrii is murky, but he apparently came from the milieu of the first. Although the Polish government and Catholic Church remained in the background, members of the Polish nobility under Jan Sapieha participated in his siege of Moscow in mid-1608. After establishing headquarters in the village of Tushino, he was joined by the wife of the first False Dmitrii, 'Tsarina Maryna', who 'recognized' the husband who had so miraculously survived. Filaret Romanov (whom the first False Dmitrii elevated to metropolitan [an ecclesiastical rank in the Orthodox Church akin to bishop], thereby facilitating a return to politics) also made his way to Tushino. As other adversaries of Vasilii also came, Tushino became the centre of a counter-government, with its own administration, and was recognized as the legitimate power by much of the realm.

Simultaneously, several towns along the upper Volga established their own army (the 'first contingent' [or "first levy"]), which proceeded to liberate Vladimir, Nizhnii Novgorod, and Kostroma. This army evidently had no ties with Vasilii, who was forced to accept the assistance of some 5,000 Swedish mercenaries.

Military Threats from Poland

Muscovy now entered phase three—the 'national crisis': in May 1609 the Polish Sejm [the parliament of the Polish nobility] approved a request by King Zygmunt III for funds to invade Russia—nominally under the pretext of repulsing a Swedish threat to Poland-Lithuania. Thus, by the autumn of 1609, two foreign armies—Swedish and Polish—were operating on Russian soil: the Poles concentrated on taking Smolensk, while the Swedes forced Vasilii to cede Korela and Livonia as compensation for their help. After some initial tensions, Moscow and Sweden soon enjoyed military success, overrunning the camp at Tushino at the end of 1609; a few months later the Swedish troops marched into Moscow. As most of the Poles retreated toward Smolensk, the second False Dmitrii settled down in Kaluga, but was slain by his own supporters at the end of 1610.

Nevertheless, Vasilii's hold on power steadily deteriorated, partly because of suspicions that the jealous tsar was responsible for the mysterious death of a popular commander, M.V. Skopin-Shuiskii. Vasilii's forces, moreover, had failed to liberate Smolensk from Polish control.

As Vasilii's power waned, in February 1610 his foes struck a deal with the king of Poland: his son Wladyslaw, successor to the Polish throne, would become tsar on condition that he promise to uphold Orthodoxy and to allow the election of a monarch in accordance with Polish customs. He also had to guarantee current landholding relations and official ranks (chiny), the legislative power of the boyar duma and an imperial council (analogues to the [Polish institutions of the] Sejm and Senate), and the preservation of peasant dependence. The agreement also provided for a military alliance between the two states. Thus, for the first time in Russian history, élites set terms for accession to the throne. These conditions were reaffirmed in a new agreement on 17 August 1610, with the added proviso that the future tsar convert to Orthodoxy.

A month earlier, the conspirators (who evidently included Filaret) had already deposed Vasilii and forced him to take monastic vows. The Polish negotiator was hetman [a tribal title of leadership] St Zólkiewski, who had conquered Moscow and, as commander of the Polish-Lithuanian occupation, held power in the capital. The agreement provided for a council of seven boyars (legitimized by an ad hoc council of the realm), which, with a changing composition, sought to govern during the interregnum [the period between rulers]. The boyars hoped to use the Polish tsar to overcome the internal strife, but their attempt would ultimately founder on the lesser nobility's fear of a boyar oligarchy.

That Muscovy obtained neither a Polish tsar nor a limited monarchy in 1610 was due to a surprising turn of events in Smolensk. There the Polish king received a 'great legation' from Moscow (with over 1,200 persons) to discuss the details of succession. Despite the mediation of Zólkiewski, the negotiations broke down as the two parties refused to compromise—chiefly over the demand by Russians (especially patriarch Germogen) that the future tsar convert to Orthodoxy, and over the Polish insistence that Moscow cede Smolensk. Zygmunt now announced that he himself wished to become tsar, which effectively eliminated any possibility of conversion to Orthodoxy. The tensions were soon apparent in Moscow, where the high-handed behaviour of the Poles and their Russian supporters triggered a popular uprising in February–March 1611. The leader of resistance was patriarch Germogen, who issued impassioned proclamations against the Poles before finally being interned. In April the king had members of the 'great legation' (including Metropolitan Filaret and the former Tsar Vasilii Shuiskii) deported to Poland and put on exhibition before the Sejm.

All this culminated in a great national uprising led by towns on the Volga. The provinces were still aflame with unrest and disorder: by mid-1611 eight pretenders claimed to be the 'true' Tsarevich Dmitrii; countless bands of peasants and Cossacks, purporting to fight for 'freedom', engulfed the land in conflict and plunder; Swedes tightened their hold on Novgorod (intended as a pawn to press other territorial demands) and ruled the entire north; and the Tatars invaded from the south.

In response Nizhnii Novgorod and Vologda raised the 'second levy', which united with the former supporters of the second False Dmitrii and advanced on Moscow. The army was led by P. Liapunov, the district governor (*voevoda*) of Riazan; like other district governors, he was originally a military commander, but had since become head of civil administration in his district. The supreme council of his army functioned as a government (for example, assessing taxes), but avoided any promise of freedom for fugitive peasants once the strife had ended. Despite written agreements, Liapunov's forces suffered from profound internal conflict, especially between peasants and petty nobles; Liapunov himself was murdered in the summer of 1611, marking an end to the 'second contingent'. The 'Council of Seven Boyars' in Moscow, meanwhile, continued to hope for the arrival of Wladyslaw.

The 'third levy', though beset with internal differences, nevertheless liberated Moscow in October 1612. This army had been created a year earlier by K. Minin, the elected head of Nizhnii Novgorod, who persuaded the population to endorse a special tax amount (up to 30 per cent of their property). Many nobles joined this army, including its commander—Prince Dmitrii Pozharskii, who established headquarters in Iaroslavl. Minin and Pozharskii later became national heroes, memorialized to this day in a monument on Red Square. But the critical factor in their victory was the decision of Cossacks under Prince Trubetskoi to join their side in the midst of the battle.

The liberation of Moscow did not mean an end to the turbulent 'Time of Troubles': for years to come, large parts of the realm remained under Swedish and Polish occupation. But it was at least possible to elect a new tsar in 1613, a date traditionally accepted as the end to the Time of Troubles. Still, the ramifications of this era were momentous and enduring, especially the large-scale intrusion of the West, which generated much commentary—and controversy—among writers such as Ivan Timofeev, Avramii Palitsyn, Semen Shakhovskoi, and Ivan Khvorostinin. And, despite the election of a new tsar, society became more self-conscious as it entered upon decades of tumult in the 'rebellious century'.

The First Romanov Tsar

In 1613 Mikhail Fedorovich Romanov—Tsar Michael in popular literature—was only one of several candidates for the throne of Muscovy. Although not yet even 17 years of age, he had already been considered for this position three years earlier. But circumstances were now more complex: in contrast to Boris's election in 1598, this time some proposed to summon a foreigner—either Archduke Maximilian of Habsburg or the Swedish prince, Karl Phillip.

Because of the patriotic mood after the expulsion of Poles from the Kremlin, however, there was nevertheless a strong preference to choose a Russian candidate. Rivalry among candidates eventually eliminated all but one—the young Romanov, widely regarded as a surrogate for his father Filaret, still in Polish detention; the latter's martyr-like captivity, in fact, contributed to his son's election. Michael came from a relatively young boyar family, which first gained prominence when it provided the first wife of Ivan the Terrible. But the old boyar clans, given to bickering among themselves, savoured this humble background—and Michael's youth, which promised to make him easier to manipulate. The electoral assembly of 700 delegates was initially unable to reach a consensus, but on 21 February 1613 finally acceded to vigorous agitation from nearby towns that Michael be chosen as the compromise candidate. In the aftermath of the Time of Troubles, when the throne had changed hands so frequently, few could have foreseen that this dynasty would remain pure-blooded until 1762 and, with the infusion of some outside (mainly German) elements, retain the throne until 1917.

In contrast to Shuiskii, Michael made no concessions to obtain the throne. Indeed, the participants themselves wanted to restore the autocracy 'of the good old days' that had ensured order and stability. In foreign policy, restoration meant expulsion of foreign foes; in domestic policy, it meant resolving the conflict between landholders and peasants, which had disintegrated into virtual chaos. Despite this call for restoration, the election did not bring an end either to popular unrest or to the intrusion of Western culture.

The re-establishment of autocracy naturally did not mean that Michael—above all, given his youth—ruled alone. Initially, he was under the influence of powerful favourites from the Mstislavskii and Saltykov clans. After 1619, when peace with Poland brought an exchange of prisoners (including Filaret), the young tsar fell under the dominance of his father, who became a virtual co-ruler and even bore the tsarist title of 'Great Sovereign': in Muscovy it was simply inconceivable that a father might occupy a lower rank than his son. This paternal dominance also corresponded to their personalities, Filaret being energetic, his son meek and pious.

Peter the Great's Governmental Reforms

By D.S. Mirsky

Czar Peter I (Peter the Great) is most frequently credited with making Russia into a modern, European-style nation. In the following article, Russian historian D.S. Mirsky analyzes the social reforms that Peter the Great made during his reign in an effort to bring Russia into line with western Europe. Peter had spent considerable time in the West during the early years of his rule and attempted to implement a number of the ideas he witnessed there in Russian culture. Mirsky looks at Peter's attempts to establish stronger control over the church—like that held by the British monarchy over the Church of England—as well as his efforts at military and industrial modernization. Mirsky also discusses the ways in which Peter's reforms opened up opportunities for those of the merchant class or civil servants (those who were neither nobles nor peasants) that had been previously denied to all but the hereditary aristocracy. Mirsky also points out, however, that the peasant classes suffered greatly under Peter's reign since his reforms created more potential masters for them.

The europeanisation of Russia took place within the twenty-seven years that Peter the Great was actual ruler of Russia (1698–1725). The process began before Peter was born, and went on after his death, but the turning-point, when the consciousness of the upper classes ceased to be Muscovite and became European, falls in these years. The classes affected by the change were the serving gentry [landowners], and a section of the commercial classes; the main mass of the tax-paying classes remained unaffected. The difference found external expression in enactments about dress and personal appearance: the gentry alone

D.S. Mirsky, *Russia: A Social History*. London: The Cresset Press, 1952.

were obliged to wear "German dress" and shave their beards, but the tax-payers might let their beards grow and dress as they liked.

In matters of form and style the Reform was drastic. Besides European dress and clean-shaven faces, European forms of social intercourse were prescribed. The women were made to appear in mixed society, and dance with men at public balls. German, Dutch, French or Latin names were given to all ranks and things in the army and navy, and to all the numerous new offices and boards. Such was the outer shell of the "Reform." Its essential content was the adoption of European technique and technical instruction, the encouragement of essential industries, the creation of a modern army and navy, and the radical secularisation of the body-politic.

The Church ceased to be a power commensurable with and sanctioning the power of the sovereign, and became a department of the administration. The Patriarchate [the rule over the Orthodox Church by a single man, the Patriarch] was abolished, and the government of the Church was vested in a "Most Holy Synod" of prelates and priests appointed by the Emperor. The new order was essentially similar to that introduced in England and in the Lutheran North by the Reformation. Peter himself was inclined to Protestantism, but as the new princes of the Church, the Ukrainian prelates, were for the most part so pliable and subservient that they made Protestant Reform superfluous, liturgy and dogma were permitted to remain unchanged. It was an Ukrainian prelate, Theophan Prokopovich, who produced the most complete and learned vindication of the new secular monarchy. Thus, with the approval of the higher clergy, the Russian theocratic monarchy was transformed into a secular absolutism of the Western type. The substitution of Western for Byzantine political thinking was symbolised by the assumption of the title of Imperator [Latin form of Emperor] instead of Tsar in 1721, and in the name of Senate given to the supreme council of government instituted in 1711.

The secularisation of the State was accompanied by the secularisation of culture. The Church ceased to be the sole depository of learning; secular schools, technical for the most part, were founded; secular books were published in increasing quantities. Russian replaced Church-Slavonic as the literary language and, to emphasise the break with ecclesiastical tradition, a new "civil" alphabet was introduced with letters approaching in form to Latin characters (1703). The old *kirilitsa* [the Cyrillic alphabet that dated back to the 9th century] and the Church-Slavonic language survived only in ecclesiastical publications.

Another aspect of Peter's Reform was militarism. The great war with Sweden for the Baltic coast filled twenty-one of the twenty-seven years of the reign (1700–1721), and most of his financial and administrative reforms are to be explained by the stress of war-time conditions. The army and navy absorbed all the resources of the country. The upper classes were, to a man, under the obligation of continuous military service. The lower classes, besides being crushed with a heavier burden of taxes and *corvees* [payment to a landlord in the form of labor] than they had ever borne, were subjected to the new burden of conscription.

The enemy, Sweden, was the most efficient military power in Europe, and began the war by utterly routing the Russian army at Narva (1700). But at the price of colossal effort an army and navy were created which won the decisive victories of Poltava (1709), and Hangöhud (1714), and which, by the end of the war were second to none in Europe.

That the country as a whole was not permanently crippled by the Swedish war, was due to the successful effort of industrialisation. The development of shipbuilding, of the iron industry in the Urals, of the leather, cloth and cordage industries in the centre, were the most important aspects of this "industrial revolution." The conquest of the Baltic coast with the ports of St. Petersburg and Riga, gave Russia a new and more advantageous outlet to the world market, and greatly increased the volume of her trade. But the economic progress of the Empire only contributed to increase the subjection and exploitation of the people.

The reforms of Peter the Great met with considerable opposition from various quarters, but it would be wrong to imagine him either as a hero struggling against fearful odds to civilise a stagnant country, or as a tyrant arbitrarily imposing an alien civilisation on an unwilling nation. The most active and vigorous forces in the land were on his side. He had the backing of almost the whole serving class, of the Ukrainian clergy, and of a small, but active, minority of the commercial class. The opposition came chiefly from the lower middle classes—urban and rural—that gravitated towards the Old Believers. The main mass of peasants was too downtrodden to do more than try to escape from taxes and forced labour into the unoccupied steppe. Nor did the opposition of the

more substantial classes take a very active form. The reign of terror maintained during the whole of this period by the secret police had innumerable victims, but few of them were guilty of anything more than words. Only in the south the *streltsy* [the standing
military] and townspeople of Astrakhan, in 1705, and the Don
Cossacks, two years later, attempted to rise in arms, but were suppressed without much difficulty and with ruthless cruelty.

THE TABLE OF RANKS

*In 1722, Peter the Great issued the Table of Ranks as a new means
for determining social status within Russian society. Until 1682,
the* mestnichestvo, *a somewhat arbitrary ranking system among
the handful of old aristocratic families, had been the sole means of
determining rank for matters such as military service or court ap-
pointments. Peter introduced the Table of Ranks to create a new nobility based primarily on government service. Given the substantial
degree of militarization in Russian society during Peter's reign, the
ability to interchange previously separate civil and military ranks
was especially important. The Table of Ranks incensed many of the
old aristocratic nobles, especially those whose status fell considerably
from where it had been under the old system, and also engendered
a great deal of bureaucratic confusion among the mass of middle-
class, would-be nobles. The Table of Ranks largely defined the Russian ruling classes until 1917.*

Class	Navy	Army	Civil
1	Admiral-General	Generalissimus; Field Marshal	Chancellor or High Privy Councillor
2	Admiral	General of: Artillery, Cavalry, & Infantry	High Privy Councillor
3	Vice-Admiral	Lieutenant-General	Privy Councillor; Procurator General
4	Rear Admiral	Major General	High State Councillor; Presidents of the Colleges
5	Commodore-Captain	Brigadier	State Councillor

The social results of Peter's reform were twofold. The policy of industrialisation and commercial development implied legislation that favoured the productive middle classes. A succession of reforms, begun as early as 1699, gave the urban and commercial classes almost complete independence from the crown administration, that is to say, from the serving class, and a predominant place in the financial government of the country. But this

Class	Navy	Army	Civil
6	Captain, First Rank	Colonel	Councillor in the Colleges; Chief Judges of Guberniia Courts
7	Captain, Second Rank	Lieutenant Colonel	Councillors in the Upper Courts
8	Fleet Lieutenant-Captain; Captain Third Rank	Major	Assessors (Vice Councillor) of the Colleges
9	Fleet Lieutenant; Artillery Lieutenant-Captain	Captain	Titular Councillor
10	Artillery Lieutenant	Staff Captain	College Secretary
11	—	—	Senate Secretary
12	Ensign; Warrant Officer	Lieutenant	Guberniia Secretary
13	Artillery Constable	Second Lieutenant	Senate Registrar
14	—	Ensign	College Registrar

To the Table of Ranks enumerated [here] we add the following points, which explain how one is obliged to act within each rank: . . .

11. All servitors, Russian and foreign, who occupy the first eight ranks, or who have in fact done so: their legitimate children and descendants in perpetuity are to be granted equal honors to the best Nobility of yore in all their dignity and advantages, although they might be of a lower kind and have never previously been elevated to Noble status or granted a coat of arms by a Crowned Head.

Daniel H. Kaiser and Gary Marker, *Reinterpreting Russian History: Readings, 860–1860s.* New York: Oxford University Press, 1994.

did not last. Peter's "bourgeois" policy was continued by Prince Dimitri Golitsyn, but the fall of that remarkable statesman in 1730 left the serf-owning and military gentry the only class of any account in political life.

It was during the reign of Peter that the serving class finally became a corporate gentry, with a definitely aristocratic class-consciousness. The transformation was not retarded by the obligation, enforced more rigorously than ever under Peter the Great, of devoting all their life to military service, for the militarism of the reign made the army and navy officer, socially and politically, a dominant figure. It was in their military capacity that the gentry were able to play their most active role. Nor did the great number of foreigners and new men admitted into the service under Peter in any way "democratise" the gentry or the administration. The famous "Table of Ranks" that divided the service into fourteen grades, open to all persons irrespective of their birth, provided for the regular infusion of new blood into the gentry, but did not diminish its corporate or hereditary character. As for the old feudal families, their influence had long ago become entirely contingent on the royal favour and their successes in the administrative career, and not in the least on birth or hereditary wealth.

The political gains of the gentry became fully apparent only after the fall of Prince Dimitri Golitsyn, but their social gains were immediate and obvious. Their estates, by the assimilation of *pomestie* [estates granted to individuals as rewards for state service] to *votchina* [inherited estates], became unconditionally hereditary property. Their serfs were assimilated with slaves, for though the law put this the other way round and transformed slaves into serfs to enable them to pay taxes, in reality their legal condition remained unchanged and that of the serfs deteriorated. Large areas of crown land were given to members of the gentry in reward for services, and the free inhabitants reduced to slavery. But the losses of the peasant class were even greater than the gains of the gentry; non-noble capitalists were given, in conditional possession, serfs to work their mines and factories; peasants supplied the forced labour used for the construction of St. Petersburg and of the canals; they paid the poll-tax (which under Peter the Great replaced the older land and house taxes), and provided the main bulk of recruits for the army and navy. All burdens were heaped on them, with no corresponding advantages; they were the slaves of both the squires and the State.

The Russian Enlightenment

BY JAMES H. BILLINGTON

Born into a noble family in the Prussian principality of Anhalt-Zerbst, Czarina Catherine II (Catherine the Great) was not originally a Russian. She became part of the ruling Romanov house when she married the future Czar Peter III in 1745, and she ascended the throne in 1762 after leading a palace revolt against her own husband. She nevertheless became one of the most successful and revered leaders in Russian history. She is often credited with bringing the ideas of the Enlightenment—a predominately western European philosophical movement that stressed reason over tradition—into Russian culture. Historian James H. Billington, who has served as Librarian of Congress since 1987, examines the ways in which Enlightenment philosophies that Catherine adapted helped transform various aspects of Russian culture. Billington describes how Catherine accelerated the process of secularizing Russian culture that Peter the Great had started a century earlier. Billington also discusses Catherine's reforms of the educational system and how they helped create a new class of educated elite, the intelligentsia, in Russian society.

The concrete achievements of Catherine's domestic program seem strangely insignificant: the introduction of vaccination, paper money, and an improved system of regional administration. Yet her impact on Russian history went far deeper than the superficial statecraft and foreign conquest for which she is justly renowned. More than any other single person prior to the Leninist revolution, Catherine cut official culture loose from its religious roots, and changed both its physical setting and its philosophical preoccupations. Important changes in architecture and ideas must thus be analyzed if one is to understand the revolutionary nature and fateful consequences of Catherine's Enlightenment.

James H. Billington, *The Icon and the Axe: An Interpretive History of Russian Culture*. New York: Alfred A. Knopf, 1966. Copyright © 1966 by James H. Billington. Reproduced by permission.

Catherine substituted the city for the monastery as the main center of Russian culture. She, and not Peter, closed down monasteries on a massive scale and tore down wooden symbols of Muscovy, such as the old summer palace of the tsars at Kolomenskoe. In some of the monasteries that remained open she placed pseudo-classical bell towers that clashed with everything else and demonstrated her inability to make even token gestures to the old religious culture of Muscovy.

Convinced that men have always honored "the memory of the founders of cities equally with the memory of lawmakers," she appointed a commission at the beginning of her reign to plan a systematic rebuilding of Moscow and St. Petersburg, and encouraged it to draw up plans for building or renovating some 416 other cities. St. Petersburg was soon transformed from an imitation Dutch naval base into a stately granite capital. New cities were built, and the over-all urban population, which had increased only slightly since the time of Peter the Great, nearly doubled between 1769 and 1782. In many of her rebuilt cities, from Tver to Tobol'sk, Catherine was able to realize her ideal of rational uniformity. Yaroslavl, second in size only to Moscow among cities of the interior, was beautifully transformed by superimposing a radiocentric grid of broad streets onto the jumbled city, and by subtly converting its ornate late-Muscovite churches into decorative terminal points for streets and promenades. The perfection and large-scale manufacture of uniform-sized bricks created new practical possibilities for rebuilding wooden provincial cities. Throughout the realm, architectural mass began to replace the florid decorative effects of both the high Muscovite style and the Elizabethan rococo. Simple, neo-classical shapes—semi-circular arches and domes and Doric columns—dominated the new urban architecture, where the design of the ensemble generally determined the proportions of the individual structure.

Of course, many of Catherine's plans for cities were completely impractical; many more were never acted on; and the percentage of total population in the cities remained minute and to a large extent seasonal. Those cities which were built conformed only to a prescribed pattern of roads and squares, and of design on important facing surfaces. Lesser streets and all block interiors were completely uncontrolled—testifying in their squalor to the superficiality of Catherine's accomplishment. Behind all the façades and profiles lay an enserfed peasantry and a swollen, disease-ridden army distracted from their collective misfortunes by a running tide of military conquest. Thousands of provincial figures—including many who were neither aristocratic nor literate—participated in building the new cities; and architecture proved in many ways as important as literature in spreading the new ideal of rational order and classical style.

Nevertheless, the majestic, artificial city of Catherine's era provided a new center and symbol for Russian culture. Catherine's new cities were not basically commercial centers, the traditional arenas for the development of a practical-minded bourgeois culture, but rather aristocratic cities: provincial showplaces for the newly acquired elegance and pro-consular power of the aristocracy. Town planners were more concerned with providing plazas for military reviews than places for trade and industry; architects devoted their ingenuity to convertible theater-ballrooms rather than convenient facilities for ordinary goods and services.

Because so many of her new cities were administrative centers for her newly created provincial governments, the city center was dominated by political rather than religious buildings. Horizontal lines replaced vertical ones as the narrow streets, tent roofs, and onion domes of the wooden cities were swept away. The required ratio of 2:1 between the width of major streets and the height of facing buildings became 4:1 in many cases. Such artificially broadened promenades and the sprawling squares visible from pseudo-classical porches and exedras gave the ruling aristocracy an imposing sense of space.

Having just conquered the southern steppe and settled on a provincial estate, the officer-aristocrat in the late years of Catherine's reign was newly conscious of the land; and its vastness seemed both to mock and to menace his pretensions. In the new cities to which he repaired for the long winter, he could feel physically secure in a way that was never before possible in Russian cities. The danger of fire was greatly reduced by the progressive elimination of wooden buildings and narrow streets; the last great peasant uprising had been quelled; and the key bases of Tatar raiders in the south were finally captured.

Yet gone also was the psychological security of the old Muscovite cities with their outer walls and inner kremlins capped by the domes and spires that lifted eyes upward. The city was now dominated by the horizontal stretch of roads leading from a central space at the heart of the city to the greater spaces that lay all around. Into such cities, the ruling aristocrats brought an inner malaise not unrelated to the limitlessness and monotony of the steppe and to the artificiality of their own position on it.

Catherine's Reform of Russian Education

A belief in the liberating and ennobling power of education was perhaps the central article of faith in the European Enlightenment. But the practical problem of providing secular education for the relatively rootless and insecure Russian aristocracy proved profoundly vexing. Both the limited accomplishments and the deeper problems are illustrated in the career of Ivan Betskoy, Catherine's principal court adviser on educational matters. His long life spanned ninety-two years of the eighteenth century; and most of his many-sided reformist activities were dedicated to the central concern of that century, the spread of education and public enlightenment.

The ideal of an expanded, Western type of school system had been present for several decades in the more advanced Western sections of the Russian Empire. German-educated Ukrainian seminarians like Gregory Teplov drew up elaborate plans; [German philosopher Johann Gottfried von] Herder, while a young pastor in Riga, dreamed of installing a system of instruction modeled on [French philosopher Jean-Jacques] Rousseau's *Émile.* Baltic German graduates of Tartu, in Esthonia, brought with them the ideas of the Enlightenment that had begun to permeate that institution. Generals like Andrew Bolotov returned from the Seven Years' War with plans for streamlining Russian aristocratic instruction along lines set down by the victorious Frederick the Great.

At first glance, Catherine's educational projects appear to be nothing more than another example of high hopes and minimal accomplishment. Encouraged by [English philosopher John] Locke's *On the Education of Children* (translated into Russian in 1761) and his *Essay Concerning Human Understanding* to think of man as a *tabula rasa* on which education is free to print any message, Catherine discussed plans for education with everyone from the encyclopedists to the Jesuits (to whom she offered shelter after the Pope abolished the Society in 1773). However, the statute for public schools in the empire, drawn up with the aid of Jankovich de Mirievo, a Serb who had reorganized public education within the Hapsburg empire, remained largely a paper proclamation. While she talked of sowing seeds of knowledge throughout the empire, she let the St. Petersburg Academy of Sciences lapse into a relatively fallow period in which little serious work was published.

Yet certain important developments did take place in education; and almost all of them were connected with Betskoy, who, like most eighteenth-century Russian aristocrats, was widely traveled, trained to think in abstract, universal terms, and almost totally without deep roots in his Russian homeland. . . .

Betskoy was born in Stockholm, educated in Copenhagen, spent most of his early life in Paris, and had close if not intimate relations with a host of minor German princesses, including the mother of Catherine the Great. Thus, when Catherine ascended to the throne, Betskoy commended himself to the young empress as a man with excellent intellectual and physiological qualifications for the court. Like Catherine's special favorites, [Grigori] Orlov and [Grigori] Potemkin, Betskoy was drawn to the Empress and her projects for reform partly because of antagonism to the more established aristocracy. Whereas most older aristocrats sympathized with [Nikita] Panin's efforts to have an aristocratic council limit tsarist authority, Betskoy and his allies sought to expand that authority as a means of furthering their own relative position in the hierarchy. Whereas the older aristocrats tended to adopt the measured rationalism of [French philosophers] Voltaire and [Denis] Diderot, Catherine's less secure courtiers tended to prefer the visionary ideas of Rousseau. There was perhaps a certain sense of identity between these relative outsiders to the Russian aristocracy and the Genevan outsider to the aristocratic Paris of the *philosophes*. Basically, however, the Russian turn from Voltaire to Rousseau reflected a general turn in intellectual fashion among European reformist circles of the 1770's and 1780's. Orlov invited Rousseau to come to Russia and take up permanent residence on his estate; one of the Potemkins became Rousseau's principal Russian translator; Catherine retreated increasingly to her own Rousseauan "Hermitage"; and the "general plan of education" which Betskoy presented to her was partly based on Rousseau's *Émile*.

Betskoy sought to create in Russia "a new breed of man" freed from the artificiality of contemporary society for a more natural way of life. The government was to assume responsibility for this new type of education, seeking to develop the heart as well as the mind, to encourage physical as well as mental development, and to place the teaching of morality at the head of the curriculum. In his search for elements suitable for remolding through pedagogical experiment he had to look no further than his own origins. Bastards and orphans—the rejected material of society—were to become the cornerstones of his new temple of humanity. On the basis of a close study of secular philanthropic activities in England and France, Betskoy set up in Moscow and Petersburg foundling homes which were to become major centers of initiation into the new Russian Enlightenment. Foundling homes are even now called "educational" (*vospitatel'nye*) homes in Russia, and these first ones were set up

> . . . to overcome the superstition of centuries, to give the people their new education and, so to speak, their new birth (*porozhdenie*).

They were to remain totally removed from the outside world in these secular monasteries from age five or six to eighteen or twenty; but, in fact, many entered at two or three, and were neither bastards nor orphans.

Betskoy was Russia's first de facto minister of education, serving as president of the Academy of Arts, organizing planner for the Smolny Monastery for women (the only one of these "monastic" schools to outlive him), and reorganizer of the curriculum for the infantry corps of cadets—as well as head of the foundling homes and an influential adviser to the Academy of Sciences and many private tutors. He was also a resourceful fund raiser, promoting special theatrical benefits and a lucrative tax for education on another favorite aristocratic recreation: playing cards. He died in 1795, just a year before his sovereign benefactor, and willed his substantial private fortune of 400,000 rubles to his educational projects. . . .

The Lasting Influence of the Enlightenment

The historical importance of the Russian Enlightenment under Catherine cannot be denied. Russians had been introduced to a new world of thought that was neither theological nor technological, but involved the remaking of the whole man in accordance with a new secular ideal of ethical activism. Moreover, the idea was established that this moral education was properly the responsibility of the government. Betskoy was thoroughly devoted to autocracy, and sought to enlist government support for his educational program on the grounds that it would serve to produce a select elite uniquely loyal to the imperial cause.

Like [French philosopher Baron de] Montesquieu in politics, Betskoy in education set the tone for much subsequent discussion in Russia, without seeing many of his practical prescriptions adopted. Betskoy's interest in using the Russian language was disregarded by academies and tutors alike, who were expected to familiarize aristocratic youth with Western European rather than Russian or Byzantine tradition. His interest in a measure of practical training in trades was never able to modify the pronounced emphasis on non-technical and broadly philosophical subjects. Time spent in higher educational institutions generally counted as state service for noblemen or for those aspiring to a title. A leisurely and dilettantish education was better preparation for life among the aristocracy than industrious specialization. Betskoy's more earnest boarding schools were remembered mainly as the object of humorous barbs, usually aimed at the "child-like Betskoy" (detskoy-Betskoy).

Betskoy's last important service to Catherine was supervising the embellishment of St. Petersburg. With characteristic thoroughness he organized expeditions to Siberia to bring back rare and decorative stones, arranged for importation of stone from Finland and the manufacture of bricks in St. Petersburg, and helped put in their final place a variety of statues, including [E.M.] Falconet's long-labored equestrian statue of Peter the Great in the Senate Square. This imposing memorial to Peter became, through [Alexander] Pushkin's famous poem "The Bronze Horseman," an enduring symbol of both the majestic power and the impersonal coldness of the new capital. Catherine's pretense in placing a monumental façade over widespread suffering seems in some ways anticipatory of the dostoprimechatel'nosti ("imposing sights") in the midst of terror in the Stalin era. Her city below Kiev on the Dnieper (Ekaterinoslav, now Dniepropetrovsk) became the site of the first and most celebrated mammoth construction project of the Soviet era: the hydroelectric dam of the 1920's.

The most important link between the Russia of Catherine and that of the revolutionary era lies, however, in the creation of a new class of secular intellectuals vaguely inclined toward sweeping reform. Betskoy had spoken of developing through education a "third rank" of citizens along with the aristocracy and the

peasantry. The educated intellectuals did indeed come to constitute a new rank in society outside the table of ranks created by
Peter. They found their solidarity, however, not as a class of enlightened state servitors, as Betskoy had hoped, but as an "intelligentsia" estranged from the state machine. This was the "new
race of men" to come out of Catherine's cultural upheaval: the
unofficial "third rank" between the ruling aristocracy and the
servile peasantry.

For Catherine's reign saw a profound and permanent change
in the source of internal opposition to imperial authority.
Whereas the first half was plagued by violent protest movements
among the lower classes, climaxing in the Pugachev uprising, the
latter half of her reign saw the first appearance of "Pugachevs
from the academies": a new kind of opposition from within the
educated aristocracy. The estrangement of these intellectuals from
their aristocratic background resulted not so much from any
changes in the sovereign's attitude toward reform as from an inner ripening of ideas within the thinking community itself. Since
this intellectual ferment was to play a vital role in subsequent
Russian history, it is important to consider the first steps on the
path of critical questioning that was to lead Russia to form an
intelligentsia, a "new Soviet intelligentsia," and perhaps something
even beyond that in the post-Stalin era.

Principles for Legislative Reform

By Catherine II

Less than five years after coming to power in Russia, Catherine II (Catherine the Great) undertook one of the most ambitious projects in Russian history. Convening a legislative commission in 1767, Catherine instructed this body to fashion a new code of laws for Russia that would embody the philosophical principles of the Enlightenment. Borrowing heavily from many of her western European influences—most notably the French political philosopher Baron de Montesquieu—Catherine produced a document, excerpts of which have been reproduced here, that was meant to guide the commission in its work. Catherine's suggestions to the commission reflect not only the Western roots of her philosophical principles as a ruler but also her unshakable belief in the virtue of an absolute form of government. The legislative commission ultimately dissolved after more than a year of meetings without producing a substantive new law code, but Catherine's instructions nevertheless represent her intention to be an enlightened autocrat, even if she was never fully able to put that intention into practice.

1. The Christian Law teaches us to do mutual Good to one another, as much as possibly we can.

2. Laying this down as a fundamental Rule prescribed by that Religion, which has taken, or ought to take Root in the Hearts of the whole People; we cannot but suppose that every honest Man in the Community is, or will be, desirous of seeing his native Country at the very Summit of Happiness, Glory, Safety, and Tranquillity.

3. And that every Individual Citizen in particular must wish to see himself protected by Laws, which should not distress him in his Circumstances, but, on the Contrary, should defend him

Catherine the Great, "Catherine the Great's Instructions to the Legislative Commission," Seton Hall University Russian and East European Studies Program. http://artsci.shu.edu.

from all Attempts of others that are repugnant to this fundamental Rule.

4. In order therefore to proceed to a speedy Execution of what We expect from such a general Wish, We, fixing the Foundation upon the above first-mentioned Rule, ought to begin with an Inquiry into the natural Situation of this Empire.

5. For those Laws have the greatest Conformity with Nature, whose particular Regulations are best adapted to the Situation and Circumstances of the People for whom they are instituted. . . .

6. Russia is an European State.

7. This is clearly demonstrated by the following Observations: The Alterations which Peter the Great undertook in Russia succeeded with the greater Ease, because the Manners, which prevailed at the Time, and had been introduced amongst us by a Mixture of different Nations, and the Conquest of foreign Territories, were quite unsuitable to the Climate. Peter the First, by introducing the Manners and Customs of Europe among the European People in his Dominions, found at that Time such Means as even he himself was not sanguine enough to expect.

Monarchy as the Sensible Form of Russian Government

8. The Possessions of the Russian Empire extend upon the terrestrial Globe to 32 Degrees of Latitude, and to 165 of Longitude.

9. The Sovereign is absolute; for there is no other authority but that which centers in his single Person that can act with a Vigour proportionate to the Extent of such a vast Dominion.

10. The Extent of the Dominion requires an absolute Power to be vested in that Person who rules over it. It is expedient so to be that the quick Dispatch of Affairs, sent from distant Parts, might make ample Amends for the Delay occasioned by the great Distance of the Places.

11. Every other Form of Government whatsoever would not only have been prejudicial to Russia, but would even have proved its entire Ruin. . . .

13. What is the true End of Monarchy? Not to deprive People of their natural Liberty; but to correct their Actions, in order to attain the supreme Good.

14. The Form of Government, therefore, which best attains this End, and at the same Time sets less Bounds than others to

natural Liberty, is that which coincides with the Views and Purposes of rational Creatures, and answers the End, upon which we ought to fix a steadfast Eye in the Regulations of civil Polity.
15. The Intention and the End of Monarchy is the Glory of the Citizens, of the State, and of the Sovereign.
16. But, from this Glory, a Sense of Liberty arises in a People governed by a Monarch; which may produce in these States as much Energy in transacting the most important Affairs, and may contribute as much to the Happiness of the Subjects, as even Liberty itself. . . .

Four Categories of Crimes

68. Crimes are divisible into four classes: against religion, against manners [morality], against the peace, against the security of the citizens. . . .
74. I include under the first class of crimes [only] a direct and immediate attack upon religion, such as sacrilege, distinctly and clearly defined by law. . . . In order that the punishment for the crime of sacrilege might flow from the nature of the thing, it ought to consist in depriving the offender of those benefits to which we are entitled by religion; for instance, by expulsion from the churches, exclusion from the society of the faithful for a limited time, or for ever. . . .
76. In the second class of crimes are included those which are contrary to good manners.
77. Such [include] the corruption of the purity of morals in general, either public or private; that is, every procedure contrary to the rules which show in what manner we ought to enjoy the external conveniences given to man by Nature for his necessities, interest, and satisfaction. The punishments of these crimes ought to flow also from the nature of the thing [offense]: deprivation of those advantages which Society has attached to purity of morals, [for example,] monetary penalties, shame, or dishonor . . . expulsion from the city and the community; in a word, all the punishments which at judicial discretion are sufficient to repress the presumption and disorderly behavior of both sexes. In fact, these offenses do not spring so much from badness of heart as from a certain forgetfulness or mean opinion of one's self. To this class belong only the crimes which are prejudicial to manners, and not those which at the same time violate public security, such as carrying off by force and rape; for these are crimes of the fourth class.

78. The crimes of the third class are those which violate the peace and tranquillity of the citizens. The punishments for them ought also to flow from the very nature of the crime, as for instance, imprisonment, banishment, corrections, and the like which reclaim these turbulent people and bring them back to the established order. Crimes against the peace I confine to those things only which consist in a simple breach of the civil polity.

Catherine II

79. The penalties due to crimes of the fourth class are peculiarly and emphatically termed Capital Punishments. They are a kind of retaliation by which Society deprives that citizen of his security who has deprived, or would deprive, another of it. The punishment is taken from the nature of the thing, deduced from Reason, and the sources of Good and Evil. A citizen deserves death when he has violated the public security so far as to have taken away, or attempted to take away, the life of another. Capital punishment is the remedy for a distempered society. If public security is violated with respect to property, reasons may be produced to prove that the offender ought not in such a case suffer capital punishment; but that it seems better and more comfortable to Nature that crimes against the public security with respect to property should be punished by deprivation of property. And this ought inevitably to have been done, if the wealth of everyone had been common, or equal. But as those who have no property are always most ready to invade the property of others, to remedy this defect corporal punishment was obliged to be substituted for pecuniary. What I have here mentioned is drawn from the nature of things, and conduces to the protection of the liberty of the citizens. . . .

Punishments That Are Consistent, Not Cruel

81. The Love of our Country, Shame, and the Dread of public Censure, are Motives which restrain, and may deter Mankind from the Commission of a Number of Crimes.

82. The greatest Punishment for a bad Action, under a mild Administration, will be for the Party to be convinced of it. The civil Laws will there correct Vice with the more Ease, and will not be under a Necessity of employing more rigorous Means.

83. In these Governments, the Legislature will apply itself more to prevent Crimes than to punish them, and should take more Care to instil Good Manners into the Minds of the Citizens, by proper Regulations, than to dispirit them by the Terror of corporal and capital Punishments.

84. In a Word, whatever is termed Punishment in the Law is, in Fact, nothing but Pain and Suffering.

85. Experience teaches us that, in those Countries where Punishments are mild, they operate with the same Efficacy upon the Minds of the Citizens as the most severe in other Places.

86. If a sensible Injury should accrue to a State from some popular Commotion, a violent Administration will be at once for a sudden Remedy, and instead of recurring to the ancient Laws, will inflict some terrible Punishment, in order to crush the growing Evil on the Spot. The Imagination of the People is affected at the Time of this greater Punishment, just as it would have been affected by the least; and when the Dread of this Punishment gradually wears off, it will be compelled to introduce a severer Punishment upon all Occasions.

87. The People ought not to be driven on by violent Methods, but we ought to make Use of the Means which Nature has given us, with the utmost Care and Caution, in order to conduct them to the End we propose.

88. Examine with Attention the Cause of all Licentiousness; and you will find that it proceeds from the Neglect of punishing Crimes, not from the Mildness of Punishments. . . .

Making Punishments Fit Their Crimes

209. Is the punishment of death really useful and necessary in a community for the preservation of peace and good order?

210. Proofs from fact demonstrate to us that the frequent use of capital punishment never mended the morals of a people. . . . The death of a citizen can only be useful and necessary in one case: which is, when, though he be deprived of liberty, yet he has such power by his connections as may enable him to raise disturbances dangerous to the public peace. This case can happen only when a People either loses or recovers their liberty, or in a

time of anarchy, when the disorders themselves hold the place of laws. But in a reign of peace and tranquillity, under a Government established with the united wishes of a whole People, in a state well fortified against external enemies and protected within by strong supports, that is, by its own internal strength and virtuous sentiments rooted in the minds of the citizens, and where the whole power is lodged in the hands of a Monarch: in such a state there can be no necessity for taking away the life of a citizen. . . .

220. A Punishment ought to be immediate, analogous to the Nature of the Crime and known to the Public.

221. The sooner the Punishment succeeds to the Commission of a Crime, the more useful and just it will be. Just; because it will spare the Malefactor the torturing and useless Anguish of Heart about the Uncertainty of his Destiny. Consequently the Decision of an Affair, in a Court of Judicature, ought to be finished in as little Time as possible. I have said before that Punishment immediately inflicted is most useful; the Reason is because the smaller the Interval of Time is which passes between the Crime and the Punishment, the more the Crime will be esteemed as a Motive to the Punishment, and the Punishment as an Effect of the Crime. Punishment must be certain and unavoidable.

222. The most certain Curb upon Crimes is not the Severity of the Punishment, but the absolute Conviction in the People that Delinquents will be inevitably punished.

223. The Certainty even of a small, but inevitable Punishment, will make a stronger impression on the Mind than, the Dread even of capital Punishment, connected with the Hopes of escaping it. As Punishments become more mild and moderate; Mercy and Pardon will be less necessary in Proportion, for the Laws themselves, at such a Time, are replete with the Spirit of Mercy. . . .

Making Laws That Are Understandable to Everyone

448. Each law ought to be written in so clear a style as to be perfectly intelligible to everyone, and, at the same time, with great conciseness. For this reason explanations or interpretations are undoubtedly to be added (as occasion shall require) to enable judges to perceive more readily the force as well as use of the law. . . .

449. But the utmost care and caution is to be observed in adding these explanations and interpretations, because they may sometimes rather darken than clear up the case; of which there

are many instances [in the existing laws].

450. When exceptions, limitations, and modifications are not absolutely necessary in a law, in that case it is better not to insert them; for such particular details generally produce still more details.

451. If the Legislator desires to give his reason for making any particular law, that reason ought to be good and worthy of the law. . . .

452. Laws ought not to be filled with subtile distinctions, to demonstrate the brilliance of the Legislator; they are made for people of moderate capacities as well as for those of genius. They are not a logical art, but the simple and plain reasoning of a father who takes care of his children and family.

453. Real candor and sincerity ought to be displayed in every part of the laws; and as they are made for the punishment of crimes, they ought consequently to include in themselves the greatest virtue and benevolence.

454. The style of the laws ought to be simple and concise: a plain direct expression will always be better understood than a studied one.

Napoleon's Invasion of Russia

By J.N. Westwood

The French emperor Napoleon's invasion of Russia in 1812 represents one of the most momentous occasions in Russian history. J.N. Westwood, honorary research fellow at the University of Birmingham in England, takes a close look at the events just prior to and during Napoleon's ill-fated campaign. Westwood begins by detailing a number of diplomatic and military missteps on the part of Czar Alexander I that helped set the stage for the French invasion. He then recounts the early months of the fighting, when the Russian army was repeatedly forced to retreat further into the Russian heartland. Westwood explains how the Russian military strategy of forcing Napoleon to chase their retreating armies stretched his resources too thin and ultimately caused his defeat, although not without the fiery sacrifice of the capital city of Moscow. Westwood claims that the unity shown by the Russian people in repulsing Napoleon's attack marked the starting point of a modern, cohesive Russian state.

When Russians talk of the war of 1812 they do not mean the war in which Washington was burned by the British, but the war in which, apparently, Moscow was burned by the Russians. This war between the French republican empire and the Russian tsarist empire was as remarkable a high-spot in the history of the latter as it was a low-spot in the history of Napoleon. For Russia, it was one of those rare moments in history when almost all people, serfs and lords, merchants and bureaucrats, put aside their enmities and realized that they were all Russians. Russia, sometimes called 'a state without a people', seemed to become, for a few precious months, one people, and never quite forgot the experience.

Five years previously, in 1807, Tsar Alexander I had made

J.N. Westwood, *Endurance and Endeavor: Russian History, 1812–1992.* Oxford: Oxford University Press, 1993. Copyright © 1993 by Oxford University Press. Reproduced by permission.

peace with Napoleon after losing more battles than he could afford and after becoming dissatisfied with his British allies. This peace was made at the celebrated meeting on a river raft at [the Polish town of] Tilsit, and entailed Russia's desertion of her ally Prussia, as well as her adherence to Napoleon's Continental System. Neither of these elements were approved by Alexander's subjects, and both he and the treaty became unpopular in Russian society. Betrayal of Prussia was regarded as dishonourable, while the Continental System, which meant the virtual cessation of Anglo-Russian trade, damaged many influential merchants and landowners, for Russia was already becoming a grain exporter, and north Russia traditionally supplied the British navy with its masts, rope, and sails.

True, the Treaty of Tilsit gave Alexander a free hand in Finland. He conquered that territory from the Swedes, and from 1809 until 1917 Finland was part of the Russian Empire, having a semi-independent status as a grand duchy. But this success did not mollify Alexander's critics at home. The Tsar, moreover, was himself becoming more and more wary of his new friend Napoleon, and in any case it is probably true that he had signed the treaty only because he had little choice and wanted time to gain strength for a final struggle against the French. For his part, Napoleon had several real and imagined grievances, and it soon became evident that the fine sentiments expressed at Tilsit had lost their meaning. Alexander prepared for the conflict by securing his flanks; he signed a treaty with Sweden and brought to a temporary close Russia's Danubian quarrel with Turkey. Napoleon prepared an invasion army and in June 1812 led it into eastern Poland, where he met Alexander's final peace envoy and sent him back with a negative answer.

Divisions of Command Among the Russians

Alexander had chosen to appoint himself commander-in-chief of the Russian armies in the field. But his advisers, remembering Alexander's disastrous intervention in 1805 which had given Napoleon his great victory at Austerlitz, persuaded him that he could do most good by going to Moscow and rallying the country. This left the minister of war, [Prince Mikhail] Barclay de Tolly, in command. Barclay was with the 1st Western Army, and the 2nd Western Army was under [Prince Peter] Bagration. The latter, senior to Barclay in military rank, was now subordinate to him by virtue of Barclay's ministerial rank. This situation was no doubt the basic cause of Bagration's hostility to his commander, expressed in occasional backbiting and intrigue.

Bagration was not a Russian, but a Georgian. He had learned the military trade fighting in what were already Russia's traditional battlegrounds. He had fought in the Caucasus against tribes resisting Russian encroachment, against the Turks on the south-western frontier, and against Sweden; Russia at the turn of the century was still expanding and meeting resistance as she did so. But Bagration's greatest glory, and one which probably made him feel superior to Barclay, was his outstanding record as a commander under the greatest of all Russian generals, [Prince Alexander] Suvorov, in the Italian and Swiss campaigns of 1799. Unlike Barclay, he had the reputation of a fiery and irrepressible warrior, but Barclay's contribution to the Russian army was far greater. Although no stranger to the battlefield, Barclay was more an organizer and thinker. In 1809, after service against the Turks, French and Swedes, and having attained the rank of General of Infantry, he became governor of the Finland he had just helped to conquer. Then in 1810 he became war minister and immediately began to strengthen the army; he wrote a manual of generalship, tightened army organization, built strongpoints, and doubled the size of the army. Like Bagration, Barclay was not a true Russian. His Scottish ancestors had been among the hundreds of skilled foreigners recruited by Russian rulers in the seventeenth century to serve as officers, technicians, or administrators. His family had settled at Riga in the Baltic provinces where the gentry, which was the ruling class and which provided the Russian Empire with many of its most notable administrators, was of German origin. Barclay could speak Russian only badly, although this was less of a handicap than it might seem, for Russia's upper gentry, the class which provided high officers and administrators, regarded Russian as the language of the common people. Top people spoke French, or if not French, German.

As Barclay's army slowly retreated eastwards from Vilna, it was joined by the 2nd Army retreating north-eastwards. Under Bagration's skilful leadership the 2nd Army had beaten off attacks by its French pursuers; thus Napoleon had failed in his attempt to prevent the union of the two main Russian armies. However, the Emperor of the French still hoped to achieve his original intention, to win an early decisive victory and thereby persuade Alexander to become his ally again. The French army was now approaching Smolensk, the westernmost city of Russia proper (as distinct from White Russia). Napoleon expected that the Russians would make a real stand here, but they did not. Barclay merely fought a very stiff rearguard action and after fighting withdrew from the city, having burned much of it.

In the circumstances the policy of retreating and avoiding a decisive battle was the only possible course. Although intensive recruiting was being carried out it would obviously be some time before Russia could convert her manpower superiority into military superiority. In the meantime, withdrawal forced Napoleon either to abandon his enterprise or to push on and thus extend his supply lines. The Russian military leaders were familiar with Wellington's strategy in the Peninsular campaign and realized it was well suited for Russia. Both Barclay and Alexander favoured a policy of retreat well before the 1812 campaign started. But neither Alexander nor Barclay had anticipated the strength of public opposition to their strategy. In St. Petersburg, Alexander was now at the lowest point of his popularity. He was blamed for making peace with Napoleon in 1807, a peace which had dishonoured Russia and had not finally saved the country from French attack, and he was blamed for retreating before Napoleon. Especially was he criticized for entrusting his armies to Barclay, a foreigner who did not understand how precious was every inch of Russian soil. After Smolensk had been relinquished without any attempt at what the St. Petersburg gentry considered a proper fight, Barclay's position became untenable. Alexander replaced him with General [Mikhail] Kutuzov. However, Barclay continued to serve under Kutuzov and his policy was not abandoned. Kutuzov, a hero of the Turkish wars and a self-styled pupil of Suvorov, was by this time too old for his job. He was sixty-seven, so fat that he could hardly walk, gluttonous, in ill-health and within eight months of death. But he had the virtue of being really Russian and of enjoying the complete confidence of public opinion. St. Petersburg society and the army officers would accept a retreat ordered by Kutuzov more readily than a retreat ordered by Barclay.

The Two Armies Face Off at Borodino

Meanwhile, Napoleon's Grande Armée was shambling across the Russian plains. It was a long, hot summer and thousands of soldiers succumbed to heat exhaustion before it was decided to march only at night. Discipline had degenerated. Supplies were short. Evidently, Napoleon's quartermasters had counted on scavenging to meet a large part of their daily requirements, but the retreating Russians left behind them little that was edible. Most

THE BURNING OF MOSCOW

Leo Tolstoy's epic novel War and Peace *centers around Napoleon's 1812 invasion of Russia and the effects it had on people from many different walks of life. One of the most memorable passages from this mammoth novel is the French army's entry into Moscow after their costly victory at Borodino. Tolstoy describes the manner in which the city had been abandoned and also openly challenges both the conventional notions that the Russians had either nobly sacrificed the city or that Napoleon had burned it out of spite upon his retreat.*

Though tattered, hungry, worn out, and reduced to a third of their original number, the French entered Moscow in good marching order. It was a weary and famished, but still a fighting and menacing army. But it remained an army only until its soldiers had dispersed into their different lodgings. As soon as the men of the various regiments began to disperse among the wealthy and deserted houses, the army was lost forever and there came into being something nondescript, neither citizens nor soldiers but what are known as marauders. . . .

Order after order was issued by the French commanders that day forbidding the men to disperse about the town, sternly forbidding any violence to the inhabitants or any looting, and announcing a roll call for that very evening. But despite all these measures the men, who had till then constituted an army, flowed all over the wealthy, deserted city with its comforts and plentiful supplies. As a hungry herd of cattle keeps well together when crossing a barren field, but gets out of hand and at once disperses uncontrollably as soon as it reaches rich pastures, so did the army disperse all over the wealthy city.

successes that were achieved in foraging were made by the more experienced French soldiers and this, added to the stingy paternalism of the French quartermasters when distributing supplies to the contingents of their allies, intensified the hostility of the non-French towards the French. The horses suffered even more

No residents were left in Moscow, and the soldiers—like water percolating through sand—spread irresistibly through the city in all directions from the Kremlin into which they had first marched. . . . Before they had had time to secure quarters the soldiers ran out into the streets to see the city and, hearing that everything had been abandoned, rushed to places where valuables were to be had for the taking. The officers followed to check the soldiers and were involuntarily drawn into doing the same. . . . When water is spilled on dry ground both the dry ground and the water disappear and mud results; and in the same way the entry of the famished army into the rich and deserted city resulted in fires and looting and the destruction of both the army and the wealthy city. . . .

However tempting it might be for the French to blame [Russian general Fyodor] Rostopchin's ferocity and for Russians to blame the scoundrel [Napoleon] Bonaparte, or later on to place an heroic torch in the hands of their own people, it is impossible not to see that there could be no such direct cause of the fire, for Moscow had to burn as every village, factory, or house must burn which is left by its owners and in which strangers are allowed to live and cook their porridge. Moscow was burned by its inhabitants, it is true, but by those who had abandoned it and not by those who remained in it. Moscow when occupied by the enemy did not remain intact like Berlin, Vienna, and other towns, simply because its inhabitants abandoned it and did not welcome the French with bread and salt, nor bring them the keys of the city.

Leo Tolstoy, *War and Peace*, translated by Aylmer Maude and George Gibian. New York: Norton, 1996, pp. 797–98.

from the supply shortage; many of them died from bad feeding, while others were themselves eaten by the soldiers. By the end of August many of the non-French troops were barefoot and their dust-caked uniforms little better than rags. Stragglers were numbered in the thousands; some of these were merely ill, for typhus and dysentery were spreading, but the majority were lagging behind voluntarily as a tactical preliminary to desertion and return home. Above all, water was short. The few good sources were usually tainted; occasionally a corpse or an amputated limb would be found in a spring or pond, deposited by the retreating Russians and perhaps recalling to the French soldiers Napoleon's utterance at Smolensk: 'how sweet smells the corpse of an enemy!'

Thus, despite the legend of the subsequent retreat from Moscow, it was the advance which caused most damage to the invaders. There was never any need for the Russian army to fight a set-piece battle, for Napoleon's forces were disintegrating day by day. However, Kutuzov was persuaded by public opinion, pressure from St. Petersburg, and the enthusiasm of his junior officers, to make one stand before Moscow. Thus occurred the battle of Borodino, a bloody contest which was strategically quite unnecessary but which was undertaken because to surrender Moscow without a fight was unthinkable. Although Peter the Great had made St. Petersburg the official capital, in the minds of Russians Moscow was still the traditional capital.

So in early September the Russian army stopped retreating and formed up in a defensive position on high ground near the village of Borodino, commanding the Smolensk-Moscow highway about seventy miles west of Moscow. The Russian forces numbered about 120,000, of whom 10,000 were hastily raised and half-trained militia sent out from Moscow. Barclay commanded the right wing and Bagration the left, with the Russian HQ in the centre. Wisely, Kutuzov passed the battle well out of cannon range, consuming cold chicken and champagne.

By this time the French army had shrunk from the half-million, with which it had begun the campaign, to a mere 130,000, and was already slightly inferior to the Russians in artillery. Napoleon decided to make a frontal attack on the opposing positions, probably fearing that otherwise the Russians would be tempted to retreat once more and deny him his long-desired victory. At the end of a hard-fought day, in which positions changed hands time after time, the Russians began a slow and orderly withdrawal. Although the French had won the battlefield they had not won the war, for they had not destroyed the opposing army. At Borodino, which Napoleon later adjudged his most expensive and terrible battle, the French suffered 30,000 casualties and the Russians 40,000 (some Russian historians give the French casualties as 68,000; some French historians give the Russian casualties as 60,000). Bagration was mortally wounded and died some weeks later at his country estate. Barclay, as though conscious of his recent unpopularity, deliberately exposed himself in the battle, emerging a hero and uninjured.

Why Napoleon failed to win his expected victory has remained a controversial issue, which some historians have avoided by claiming that Borodino was in fact a French victory. The fundamental fact is that the two armies were closely matched in strength and that Napoleon on this occasion was not able to win a smashing victory by taking advantage of poor generalship on the part of his opponent. There was one critical point in the battle when Napoleon could have turned the tide by committing his reserve, the Imperial Guard. However, despite the urgings of his generals, he did not do this and lost his chance. It has to be remembered, too, that Napoleon was unwell at the time. Moreover, the greater part of his army had been afflicted with chronic diarrhoea since entering Russia. This ailment was almost catastrophic for the cavalry, for reasons which do not need to be explained. One French cavalry lieutenant, writing to his wife about the battle, made this comment:

> I had again become afflicted by the diarrhoea which had so tortured me at Smolensk, and this day I experienced one of the worst imaginable agonies. For I wanted neither to leave my post nor dismount. I dare not say what I did to get rid of that which was tormenting me, but in the process I lost two handkerchiefs.

The Occupation and Burning of Moscow

A week after Borodino, Napoleon stood on a hill overlooking Moscow and, according to an eye-witness, was exceedingly contented. With Moscow in his grasp, he thought that Alexander would sue for peace, leaving him free to master the rest of the world. This showed a crucial misjudgement of Alexander and of Russia; shortly after this the Tsar told one of Napoleon's peace envoys that he would rather grow potatoes in Siberia than submit to the French Emperor.

By arrangement between the two sides, the Russian army left Moscow through one gate while the French entered it through another. Instead of crowds on the streets and a welcoming deputation, Napoleon met empty streets and silence. Almost all the population of Moscow had left, taking the most transportable valuables and food along with them. This was an unusual and unnerving experience for Napoleon, and so was the fire of Moscow which broke out shortly after the French arrived. Moscow was built of wood, except for a few mansions and public buildings. After four days of burning, during which a lack of fire pumps and the indiscipline of the occupying troops made fire-fighting ineffectual, about four-fifths of the city was uninhabitable. The difficulty in properly housing his troops, added to the anxiety about his supply lines, forced Napoleon to quit Moscow. He waited a few weeks, hoping that Alexander would negotiate, then gave the order to leave.

The Russians believed (and still do) that it was the French who set fire to Moscow to vent their frustration at finding so little to loot and to eat in the city. Among Russia's allies, the belief grew that the fire was an act of noble self-sacrifice on the part of the Russians, prepared to destroy what they valued most for the sake of defeating Napoleon. After the war the then governor of Moscow, [Count Fyodor] Rostopchin, found himself lionized in European society, which believed that it was he who had issued the order for the burning. Responding to this flattery, Rostopchin openly claimed that he had been responsible. However, on returning to Russia, where the fire of Moscow was regarded as a dastardly act, he found that his claim had made him very unpopular. Accordingly, he denied his complicity. The truth of the matter has never been reliably established, but the balance of probability suggests that it was indeed Rostopchin who was responsible. After all it was he who, before leaving Moscow, ignited his own house and ordered the removal of the city's fire pumps.

The French Retreat

The French left Moscow in mid-October, with the intention of returning west by a route more southerly than their approach road. The Russian army when it abandoned Moscow had not moved north, so as to cover St. Petersburg, but had chosen a far

better strategy, moving south and then west so as to threaten
Napoleon's communications and to have access to the food supplies of the fertile south. The French Emperor hoped that *en route*
he would meet the Russian army and win a victory which might
not be decisive but would at least camouflage his humiliation. On
leaving Moscow he ordered the blowing-up of the Kremlin, but
this order was not fulfilled, because the fuses were wet. Another
unfulfilled order forbade officers and men to burden themselves
with loot; when the *Grande Armée* left Moscow it resembled more
a caravan of carpet traders than an army. Some officers had found
Russian carts and carriages which they loaded with all kinds of
furniture, pictures, and wines.

A week after leaving Moscow there was a heavy engagement
with Kutuzov, resulting in both sides retiring to lick their
wounds. Napoleon was forced to retreat along the road by which
he had advanced, via Borodino with its still-unburied corpses.
Although Kutuzov, to the disgust of the British general who was
attached to his headquarters, avoided close engagements with his
retreating opponent, Cossacks and partisans were quick to bring
a bestial death to stragglers or lagging detachments. The first
snow fell in the first week of November. Neither the cavalry nor
the artillery had been supplied with winter horseshoes and it was
not long before most of the army's horses disappeared. Without
horse transport the supply situation became catastrophic and
more men dropped out by the roadside. At the end of November the Russians were outmanoeuvred for a few precious hours,
enabling most of the army to cross the river Berezina, but thousands of stragglers and camp followers were killed at this point,
drowned, trampled underfoot by their comrades, or massacred by
Russian guns. It was not until early December that the really cold
weather set in. Contrary to the impression given by Napoleon's
apologists, there was no early winter that year and the French
were not defeated by the cold. The cold, when it came, only finished the job. In the final count, probably four-fifths of the half
million men who followed Napoleon into Russia were lost, and
only a few of these died from cold.

After the crossing of the Berezina and the onset of below-zero
temperatures, Napoleon left the remains of his army and went
on ahead back to France. 1812 had not been a good year for him.
For Alexander and for Russia, on the other hand, 1812 had been
a great year. It was not simply a military triumph; it seemed to be

a demonstration of moral strength. Earlier, the government had feared that invasion would spark off widespread peasant revolts, but this had not happened and the people and government had, for once, stood shoulder to shoulder. Thus the Russians were right to call this campaign the Patriotic War, and there is some justification for choosing 1812 as the starting point for a history of modern Russia.

THE HISTORY OF NATIONS
Chapter 3

Revolutionary Times

The Emancipation Manifesto

By Alexander II

The institution of serfdom had been the unchallenged basis of the Russian agricultural system since the early seventeenth century (and had existed to a lesser extent for centuries prior to that). Under this system, peasants were bound together with the land on which they worked and could be sold along with that land by their landlord. Though not technically slavery, this system made the peasantry entirely dependent on the landowning classes and subjected them to frequent abuses. By 1861, a substantial outcry had arisen among the more progressive elements of the Russian government and intelligentsia for the abolition of serfdom. Czar Alexander II responded to this sentiment by issuing the Emancipation Manifesto on March 3, 1861, which freed the serfs from their obligations to their landowners. Although it stopped well short of granting the peasantry equal status in society, this proclamation began a process of radical transformation of Russia and its economy that lasted for the remaining twenty years of Alexander II's reign.

By the Grace of God We [like many other "divine-right" monarchs, the Russian tsars used the "royal we" when referring to themselves], Alexander II, Emperor and Autocrat of All Russia, King of Poland, Grand Duke of Finland, etc., make known to all our faithful subjects:

Called by Divine Providence and by the sacred right of inheritance to the throne of Our Russian ancestors, We vowed in Our heart to respond to the mission which is entrusted to Us and to surround with Our affection and Our Imperial solicitude all Our faithful subjects of every rank and condition, from the soldier who nobly defends the country to the humble artisan who works in industry; from the career official of the state to the plowman who tills the soil.

Examining the condition of classes and professions compris-

Alexander II, "The Emancipation Manifesto, March 3, 1861," *Imperial Russia: A Source Book, 1700–1917*, edited by Basil Dmytryshyn. New York: Holt, Rinehart and Winston, 1967.

ing the state, We became convinced that the present state legislation favors the upper and middle classes, defines their obligations, rights, and privileges, but does not equally favor the serfs, so designated because in part from old laws and in part from custom they have been hereditarily subjected to the authority of landowners, who in turn were obligated to provide for their well being. Rights of nobles have been hitherto very broad and legally ill defined, because they stem from tradition, custom, and the good will of the noblemen. In most cases this has led to the establishment of good patriarchal relations based on the sincere, just concern and benevolence on the part of the nobles, and on affectionate submission on the part of the peasants. Because of the decline of the simplicity of morals, because of an increase in the diversity of relations, because of the weakening of the direct paternal attitude of nobles toward the peasants, and because noble rights fell sometimes into the hands of people exclusively concerned with their personal interests, good relations weakened. The way was opened for an arbitrariness burdensome for the peasants and detrimental to their welfare, causing them to be indifferent to the improvement of their own existence.

These facts had already attracted the attention of Our predecessors of glorious memory, and they had adopted measures aimed at improving the conditions of the peasants; but these measures were ineffective, partly because they depended on the free, generous action of nobles, and partly because they affected only some localities, by virtue of special circumstances or as an experiment. Thus Alexander I issued a decree on free agriculturists, and the late Emperor Nicholas, Our beloved father, promulgated one dealing with the serfs. In the Western *gubernias* [administrative units, somewhat akin to states in the United States], inventory regulations determine the peasant land allotments and their obligations. But decrees on free agriculturists and serfs have been carried out on a limited scale only.

We thus became convinced that the problem of improving the condition of serfs was a sacred inheritance bequeathed to Us by Our predecessors, a mission which, in the course of events, Divine Providence has called upon Us to fulfill.

We have begun this task by expressing Our confidence toward the Russian nobility, which has proven on so many occasions its devotion to the Throne, and its readiness to make sacrifices for the welfare of the country.

We have left to the nobles themselves, in accordance with their own wishes, the task of preparing proposals for the new organization of peasant life—proposals that would limit their rights over the peasants, and the realization of which would inflict on them [the nobles] some material losses. Our confidence was justified. Through members of the *gubernia* committees, who had the trust of the nobles' associations, the nobility voluntarily renounced its right to own serfs. These committees, after collecting the necessary data, have formulated proposals on a new arrangement for serfs and their relationship with the nobles.

These proposals were diverse, because of the nature of the problem. They have been compared, collated, systematized, rectified and finalized in the main committee instituted for that purpose; and these new arrangements dealing with the peasants and domestics of the nobility have been examined in the Governing Council.

Having invoked Divine assistance, We have resolved to execute this task.

The New Rights of the Peasantry

On the basis of the above mentioned new arrangements, the serfs will receive in time the full rights of free rural inhabitants.

The nobles, while retaining their property rights on all the lands belonging to them, grant the peasants perpetual use of their domicile in return for a specified obligation; and, to assure their livelihood as well as to guarantee fulfillment of their obligations toward the government, [the nobles] grant them a portion of arable land fixed by the said arrangements, as well as other property.

While enjoying these land allotments, the peasants are obliged, in return, to fulfill obligations to the noblemen fixed by the same arrangements. In this state, which is temporary, the peasants are temporarily bound.

At the same time, they are granted the right to purchase their domicile, and, with the consent of the nobles, they may acquire in full ownership the arable lands and other properties which are allotted them for permanent use. Following such acquisition of full ownership of land, the peasants will be freed from their obligations to the nobles for the land thus purchased and will become free peasant landowners.

A special decree dealing with domestics will establish a temporary status for them, adapted to their occupations and their needs. At the end of two years from the day of the promulgation of this decree, they shall receive full freedom and some temporary immunities.

In accordance with the fundamental principles of these arrangements, the future organization of peasants and domestics will be determined, the order of general peasant administration will be established, and the rights given to the peasants and to the domestics will be spelled out in detail, as will the obligations imposed on them toward the government and the nobles.

Although these arrangements, general as well as local, and the special supplementary rules affecting some particular localities, estates of petty nobles, and peasants working in factories and enterprises of the nobles, have been as far as possible adapted to economic necessities and local customs; nevertheless, to preserve the existing order where it presents reciprocal advantages, we leave it to the nobles to reach a friendly understanding with the peasants and to reach agreements on the extent of the land allotment and the obligations stemming from it, observing, at the same time, the established rules to guarantee the inviolability of such agreements.

This new arrangement, because of its complexity, cannot be put into effect immediately; a time of not less than two years is necessary. During this period, to avoid all misunderstanding and to protect public and private interests, the order actually existing on the estates of nobles should be maintained until the new order shall become effective.

Towards that end, We have deemed it advisable:

1. To establish in each *gubernia* a special Office of Peasant Affairs, which will be entrusted with the affairs of the peasant communes established on the estates of the nobility.

2. To appoint in every district justices of the peace to solve all misunderstandings and disputes which may arise from the new arrangement, and to organize from these justices district assemblies.

3. To organize Peace Offices on the estates of the nobles, leaving the village communes as they are, and to open volost offices in the large villages and unite small village communes under one volost office.

4. To formulate, verify, and confirm in each village commune or estate a charter which would enumerate, on the basis of local conditions, the amount of land alloted to the peasants for per-

manent use, and the scope of their obligations to the nobleman for the land as well as for other advantages which are granted.

5. To put these charters into practice as they are gradually approved on each estate, and to put them into effect everywhere within two years from the date of publication of this manifesto.

6. Until that time, peasants and domestics must be obedient towards their nobles, and scrupulously fulfill their former obligations.

7. The nobles will continue to keep order on their estates, with the right of jurisdiction and of police, until the organization of volost and of volost courts.

Aware of the unavoidable difficulties of this reform, We place Our confidence above all in the graciousness of Divine Providence, which watches over Russia.

We also rely upon the zealous devotion of Our nobility, to whom We express Our gratitude and that of the entire country as well, for the unselfish support it has given to the realization of Our designs. Russia will not forget that the nobility, motivated by its respect for the dignity of man and its Christian love of its neighbor, has voluntarily renounced serfdom, and has laid the foundation of a new economic future for the peasants. We also expect that it will continue to express further concern for the realization of the new arrangement in a spirit of peace and benevolence, and that each nobleman will realize, on his estate, the great civic act of the entire group by organizing the lives of his peasants and his domestics on mutually advantageous terms, thereby setting for the rural population a good example of a punctual and conscientious execution of state regulations.

The examples of the generous concern of the nobles for the welfare of peasants, and the gratitude of the latter for that concern, give Us the hope that a mutual understanding will solve most of the difficulties, which in some cases will be inevitable during the application of general rules to the diverse conditions on some estates, and that thereby the transition from the old order to the new will be facilitated, and that in the future mutual confidence will be strengthened, and a good understanding, and a unanimous tendency towards the general good will evolve.

To facilitate the realization of these agreements between the nobles and the peasants, by which the latter may acquire in full ownership their domicile and their land, the government will lend assistance, under special regulations, by means of loans or transfer of debts encumbering an estate.

We rely upon the common sense of Our people. When the government advanced the idea of abolishing serfdom, there developed a partial misunderstanding among the unprepared peasants. Some were concerned about freedom and disconcerned about obligations. But, generally, the common sense of the country has not wavered, because it has realized that every individual who enjoys freely the benefits of society owes it in return certain positive obligations; according to Christian law every individual is subject to higher authority (Romans, chap. xiii., 1); everyone must fulfill his obligations, and, above all, pay tribute, dues, respect, and honor (Ibid., chap. xiii., 7). What legally belongs to nobles cannot be taken away from them without adequate compensation, or through their voluntary concession; it would be contrary to all justice to use the land of the nobles without assuming responsibility for it.

And now We confidently expect that the freed serfs, on the eve of a new future which is opening to them, will appreciate and recognize the considerable sacrifices which the nobility has made on their behalf.

They should understand that by acquiring property and greater freedom to dispose of their possessions, they have an obligation to society and to themselves to live up to the letter of the new law by a loyal and judicious use of the rights which are now granted to them. However beneficial a law may be, it cannot make people happy if they do not themselves organize their happiness under protection of the law. Abundance is acquired only through hard work, wise use of strength and resources, strict economy, and above all, through an honest God-fearing life.

The authorities who prepared the new way of life for the peasants and who will be responsible for its inauguration will have to see that this task is accomplished with calmness and regularity, taking the timing into account in order not to divert the attention of cultivators away from their agricultural work. Let them zealously work the soil and harvest its fruits so that they will have a full granary of seeds to return to the soil which will be theirs.

And now, Orthodox people, make the sign of the cross, and join with Us to invoke God's blessing upon your free labor, the sure pledge of your personal well being and the public prosperity.

Given at St. Petersburg, March 3, the year of Grace 1861, and the seventh of Our reign.

Alexander

Alexander II: The Ambiguous Czar

By W.E. Mosse

Although Alexander II's reign from 1855 to 1881 is often cited as one of the most liberal periods in Russian history—largely because of the end of serfdom—the lasting effects of Alexander's attempts at reform were often diminished either by his own lack of genuine liberal sentiment or by the strong opposition that he faced. W.E. Mosse, professor emeritus of European history at the University of East Anglia in Norwich, England, argues that Alexander II was, despite a number of good intentions, ultimately a failure both as a liberal and as an autocrat. Mosse argues that Alexander II's personality prevented him from being as genuinely liberal as his more reform-minded friends and advisers wanted him to be. Furthermore, he argues that Alexander's inability to exert his authority when he needed to caused him problems among the more scheming and reactionary members of his court, including his son, the future czar Alexander III. Mosse concludes that Alexander achieved some noble and noteworthy deeds during his reign, but that he ultimately disappointed the expectations of both liberals and conservatives in Russia.

T he circumstances of Alexander's death underline his tragic personal failure. Except at brief moments during the liberation struggle [i.e., the national debate over ending serfdom], and later during the Polish insurrection [of 1863], he had never been a popular ruler. His personality—however charming in an intimate circle, and particularly in the company of children—was reserved and haughty. The pleasantness and suavity of his manner was broken all too easily by outbursts of temper. Both the Tsar's private life and that of his entourage brought the dynasty reproach. Nor did Alexander possess many of the qualities indispensable to a successful ruler. From his childhood he had tried to evade difficulties, to find an easy escape

W.E. Mosse, *Alexander II and the Modernization of Russia*. London: I.B. Taurius & Co. Ltd., 1992. Copyright © 1992 by W.E. Mosse. Reproduced by permission.

from complex situations. What had been a venial sin in the pupil of [Alexander's tutor Karl] Merder and [Russian intellectual Vasily] Zhukovsky, became a serious fault in the autocratic Emperor of All the Russias. A sense of duty instilled by his father had prevented the Tsar from becoming *Alexandre le Bien Aimé* [Alexander the Well-Loved]—another Louis XV—but the tenacity and concern for the public welfare shown in the struggle for liberation later evaporated. A sense of insecurity and apprehension made Alexander the 'prisoner' first of [head of the secret police Pyotr] Shuvalov and [governor-general of St. Petersburg Fyodor] Trepov, later of [interior minister Mikhail] Loris-Melikov. His ill-starred infatuation for Catherine Dolgoruky [a young aristocrat with whom Alexander had a lengthy affair] became a scandal to the state which undermined his own authority and destroyed the respect of his subjects.

Alexander's personal failings aggravated his already difficult task of reconciling the increase of freedom with the preservation of imperial authority. Peter the Great, Nicholas I, and [Vladimir] Lenin did not experience this conflict: they were autocrats who knew not the meaning of liberty. Alexander, on the other hand, although not a liberal himself, was born into an age when liberalism was in the ascendant. The teachings of Zhukovsky, reaction against the régime of Nicholas [Alexander's father and predecessor], popular expectations and demands, combined with the impetuosity of the Grand-Duke Constantine [Alexander's brother and a relative liberal], carried him into concessions to the liberal *Zeitgeist* ["spirit of the age"] against his inclination. These concessions, half-hearted though they were, produced the general ferment of opinion inseparable from a Russian 'thaw'. Alexander's 'mildness' led to a general loosening of the reins of government. The Russian public, unprepared for freedom, indulged in extravagant criticism which threatened to undermine the authority of the Tsar and his government. By 1861, with student and peasant unrest, subversion in the army, incipient rebellion in Poland, and incendiarism in the capital, it appeared that Russia was slipping into chaos; liberty was degenerating into licence.

Yet Alexander was a pupil of Nicholas much more than a pupil of Zhukovsky. He was at heart a believer in order, authority, and autocracy. In his view everything at home must come from above and be carefully controlled and supervised; abroad, there must be order, authority, and a respect for existing rights and obligations. With a disposition in itself autocratic, Alexander naturally turned to reaction—some would say the defence of his legitimate authority—when subversive movements made their appearance.

Alexander II as Failed Autocrat

It was, however, precisely as an autocrat that Alexander was the greatest failure. Throughout his reign order was not effectively maintained, authority never secure. Characteristically, he flouted the wishes of his parents by his marriage to the Princess Mary. Again, in his private and family life he failed to set an example of order. Leading an irregular life himself he was unable to rebuke others—in this way very much unlike his father. The absence of a firm paternal or fraternal authority in the imperial family became notorious. Nor could the Emperor's entourage—from the gambler Sasha Adlerberg to Catherine's stock-jobbing friends—inspire much respect. The Tsarevich [Alexander's son, the future tsar Alexander III] consistently opposed Alexander in his later years, and did not scruple to criticize his father's private and public conduct. The Tsar was never master in his own house. A court rent by factions and intrigues can be no secure basis of authority for an absolute government in troubled times.

The disorder spread outwards from the centre. There was no unity in the government. Ministers of divergent views fought and intrigued against each other; important political decisions were made according to the constellation of the moment. The Emperor, it was said, gave his voice to whoever had spoken to him last. Alexander had no [Cardinal] Richelieu [noted adviser to French King Louis XII] or [German chancellor Otto von] Bismarck, but only a [foreign minister Alexander] Gorchakov. Shuvalov, his ablest Minister, fell victim to an intrigue engineered by the Princess Catherine [Dolgoruky]. Loris's power was based on a precarious coalition brought about by an emergency. If there was no cohesion in the government in distant St. Petersburg, there could be no order among its local agents scattered over the vast empire. Alexander could exercise effective control neither over the powerful proconsuls [regional government officials] in Tiflis and Tashkent [major cities in Georgia and Central Asia, respectively], nor yet over [Mikhail] Katkov [a powerful conservative newspaper editor], the eloquent demagogue, ambitious liars like [Russian ambassador to the Ottoman Empire Nikolai] Ignatiev, or even a windy adventurer like [military commander Mikhail] Cherniaev. Acts of defiance and insubordination enough to cause Nicholas I to turn in his grave were committed with impunity every day. Alexander proved himself not only a disappointing 'liberal'— if indeed that term can be applied to him—but, more seriously, an inefficient autocrat. While he would not give his educated subjects the constitution for which they clamoured, he failed to use to advantage the autocratic powers which he felt impelled to retain. He merely succeeded in proving that a pseudo-liberal autocrat is an unhappy hybrid unlikely to achieve political success. The narrow principles of Nicholas I or Alexander III, for whom Alexander's problems did not exist, proved—on a short-term view—more effective than the unsuccessful attempt to combine authority and freedom.

Yet Alexander's policy of combining reform with control from above was not, in itself, unsound. He was right in initiating long-overdue reforms; one cannot blame him for trying to carry them into effect through the existing machinery of government. Such a policy, however, was likely to be opposed from two different directions. Reform could not but hurt the vested interests of landowners, merchants, and officials; refusal to admit the participation of the public in government could not but antagonize the liberals. Alexander's reign combined reform and repression; the combination pleased no important section of the population. Conservatives would have preferred less reform and more control; the liberals the opposite. Alexander, working for the public welfare according to his lights, succeeded in antagonizing both groups at the same time. A gulf began to open between the Russian government and the public never again to be closed. Loris's administration—so nearly successful yet, in the event, so tragically abortive—was the last attempt of tsarism to come to terms with liberal Russian opinion. Could Loris have succeeded in his policy of organic institutional development? Could even he have successfully counteracted the effects of the Tsar's unpopular liaison and Catherine's probable coronation? It seems more than likely that, had Alexander once again escaped the assassin, he would have fallen to a peaceful palace 'revolution' and abdicated in favour of his son. The end would still have been Alexander III, [Alexander's arch-conservative adviser Konstantin] Pobedonostsev, and Katkov.

Did Alexander's Reforms Face Insurmountable Obstacles?

If the seeds of Alexander's tragedy lay in his personal character and the resulting inability to combine freedom and authority, it is true that unfavourable circumstances made his difficulties almost insuperable. The Tsar was fated to preside over one of the recurring and normally abortive 'liberal' interludes in the history of Russia. After the reign of Nicholas, as after those of Peter I, Paul I, or [Josef] Stalin, a 'thaw' had become an imperative necessity. The new government must throw off the odium accumulated by the preceding despotism. Yet, as soon as Alexander lifted the tight lid of repression, the compressed steam began to escape with powerful effect. Conditions developed enough to frighten even a ruler less naturally insecure than Alexander. Not for nothing did the great [French statesman Alexis de] Tocqueville observe that the most dangerous moment for a bad government usually comes when it begins to reform itself. By 1862 the dangers of the 'thaw' were clearly apparent to all, and repression, never completely abandoned, again came into its own.

Alexander has been criticized for 'abandoning' his earlier course. Yet what could the Emperor have done? The establishment of a democratic form of freedom was surely out of the question in the conditions of nineteenth-century Russia. Oligarchic rule [government by a small, powerful élite], as demanded by the disgruntled gentry? Complete freedom for the radical press and its revolutionary supporters? Could the Poles be given their freedom—within the boundaries of 1772 which they claimed? If not, what course was left but repression once Wielopolski's policy [Alexander Wielopolski, a Polish nobleman, advocated limited autonomy for Poland, but his strategy was rejected by both Polish and Russian nationalists.] had failed? Real freedom in the Russian empire was an impossibility. So, regrettably from Alexander's point of view, was a policy of effective repression—except in Poland and Lithuania after the suppression of the insurrection [in 1863]. Alexander was not by nature a 'stern reactionary' like his father or his son. His hankering after popularity sometimes introduced an element of weakness and hesitation into a repressive system. In any case, the zemstvos [local assemblies that were empowered by Alexander II to help administer the country] and the new courts, supported by the weight of public opinion, made 'black repression' of the type [Siberian governor-general Nikolai] Muraviev and [minister of justice Vladimir] Panin might have favoured a practical impossibility. Finally, except for a time under Shuvalov, the police organization was weak and inefficient. The weapons of the modern totalitarian state were not at the Tsar's disposal. Complete repression was no more practicable than complete freedom. Only a compromise policy was possible.

It is here that the Tsar's course is open to criticism. The compromise to which, under pressure, he consented at the end of his reign might have been greeted with acclamation if it had followed the introduction of the zemstvo and judicial reforms. Instead, frightened by Karakozov's attempt [a failed assassination attempt by a former university student named Dmitry Karakosov in 1866], the Tsar, rather than listen to [his reform-minded interior minister Pyotr] Valuiev and the Grand-Duke Constantine, handed over power to Shuvalov and Trepov. It was a fateful decision. The wiser course *might*, if adopted, have led Russia along the road of peaceful constitutional development.

Could Alexander have prevented the Turkish War which finally helped to destroy his system? The conclusion would appear to be that the pressure for warlike action, although powerful, was not irresistible. The Tsar—half-unwillingly—allowed himself to be dragged along the road which might lead to Constantinople. Public opinion did not force him into war; when he made his decision the Pan-Slav agitation [Following the brutal repression of an uprising by the Turks in Bulgaria—a part of the Ottoman Empire at the time—many Russians clamored for a war with the Turks on the basis that Bulgarians were fellow Slavs.] had passed its peak. What Alexander hoped for—perhaps understandably—was a military walk-over to bolster up his shaken régime. A century-old ambition of the Russian people might be realized. Osman Pasha's unexpected resistance at Plevna upset the Russian plans. What might have been a brilliant Russian triumph became a disappointing compromise. Circumstances, as well as the flaws in his personal character, were responsible for the failures of Alexander's reign.

Alexander II's Legacy

And yet even though Alexander cannot be termed a successful ruler, the results of his reign challenge comparison with the more spectacular achievements of Peter the Great and Lenin. The policy of 'modernization' applied to almost every sphere of Russian life made Alexander one of Russia's great 'westernizers'. In his reign, and in no small degree as the result of official policy, the Russian empire passed from the semi-feudal to the early capitalist stage of its development. Far-reaching social changes resulted. In a different sphere, the reforms of Alexander II helped to assure Russia's survival as a major power after her collapse in the Crimean War [in 1856]. Under him, the bounds of the empire were enlarged. Finland and Bulgaria were set on the road to nationhood, the economic and social structure of Poland was transformed. Finally, although Alexander was not himself a distinguished patron of the arts, it was in his reign that [authors Ivan] Turgeniev, [Fyodor] Dostoevsky and [Leo] Tolstoy, [and composers Modest] Mussorgsky, [Pyotr] Chaikovsky and [Nikolai] Rimsky-Korsakov, wrote and composed their masterpieces. The foundations were being laid for Russia's cultural 'conquests'.

In fact, there was more than a little truth in the remarks made by one French diplomat to another during Alexander's funeral:

"Have a good look at this martyr. He was a great tsar and deserved a kinder fate. . . . His was not a great intellect, but he had a generous soul, very upright and very lofty. He loved his people and his solicitude for the humble and the suffering was unbounded. . . . Remember the reforms he introduced. Peter the Great was the author of none more deeply reaching, and he put into them less of his heart. . . . Think of all the resistance he had to overcome to abolish serfdom and restore the foundation of rural economy. Think that thirty million men owe their affranchisement to him. . . . And his administrative reforms! He aimed at nothing less than the destruction of the arbitrary bureaucracy and social privilege. In the judicial sphere he established equality before the law, assured the independence of the magistrates, abolished corporal punishment, instituted the jury. And this was done by the immediate successor of the despot Nicholas I! . . . In foreign politics his work is on the same scale. He followed the line taken by Catherine II on the Black Sea; he wiped out the humiliations of the Treaty of Paris [which ended the Crimean War in 1856]; he brought the eagles of Muscovy to the shores of the Propontis [the Sea of Marmara, a traditional boundary between Europe and Asia, now located in Turkey], the very walls of Constantinople; he delivered the Bulgar; he established Russian dominion in the heart of Central Asia. . . . Finally, on the morning of his death, he was working on a reform which would have surpassed all the others, would have launched Russia irrevocably along the track of the modern world: the granting of a parliamentary charter. . . . And the Nihilists have killed him! [Alexander II was assassinated in March 1881 by members of a revolutionary group known as "the People's Will."] . . . But mark the odd coincidence of history, the strange irony of things. Lincoln, the emancipator of the American negroes, was also assassinated. Now, it was the deliverance of the negroes which brought in its train, on the other side of the world, the affranchisement of the *moujiks* [Russian peasants]. Alexander did not intend that Russia should remain the only serf-holding nation in the Christian world [in fact, serfdom in Russia ended before slavery was abolished in the United States]. . . . Oh, a liberator's is a dangerous job!"

The October Manifesto

By Nicholas II

*The reign of Alexander III (1881–1894) and the first decade of
Nicholas II's reign were notable for the extent to which they backtracked
from the liberalizing reforms that had been made earlier in the nineteenth
century. Following the assassination of Alexander II by anarchists in
1881, his successor Alexander III blamed the unrest in the country predominantly on the loosening of the reins of power that had occurred during his father's tenure as czar and instituted a number of policies designed to restore the unquestioned power of the monarchy. Nicholas II
continued this practice of severe reaction against any opposition elements
in Russian society, but the harshness of his reprisals, coupled with a general downturn in Russia's economic and military fortunes, ultimately led
to a mass uprising in 1905. Workers, peasants, members of ethnic minorities, reformist intellectuals, and disgruntled soldiers clamored for a
more representative constitutional government and threatened widespread
violence. Although the actual fighting was fairly limited, Nicholas II succumbed to the pressure of the revolutionaries and announced on October
30, 1905, the formation of a democratically elected parliament (the
Duma) to help govern Russia. The October Manifesto was the end of
absolute monarchy in Russia and the monarchy itself would cease to exist twelve years later after the larger, successful Bolshevik Revolution.*

By the grace of God, We Nicholas II, Emperor and Autocrat of all Russia, Tsar of Poland, Grand Duke of Finland, etc.

Make known to all Our loyal subjects: Rioting and disturbances in the capitals and in many localities of Our Empire fill
Our heart with great and heavy grief. The well-being of the
Russian Sovereign is inseparable from the national well-being;
and the national sorrow is His sorrow. The disturbances which

Nicholas II, "Concessions of Nicholas II in the Revolution of 1905," *Imperial Russia: A Source Book, 1700–1917*, edited by Basil Dmytryshyn. New York: Holt, Rinehart and Winston, 1967.

have appeared may cause a grave national tension that may endanger the integrity and unity of Our State.

By the great vow of Tsarist service We are obligated to use every resource of wisdom and Our authority to bring a speedy end to an unrest dangerous to Our State. We have [already] ordered the responsible authorities to take measures to terminate direct manifestations of disorder, lawlessness, and violence, and to protect peaceful people who quietly seek to fulfill the duties incumbent upon them. To successfully fulfill general measures which We have designed for the pacification of State life, We feel it is essential to coordinate the activity of the higher government.

We impose upon the government the duty to execute Our inflexible will:

1. To grant the population the inviolable foundations of civic freedom based on the principles of genuine personal inviolability, freedom of conscience, speech, assemblies and associations.

2. Without postponing the scheduled elections to the State Duma [the legislative body of tsarist Russia], to admit in the participation of the Duma insofar as possible in the short time that remains before its scheduled meeting all those classes of the population which presently are completely deprived of voting rights, and to leave further development of general elective law to the future legislative order;

3. To establish as an unbreakable rule that no law shall become effective without the confirmation by the State Duma, and that the elected representatives of the people shall be guaranteed an opportunity of real participation in the supervision of the legality of the acts by authorities whom We shall appoint.

We summon all loyal sons of Russia to remember their duties towards their country, to assist in terminating this unprecedented unrest, and together with Us to make every effort to restore peace and tranquility in Our native land.

Given in Peterhof, October 30, the year of Our Lord 1905, and eleventh of Our reign.

Nicholas

The Two Revolutions of 1917

By Geoffrey Hosking

The czarist period of Russian history ended abruptly in February 1917 when Nicholas II abdicated and the Provisional Government, made up of representatives of several different revolutionary groups, took over power. Over the course of the next eight months, the power of the Provisional Government was increasingly challenged by the Bolsheviks, who believed that it stopped short of accomplishing a genuine Communist revolution. Geoffrey Hosking, professor of history at the School of Slavonic and Eastern European Studies at the University of London, looks at the struggle for power that took place between the two revolutions of 1917. He begins by comparing the relative strengths and weaknesses of the Provisional Government and the Bolsheviks as of February 1917 and discusses the ways in which both attempted to harness the sense of dissatisfaction among the peasants, the urban working class, and the military. Next he chronicles the series of events that led to the overthrow of Alexander Kerensky's government by Lenin and the Bolsheviks. The Bolsheviks' success in ousting Kerensky and the Provisional Government led to the establishment of the Soviet Union and the eventual dominance of the Bolshevik model of communism for the next seven decades.

I t was a mark of the abruptness of political change in Russia that when the monarchy fell [in 1917], what replaced it was not one regime, but two. On the one hand, the politicians surviving from the Duma [the parliamentary body during the last years of the tsars] established a Provisional Government, in which the principal parties were at first the Kadets [the Constitutional Democratic Party], later the Mensheviks [the non-Bolshevik Communist minority] and Socialist Revolutionaries. It was called 'provisional' because it was to exercise power only until a Constituent Assembly could be convened, elected by all the people.

Geoffrey Hosking, *The First Socialist Society: A History of the Soviet Union from Within.* Cambridge, MA: Harvard University Press, 1993. Copyright © 1993 by Geoffrey Hosking. Reproduced by permission of the publisher.

On the other hand, the workers of Petrograd (as St Petersburg was now called) hastened to revive their memories of the days of freedom in 1905 by re-establishing the Petrograd Soviet. They were joined by the soldiers of the capital city's garrison, active participants in the revolution for the first time, and their joint tribune was known as the Soviet of Workers' and Soldiers' Deputies.

But government and soviet refrained from trying to oust each other—for good reason. The Provisional Government, which began by abolishing the tsarist police and security services, had no effective power of coercion, and therefore had to tolerate the soviets as expressions of the popular will, at least in the big cities. As the minister of war, [Alexander] Guchkov, said, 'The Provisional Government does not possess any real power; and its directives are carried out only to the extent that it is permitted by the Soviet of Workers' and Soldiers' Deputies, which enjoys all the essential elements of real power, since the troops, the railroads, the post and telegraph are all in its hands.' The leaders of the soviets, for their part, recognized that the Provisional Government contained experienced politicians, that it could command the loyalty of the army officers, reduce the chances of counterrevolution, and gain international recognition. The theoretically inclined among them regarded the Provisional Government as a 'bourgeois' [that is, a remnant of the old order] institution, which the soviets would 'supervise', on the workers' behalf, until such time as the socialist revolution became possible.

The Provisional Government was from the start in a very difficult, arguably an untenable position. It had not been brought to power by election, but nor could it claim direct descent from the old imperial government or the Duma. Prince [Georgy] Lvov, its first prime minister, proclaimed that it had been created by the 'unanimous revolutionary enthusiasm of the people'. That was to prove a shaky basis, especially since the new government found itself in a situation where it was unable to carry out the reforms that the 'people' were expecting. The fundamental difficulty was the war. The peasants might be crying out for a redistribution of the land in their favour, but could such a complex operation be carried out equitably without first a thorough land survey, and while millions of peasant-soldiers, with an impeccable claim to their own shares, were far away from the village at the front, and unable to take part in the share-out? The workers began to organize themselves to exercise a greater share in the running of factories and enterprises, but was it responsible to attempt such intricate reorganization in the middle of keeping up industrial output for the war effort? Could the supplies problems, which had brought the tsarist government down, be solved while the war was on? Most important of all, was the soldiers' demand to elect their own committees and to take part in the running of their units compatible with the discipline needed at the front line?

While the war continued, none of these questions could be solved without serious and damaging political conflict. And yet, to stop the war proved almost impossible. . . . The leaders of the Petrograd Soviet tried to organize a conference of socialists from all the combatant states, to put pressure on their governments to negotiate a peace 'without annexations or indemnities'. The British and French governments, however, put paid to this plan by refusing to allow representatives from their parliaments to attend. The alternative would have been to sign a separate peace with Germany and Austria-Hungary, but this would have amounted to a capitulation, and not until the Provisional Government was in its final days did any of its members recommend such a desperate step. So the war went on. Its problems continued to undermine the Provisional Government's efforts to establish a new political system, until the popular expectations aroused by the February revolution finally brought the Bolsheviks to power.

New Opportunities After February 1917

The new-found freedoms of February caused a tremendous upsurge in the ordinary people's capacity to organize themselves. It is often supposed that the Russians are a passive people, accustomed to doing what their rulers tell them. Actually, this is far from being the case. Partly because of the huge distances, many Russian communities remained, at least up to the early twentieth century, relatively unaffected by central government, and had to improvise their own arrangements. But even where government has been near and ever-pressing, Russians have always been highly inventive in devising social forms such that they appear to be obeying their rulers, whilst in fact running matters as far as possible to their own advantage. This was the centuries-old basis of the peasant commune, which the government had always intended as an agency for taxation and military recruitment. Now, in 1917, with government repression suddenly removed, there was a veritable explosion of 'self-help' organizations among Russian workers, peasants and soldiers, each with their own, often exaggerated demands.

The peasants saw in the February revolution an opportunity to rectify what they considered a very longstanding injustice, that much of the land they worked did not belong to them. As a resolution from Samara province put it, 'The land must belong to those who work it with their hands, to those whose sweat flows.' Peasants were prepared to support the Provisional Government as long as it appeared to be actively promoting a wholesale transfer of land to them. As the months passed, and the Provisional Government did nothing, they lost interest in it and turned instead to direct action. Ironically, the government helped them to create the institutions which made this possible: the local land committees, which it set up to carry out a land survey and prepare for the ultimate land reform, actually became dominated at the lowest level by the peasants themselves, and increasingly proceeded to direct land seizures. This was especially the case after the army began to break up. A typical scenario was for a deserter to return to the village from the front, bringing news of land seizures elsewhere. The peasants would gather in their traditional *mir* assembly, or use the facade of the local land committees; they would discuss the situation and decide to take the local landowner's estate for themselves. They would then all march together up to the steward's office, demand the keys, proclaim the land, tools and livestock sequestered and give the owners forty-eight hours to leave. Then they would divide up the land among themselves, using the time-honoured criteria employed in the *mir,* the 'labour norm' or the 'consumption norm' (i.e. the number of working hands available, or the number of mouths to feed), whichever prevailed in local custom. They used violence where they thought it necessary, or where things got out of hand. . . .

Nowhere was the exuberant improvisation of the revolutionary period so evident as in the multiplicity of organizations created by the workers of Russia's cities. Pride of place, of course, belonged to the soviets, to which the workers of Petrograd streamed back as soon as they had a chance in February 1917. It cannot be said, however, that the Petrograd Soviet, or any other large city soviet, lived up to its original ideals. Perhaps that was impossible. The Petrograd Soviet's plenary assembly consisted of three thousand members, and even its executive committee soon grew to an unmanageable size, so that many of its functions had to be delegated to a bureau of twenty-four members, on which each of the main socialist parties had a prearranged quota of representatives. Naturally enough, these representatives tended to be established politicians and professional men rather than workers or soldiers. In fact, the attempt to introduce direct democracy led to an engaging but unproductive chaos, so that the real business had to be transferred upstairs to a small number of elected officials. This engendered a feeling among the rank and file that their voices no longer counted for anything. As we shall see, this discontent played an important part in the events of 1917, and helped to provide the Bolsheviks with the impetus that carried them to power. . . .

Where the Bolsheviks Stood in February 1917

At the time of the February revolution the Bolsheviks numbered, at the highest estimate, no more than 20,000, and their leaders were scattered in exile, at home and abroad. For that reason they had even more difficulty than the other parties in adjusting to the sudden changes. They were seriously divided about what to do, but the dominant figures inside Russia, notably [Lev] Kamenev and [Joseph] Stalin, inclined towards cooperation with the other socialist parties in the soviets in exercising 'vigilant supervision' over the Provisional Government. Some even talked of a rapprochement with the Mensheviks.

[Vladimir] Lenin had quite different ideas. He was still in Switzerland in February. He returned to Russia with the help of the German High Command, taking a specially provided 'sealed train' through Germany to Sweden. The Germans were anxious to facilitate his return, so that he could begin fomenting unrest inside Russia and spread his idea of a separate peace. They also provided the Bolsheviks with considerable funds thereafter, which helped to pay for the newspapers and political agitators who proved so effective among the soldiers and workers.

As soon as he arrived back in Petrograd, Lenin poured scorn on the notion of 'revolutionary defencism' [the idea that Russia should continue to fight in World War I to defend the gains of the revolution against aggression], conditional support for the Provisional Government, or cooperation with the other socialist parties. The 'bourgeois' stage of the revolution, he maintained, was already over, and it was time for the workers to take power, which they could do through the soviets. Russia should unilaterally pull out of the war, calling on the workers of all the combatant nations to convert it into an international civil war by rising against their rulers. Landed estates should be expropriated forthwith, and all other land nationalized and put at the disposal of 'Soviets of Agricultural Labourers and Peasant Deputies'.

Lenin's new programme should not have been a complete surprise to those who had read his writings since 1905, but all the same it did represent something of a shift in his thinking. His study of imperialism had led him to the view that the socialist revolution would take place on an international scale, with the colonized nations of the world rising against their exploiters. In this perspective, Russia, as the weakest of the imperialist powers, but also the strongest of the colonies (in the sense that it was exploited by French, German and other capital), was the natural setting for the initial spark of the revolution—though it would need swift support from within economically stronger nations if it was not to die away. Lenin, in fact, had moved close to the position of [Leon] Trotsky, who since 1905 had been preaching 'permanent revolution' on an international scale. Trotsky acknowledged this rapprochement by joining the Bolsheviks in the course of the summer. . . .

Initially, the Bolsheviks' position in the new popular institutions was very weak. With the disappointments of the summer and autumn, however, some existing delegates swung over towards the Bolsheviks, while new ones were elected on a Bolshevik mandate. The appeal of the Bolsheviks lay in their programme of 'peace, land and bread'. Facing a Provisional Government which could not end the war, and which was therefore incapable of carrying out land reform or ensuring food supplies either, the Bolsheviks were able to offer something which nearly all workers, peasants and soldiers wanted. Bearing these promises in their hands, Bolshevik speakers were often able to win over audiences and gradually the new grass-roots popular insitutions as well. This was the case first of all in the factory committees, then in the soviets of workers' deputies, then in the soldiers' committees and in some of the trade unions. The failure of the July uprising [unrest among the soldiers and workers in Petrograd that had been stirred up by the Bolsheviks] and the public revelations about German backing for Lenin reduced this support for a time, but it revived and redoubled with the Kornilov affair at the end of August.

The Kornilov Affair and Its Consequences

This affair has been the subject of much historical controversy, and it cannot be said that it is clear even now exactly what happened. In the last week of August General [Lavr] Kornilov, commander-in-chief of the Russian army, sent troops from the front to Petrograd, evidently with the intention of dispersing the soviets and arresting all the leading Bolsheviks, probably in order to set up a military government. He was thwarted by the action of [Alexander] Kerensky (now prime minister) in declaring him under arrest, by the railwaymen, who blocked the passage of his troops, and by the soldiers of the garrisons south and west of Petrograd, who fraternized with Kornilov's troops and persuaded them they were fighting on the wrong side. General [Nikolai] Krymov, their commander, committed suicide at this disgrace. . . .

What is quite certain is that this fiasco dramatically revived the fortunes of the Bolsheviks. It left the [military] High Command confused, demoralized and resentful of the Provisional Government. [Mikhail] Alexeyev, Kornilov's immediate successor, resigned in disgust in the middle of September, saying, 'We have no army', and describing his fellow officers as 'martyrs' in the face of the general indiscipline. By contrast, the workers' militias, especially in Petrograd itself, gained enormously in status and self-esteem: under their new name of 'Red Guards' they gained many new recruits during September and October. The Bolsheviks' view of events generally seemed to have been vindicated, and nearly all popular institutions, especially the soviets, swung sharply in their direction. From the beginning of September the Bolsheviks had a majority in the crucial Petrograd Soviet, and Trotsky became its chairman. Moscow soon followed suit, and it became clear that the elections to the second All-Russian Congress of Soviets would result in the Bolsheviks becoming the largest single party.

To forestall any possible repeat of the Kornilov affair, the Petrograd Soviet established on 9 October a Military Revolutionary Committee (MRC), to organize the 'revolutionary defence' of the capital against either a military putsch or Kerensky's reported intention of evacuating the city and letting the Germans (already in Riga, only 300 miles away) occupy it and crush the soviet. The motion to establish MRC was supported by left-wing Mensheviks and Socialist Revolutionaries; its first chairman was a Socialist Revolutionary. All the same, the majority of its members were Bolsheviks. The new body immediately set about coordinating the Red Guards and, helped by the impassioned oratory of Trotsky, persuading the garrison troops to recognize *it* rather than the Provisional Government as their ultimate source of authority.

Throughout September, Lenin, at first from the safety of Finland (a warrant had been out for his arrest since the July Days), then from hiding in Petrograd, bombarded the party Central Committee with letters urging that the moment for the insurrection had come. He cited as evidence the Bolshevik majorities in the soviets, the rising wave of peasant unrest, the intended surrender of Petrograd, and in the international dimension the recent mutiny in the German Baltic Fleet. Once MRC was in existence, that seemed to him the appropriate instrument for the seizure of power. And indeed, it was on the day after its establishment, 10 October, that he at last persuaded his colleagues on the Central Committee that a rising was 'on the agenda'. . . .

The Bolsheviks Seize Power

[What] finally provoked the seizure of power was Kerensky's action, on the night of 23–24 October, in trying to close down two Bolshevik newspapers and to arrest some Bolsheviks on charges of antigovernment agitation. On the initiative of Trotsky, MRC responded by reopening the newspaper offices, and then, to ensure the safety of the second All-Russian Congress of Soviets, due to open the next day in Petrograd, its troops began to occupy bridges, road junctions and railway stations, moving on to take over telegraph offices and government ministries during the following night. Lenin came out of hiding and went to the Smolny Institute, now the headquarters of MRC, to persuade them not to confine themselves to a defensive operation, but to carry on and arrest the Provisional Government. This is certainly what happened, whether because of Lenin's influence or from the natural dynamic of events. MRC called in Baltic sailors from Kronstadt and Helsingfors, while Kerensky's attempts to raise units from the front line were almost wholly unavailing, so low was the stock of the Provisional Government among army officers. In the end Kerensky slipped out of the city in a car to continue his efforts in person. The rest of the Provisional Government was duly arrested in the Winter Palace late on the night of the 25th–26th.

Already on the 25th Lenin felt able to issue a proclamation announcing that power had passed into the hands of the soviets. He did not, however, significantly, identify the Congress of Soviets or even the Petrograd Soviet as the new source of authority, but rather MRC, 'which has placed itself at the head of the proletariat and the garrison of Petrograd'. He thus specifically located power in the institution where the Bolsheviks had perhaps the greatest weight. When the Congress of Soviets met that evening, a large and influential group of Mensheviks and Socialist Revolutionaries, including most of the members of the executive committee of the First All-Russian Congress of Soviets (back in June), condemned this step as a usurpation and walked out of the assembly, to form a Committee of Public Safety and to try to organize resistance to unilateral Bolshevik rule. A few Mensheviks remained behind, while the much larger number of Socialist Revolutionaries who did so reconstituted themselves as the Left Socialist Revolutionary party, finalizing a break which had existed for some months in all but name.

Now that power was in the hands of the soviets, one might have expected that it would be exercised by the All-Russian Executive Committee (VTsIK), which was elected by the congress to conduct its business between sessions and to hold authority in the soviet movement. This, of course, contained representatives of several socialist parties. Lenin, however, announced that the supreme body in the new 'Workers' and Peasants' Government' would be the so-called Council of People's Commissars (*Sovnarkom*), a kind of 'council of ministers', whose members would all be Bolshevik. The Left Socialist Revolutionaries were invited to participate, but were unwilling to do so without other socialist parties also being represented.

As a result of the way Lenin and the Central Committee interacted, then, the Bolsheviks had seized power under the guise of defending the soviets against a Provisional Government bent on undermining them. That was the basis on which most of the participants in the seizure of power had acted, and most of them expected a coalition socialist government to follow, resting on the authority of the soviets.

The Goals of the Bolshevik Revolution

BY V.I. LENIN

Vladimir Ilych Lenin, born Vladimir Illych Yulianov, was perhaps the single individual most responsible for the Bolshevik Revolution. A dedicated revolutionary since his university days during the reign of Alexander III, Lenin was a key figure in the development of Russian communism for more than thirty years. Although he never actually held an official position of leadership in the Soviet government that arose after the revolutions of 1917, Lenin was unquestionably the ideological leader of the Bolsheviks. The essay reprinted here is typical of Lenin's revolutionary rhetoric from the early years of the Soviet Union. Written in December 1917, less than two months after the October Revolution propelled the Soviets into power, Lenin's fiery words demonstrate his unwillingness to cooperate with any groups—from the old czarist elites to the less radical Menshevik wing of the Communist Party—that opposed the transformation of Russia into a truly Communist nation as envisioned by Karl Marx. The outcome of the revolution at the time Lenin wrote this essay was far from certain; thus, his rhetoric reflects a desire to avoid what he saw as the failures of the 1905 and February 1917 revolutions, namely an unwillingness to act decisively and violently against the classes being overthrown.

The capitalists and their supporters, witting and unwitting, are thinking, saying and writing: "The Bolsheviks have now been in power for two months, but instead of a socialist paradise we find the hell of chaos, civil war and even greater dislocation."

We reply: the Bolsheviks have been in power for only two

V.I. Lenin: Collected Works, Volume 26, September 1917–February 1918, edited by George Hanna, translated by Yuri Sdobnikov and George Hanna. Moscow: Progress Publishers, 1964.

months, but a tremendous step towards socialism has already been made. This is not evident only to those who do not wish to see or are unable to analyse the chain of historical events. They refuse to see that in a matter of weeks the undemocratic institutions in the army, the countryside and industry have been almost completely destroyed. There is no other way—there can be no other way—to socialism save through such destruction. They refuse to see that in a few weeks, the lying imperialist foreign policy, which dragged out the war and covered up plunder and seizure through secret treaties, has been replaced by a truly revolutionary-democratic policy working for a really democratic peace, a policy which has already produced such a great practical success as the armistice and has increased the propaganda power of our revolution a hundredfold. They refuse to see that workers' control and the nationalisation of the banks are being put into practice, and these are the first steps towards socialism.

Those tyrannised by capitalist routine, shocked by the thundering crash of the old world, and the blast, rumble, and "chaos" (apparent chaos) as the age-old structures of tsarism and the bourgeoisie break up and cave in cannot see the historical prospects; nor can those who are scared by the class struggle at its highest pitch when it turns into civil war, the only war that is legitimate, just and sacred—not in the clerical but in the human sense—the sacred war of the oppressed to overthrow the oppressors and liberate the working people from all oppression. Actually all these tyrannised, shocked and scared bourgeois, petty bourgeois and "those in the service of the bourgeoisie" are frequently guided, without realising it, by that old, absurd, sentimental and vulgar intellectualist idea of "introducing socialism", which they have acquired from hearsay and scraps of socialist theory, repeating the distortions of this theory produced by ignoramuses and half-scholars, and attributing to us Marxists the idea, and even the plan, to "introduce" socialism.

To us Marxists these notions, to say nothing of the plans, are alien. We have always known, said and emphasised that socialism cannot be "introduced", that it takes shape in the course of the most intense, the most acute class struggle—which reaches heights of frenzy and desperation—and civil war; we have always said that a long period of "birth-pangs" lies between capitalism and socialism; that violence is always the midwife of the old society; that a special state (that is, a special system of organised coercion of a definite class) corresponds to the transitional period between the bourgeois and the socialist society, namely, the dictatorship of the proletariat. What dictatorship implies and means is a state of simmering war, a state of military measures of struggle against the enemies of the proletarian power. The Commune [the revolutionary government of France from 1792 to 1794] was a dictatorship of the proletariat, and [German philosopher Karl] Marx and [Friedrich] Engels reproached it for what they considered to be one of the causes of its downfall, namely, that the Commune had not used its armed force with *sufficient* vigour to suppress the resistance of the exploiters.

These intellectualist howls about the suppression of capitalist resistance are actually nothing but an echo of the old "conciliation", to put it in a "genteel" manner. Putting it with proletarian bluntness, this means: continued kowtowing to the money-bags is what lies behind the howls against the present working-class coercion now being applied (unfortunately, with insufficient pressure or vigour) against the bourgeoisie, the saboteurs and counter-revolutionaries. The kind [Alexei] Peshekhonov, one of the conciliating ministers, proclaimed in June 1917: "The resistance of the capitalists has been broken." This kind soul had no inkling of the fact that their resistance must really be *broken,* and it *will* be broken, and that the scientific name for this breaking-up operation is dictatorship of the proletariat; that an entire historical period is marked by the suppression of capitalist resistance, and, consequently, by systematic application of *coercion* to an entire class (the bourgeoisie) and its accomplices.

The grasping, malicious, frenzied filthy avidity of the money-bags, the cowed servility of their hangers-on is the true social source of the present wail raised by the spineless intellectuals ... against violence on the part of the proletariat and the revolutionary peasants. Such is the objective meaning of their howls, their pathetic speeches, their clownish cries of "freedom" (freedom for the capitalists to oppress the people), etc. They would be "prepared" to recognise socialism, if mankind could jump straight into it in one spectacular leap, without any of the friction, the struggles, the exploiters' gnashing of teeth, or their diverse attempts to preserve the old order, or smuggle it back through the window, without the revolutionary proletariat responding to each attempt in a violent manner. These spineless hangers-on of the bourgeoisie with intellectualist pretensions are quite "prepared" to wade into the water provided they do not get their feet wet.

The drooping intellectuals are terrified when the bourgeoisie and the civil servants, employees, doctors, engineers, etc., who have grown accustomed to serving the bourgeoisie, go to extremes in their resistance. They tremble and utter even shriller cries about the need for a return to "conciliation". Like all true friends of the oppressed class, we can only derive satisfaction from the exploiters' extreme measures of resistance, because we do not expect the proletariat to mature for power in an atmosphere of cajoling and persuasion, in a school of mealy sermons or didactic declamations, but in the school of life and struggle. To become the ruling class and defeat the bourgeoisie for good the proletariat must be *schooled,* because the skill this implies does not come ready-made. The proletariat must do its learning in the struggle, and stubborn, desperate struggle in earnest is the only real teacher. The greater the extremes of the exploiters' resistance, the more vigorously, firmly, ruthlessly and successfully will they be suppressed by the exploited. The more varied the exploiters' attempts to uphold the old, the sooner will the proletariat learn to ferret out its enemies from their last nook and corner, to pull up the roots of their domination, and cut the very ground which could (and had to) breed wage-slavery, mass poverty and the profiteering and effrontery of the money-bags.

The strength of the proletariat and the peasantry allied to it grows with the resistance of the bourgeoisie and its retainers. As their enemies, the exploiters, step up their resistance, the exploited mature and gain in strength; they grow and learn and they cast out the "old Adam" of wage-slavery. Victory will be on the side of the exploited, for on their side is life, numerical strength, the strength of the mass, the strength of the inexhaustible sources of all that is selfless, dedicated and honest, all that is surging forward and awakening to the building of the new, all the vast reserves of energy and talent latent in the so-called "common people", the workers and peasants. Victory will be theirs.

Why the Bolsheviks Won the Russian Civil War

By Evan Mawdsley

The Bolsheviks' hold on power during the first three years of the Soviet Union was extremely tenuous, thanks to the vigorous opposition of several groups, usually lumped together as the "Whites," during the civil war that lasted from early 1918 until 1922. Evan Mawdsley, professor of modern history at the University of Glasgow in Scotland, examines several reasons why the Bolshevik "Reds" were able to triumph in the Civil War despite the opposition of deposed elites, Cossack soldiers, a substantial portion of the intelligentsia, Socialist-Revolutionaries, and other leftist groups expelled from the government by the Bolsheviks. Not even the intervention of the wartime Allies on the side of the Whites (Japan, Great Britain, France, and the United States sent a total of more than 100,000 troops to assist the White forces) could sway the battle against the Reds. Mawdsley claims that the Bolsheviks had several advantages going into the Civil War that ultimately helped them win, including control of the major cities of St. Petersburg and Moscow, having room to retreat when necessary to avoid excessive losses, and the ability to raise a large (if not always well-trained or well-equipped) fighting force through ideological appeals. Mawdsley also looks closely at the roles that Lenin and Red Army commander Leon Trotsky played in the Bolsheviks' victory.

Sunday, 7 November 1920, was the third anniversary of the October Revolution. The evening before, [Bolshevik leader Vladimir] Lenin had spoken to a large meeting in Moscow's Bolshoi Theater. "Today," he said, "we can celebrate our victory." Had the Bolsheviks been told on the night of the Petrograd ris-

Evan Mawdsley, *The Russian Civil War*. Boston: Allen and Unwin, 1987. Copyright © 1987 by Evan Mawdsley. Reproduced by permission.

ing [November 7, 1917, the night Bolshevik-led troops stormed the Winter Palace in St. Petersburg and established Soviet rule] "that, three years later what is would be, that we would have this victory of ours, nobody, not even the most incurable optimist would have believed it." (Lenin's memory failed him here; in October 1917 many Bolsheviks had expected victory not just in Russia but across all of Europe, and in a very short period.) *Pravda*, on the 7th, had banner headlines:

> For three years the Republic of Soviets has lived and fought, holding in its hands both the hammer and the rifle.
>
> For three years, hungry and cold, in fierce struggle, the worker has gone from victory to victory.
>
> He has waited for the time when his last enemies have perished, when the shackles on the hands of his foreign brothers have been broken.
>
> Forward again! No shrugging of the mighty shoulders. The hour of world victory is near.

That night the Red forces began the main attack on [White general Peter] Vrangel's army at Perekop. A week later, on the 15th, [Red general Mikhail] Frunze sent a jubilant signal from the Crimea: "Today our units entered Sevastopol. With powerful blows the Red regiments have finally crushed the south Russian counterrevolution. The tortured country now has the chance to begin to heal the wounds inflicted by the imperialist and civil wars." There was a parade of army cadets in Red Square on the 16th, but no great celebration. Soviet Russia's economic problems were nearing their winter crisis, and this was no time for relaxation. Nevertheless, the last large, organized, anti-Bolshevik force had been driven from Soviet soil. The terrible struggle was over. Soviet power, established three years earlier, was secure. Bolshevism had won.

Eliminating Some Reasons for the Bolsheviks' Victory

Was Red victory based on the political and economic policies of the Soviet government? Without doubt the Bolsheviks' early promises were a basic reason why they were able to seize and consolidate power in 1917–1918; their program of Soviet power, peace, land reform, and workers' control was widely popular. But those promises could not be kept. Economic life suffered greatly in the aftermath of the Revolution and the World War. Factories closed, towns starved. The Bolsheviks faced in 1918 a big challenge even within the working class. Urban conditions remained dreadful throughout the Civil War, as [Bolshevik stateswoman] Aleksandra Kollontai pointed out in March 1921: "To our shame, in the heart of the republic, in Moscow itself, working people are still living in filthy, overcrowded and unhygienic quarters, one visit to which makes one think that there has been no revolution at all."

Nor were peasants, the great majority of the population, satisfied. Once the gentry's land had been taken there was nothing else to offer them. And given the movement from the towns, the small size of the nobility, and the large amount of land that had been rented prior to 1917, the peasants had access to little more land than they had before. Instead the state had to take the peasants' produce for the towns and their sons for the Red Army. It has been argued that Bolshevik agrarian and food-supply policies had a worse effect than did Civil War fighting, since it was the provinces in the Soviet rear that suffered the worst decline in farm production. A frank (and secret) Soviet report of conditions in 1921 in Tambov, a typical rural province, made clear the dissatisfaction of the peasants: "what sort of Workers' and Peasants' regime is it that we have [?]" they were asking themselves, "the regime in fact is that of the workers, over the peasants."

Nor were the Bolsheviks able to create the kind of mass democracy that they had promised in 1917. The same Tambov report showed great weaknesses even after three years of continuous Soviet rule, and spoke of the "Military-Administrative character of the Soviet Regime"; "the peasantry, in their majority, have become accustomed to regarding the Soviet regime as something extraneous to themselves, something that issues only commands." "Our party," it concluded, "has put down no firm roots in the countryside." By December 1919 Lenin had seen that power had to come first, mass support second: "The proletariat must first overthrow the bourgeoisie and win *for itself* state power, and then use that state power, that is, the dictatorship of the proletariat, as an instrument of its class for the purpose of winning the sympathy of the majority of the working people."

Lenin once said that the underlying reason for "such an historical miracle," why a "weak, exhausted and backward country was able to defeat the most powerful countries in the world" was "centralization, discipline, and unparalleled self-sacrifice." But if Bolshevik success was not explained solely by popular policies it was also not explained solely by some remarkable political efficiency, going back to the Leninist tradition of the elite vanguard party. Economic and military steps were not carried out across Soviet Russia under strict control from Moscow. The Civil War will be much better understood once objective regional studies have been written, but even now it is clear that given the size of "Sovdepia" [the original, mocking name given by the Whites to the area under Bolshevik control] and the low quality of communications there could be no all-powerful economic and political center; and a great deal of the success of the armies depended on their own efforts as they advanced into the food-rich periphery; the Polish campaign of 1920 was the exception that proved the rule.

Factors That Led to Red Victory

The Soviet victory, then, must be seen as a mixture of several elements. The popularity of the Bolsheviks' economic programs was limited after the winter of 1917–1918, and they had not created a real mass democracy. (Indeed, one of the strengths of the Soviet regime was that it often knew better than to pursue unrealistic policies when they did not work.) Nor was the Soviet state highly efficient. Nevertheless, the popularity of Bolshevik programs and the effectiveness of their administration was acceptable—relative to that of their opponents. The effect of Red Terror [mass reprisals by the Bolsheviks against political opponents during the early months of the Civil War] is harder to assess. Even some Bolshevik leaders felt that terror was counterproductive, but on balance it must be seen as an additional factor leading to victory. It contained the worst effects of the dangerous economic policies and prevented a successful "internal" revolt. Red Terror ensured that no one, as Lenin feared they might, thought the Bolsheviks "old women."

The Bolsheviks kept control of the Red heartland throughout the Civil War, with the result that they outnumbered their opponents. The core territory of Sovdepia was the largest chunk of the population of the old empire, it was mostly Great Russian [i.e., not Ukrainian or Belorussian] in nationality, it contained most of the war industry, most establishments and stores of the old army and navy. Gaining and keeping control of this heartland in 1917–1918 was the decisive achievement of the Civil War. Moscow was the symbol of the heartland. [Vladimir] Lebedev, one of the SR [Socialist Revolutionaries, who were initially allies of the Bolsheviks during the Revolution but became enemies during the Civil War] leaders of the little Komuch-Czechoslovak force that took Kazan in 1918, dreamed of a further advance on Moscow: "all her resources of people, of war, of finance would now be in our hands." "In Moscow we would get masses of troops, there we would get the whole brain of our country, all her soul, all that is talented in Russia."

In fact it was the Bolsheviks who held the Aladdin's cave throughout the Civil War, and their enemies could only dream of its treasures—after Lebedev [White admiral Alexander] Kolchak, and after Kolchak [White general Anton] Denikin. Moscow too was the center of communications which enabled the embattled Reds to defeat their isolated enemies one by one. "The ancient capital," as [British statesman Winston] Churchill put it, "lay at the center of a web of railroads . . . and in the midst a spider! Vain hope to crush the spider by the advance of lines of encircling flies!" The Reds fought from this base in the winter after their revolution, and in the campaigns of 1918 and 1919. By the time of the 1920 campaign the Reds had an overwhelming numerical superiority. All that could have destroyed them was internal decay, and they were able to avoid the most serious internal crises until after their victory on the battlefront. The main campaigns were conventional military ones, and that is where their reserves of manpower gave them an enormous advantage.

They also controlled a vast territory and could give up ground without being seriously threatened. When Lenin in April 1920 listed four conditions facilitating victory, one of them was "the possibility of holding out during a comparatively long civil war, partly thanks to the gigantic size of the country and to the bad means of communication" (the other factors were the Bolshevik peace policy, imperialist disunity, and peasant revolution). Trotsky made the same point: "if we are alive today as an independent revolutionary country . . . this is due to our expanses."

Red strategy probably should not be made too much of as a cause of victory. The Polish campaign was the most complex in military terms, but [Polish general Jozef] Pilsudski said he would not contradict those who described it as "a kind of children's scuffle, a mere brawl, unworthy to be considered in the light of the high theories of the military art." "We defeated our enemies," [Bolshevik leader Leon] Trotsky admitted, "but it cost us the greatest losses. We took too long over every battle, every war, every campaign." On the whole the Reds simply responded to one attack after another. Their one great adventure, the advance to the west and the southwest in the winter of 1918–1919, possibly prevented the defeat of the Don Cossacks and certainly exposed the Soviet zone to attacks from the east and southeast. One vital decision of mid-1919, to pursue Kolchak beyond the Urals, was largely made *despite* the opinion of Main Commander-in-Chief [Ioakhim] Vatsetis. The planned southern offensive of the late summer of 1919, with the main blow coming down the Volga and through the Don Host Territory, made strategic sense, but proved impossible to execute. In the destruction of Denikin in the winter of 1919–1920 the Reds overlooked the importance of the Crimea, Vrangel's future base. The final strategic counteroffensive against Poland in the summer of 1920 was clearly pushed too far. This patchy record was only partly due to the shortcomings of the Soviet high command; the size of the country and the disruption of the railway system also made it extremely difficult to follow a more "polished" strategy.

Nevertheless, the form that the Red victory took was a military one. However much the Russian struggle may have depicted—and in fact was—a war between classes, it was fought out by armies. Ultimately, Soviet victory owed much to the raising of a mass army commanded by former officers, equipped from Imperial stocks, and manned by peasant conscripts. The acceptance of military reorganization in 1918, under the pressure of the Volga campaign, prepared the Reds for the greater onslaught. Even then, they only won because their forces were so much larger than those of their enemies. Of course, it was terribly important that the Reds were fighting for a cause and had a big propaganda apparatus, but the Whites themselves showed that a remarkable military effort could be created in Russia without an attractive ideology—beyond the supposed restoration of order.

The Role of Ideology

It must never be forgotten that for the Bolshevik leaders the international dimension was extremely important. "We have always known," Lenin said in his third anniversary speech on 6 November 1920, that "until the revolution takes place in all states . . . our victory will be only half a victory, or perhaps less." [British historian] E.H. Carr argued that "World revolution . . . was in fact imposed on the regime, not so much by doctrinal orthodoxy, as by the desperate plight of the civil war"; "World revolution" was for Carr the diplomatic counterpart of economic "war communism"; both came not from doctrine but from the war emergency. The parallel is clever, but the analysis is wrong in both cases. The stress on world revolution in 1919–1920 had little to do with the Civil War; the causes were Bolshevik utopianism and central European turmoil.

World revolution became subordinate to other strands of Soviet policy in the 1920s. This was not because the war emergency had ended, but because events had proved it to be just a dream. The basic assumptions had been wrong: Europe was not on the brink of revolution in 1919. Only in backward Russia could radicals take control. Neither the Komintern [the international organization of Communist groups designed to spread revolution] nor the Red Army gave Moscow a means of forcing the pace. The revolution could spread only by example, and the Soviet example was—on balance—negative. Karl Kautsky, the leading spokesman of western European Marxist orthodoxy, condemned the "Stenka Razin [Razin led a popular uprising against Tsar Alexis in 1670 and 1671] socialism," "barrack socialism," the "Tartar socialism" of Moscow; "Bolshevism has, up to the present, triumphed in Russia, but Socialism has already suffered a defeat." In other countries moderate leaders and mass opinion were alienated by political repression, terror, and economic chaos; and they were shocked by the Civil War. The Bolsheviks dreamed of turning world war into civil war; in the end only Russia suffered this fate.

Foreign policy was a crucial factor in the Red victory, but not in the way the Bolsheviks originally intended. The greatest single stroke, the event that more than anything else kept the Bolsheviks in power, was the separate peace that unfolded between 25 October 1917 and 3 March 1918. [Upon seizing power, the Bolsheviks immediately withdrew from World War I and concluded peace treaties with their former enemies through the Treaty of Brest-Litovsk, which was signed on March 3, 1918.] This was in many ways, as the Bolshevik Left realized, a rejection of full-

blooded internationalist principles. It also had the negative effect
of leading to anti-Bolshevik intervention by the Allies and deepening the economic crisis. But it did allow consolidation of the
Bolshevik heartland in 1918, and that made victory possible in
1919 and 1920. After 1918 internationalism had the secondary
benefit of maintaining Russian morale by putting forward the
myth of the imminent European revolution.

How Important Were Lenin and Trotsky?

Lenin's role in the Red victory was not as universal as Soviet historians now maintain. As Trotsky pointed out, he took little consistent part in military decision-making at an operational level;
he never visited the front and very seldom consulted the high
command. [Joseph] Stalin's estimate of 1946 seems about right:
"In the Civil War Lenin urged us, then young comrades from the
CC [Central Committee, the ruling council of the Communist
Party], 'Study military affairs thoroughly'. As far as he was concerned, he told us openly, it was too late to study military affairs."
Nor was Lenin's *political* judgment an unalloyed success. He was
profoundly wrong about issues that were most basic to his beliefs.
He was wrong about the ability of the masses to run the state and
the economy, his basic economic policies were untenable (some
of them were tested almost to the point of destruction in the
winter of 1920–1921), and he was wrong about the likelihood
of European revolution. On the other hand his leadership during the October Revolution and the Brest negotiations was of
central importance, and he also established a personal control over
the party and the state which prevented (after March 1918) internal instability. He was sometimes prepared, too, to back off
when he met obstacles—as in the use of the regular army and in
some aspects of peasant policy.

The historian looking at Trotsky's Civil War career must beware of two myths. The first is the Soviet view dominant ever
since his disgrace in the late 1920s that he played no beneficial
role in the Civil War. ("History," Comrade Stalin in fact pointed
out, "shows that . . . Kolchak and Denikin were beaten by our
troops *in spite* of Trotsky's plans.") The second might be called
the "Trotskyist" myth that exaggerates his importance. The truth
lies in between the two, but given the state of Western histori-
ography it is perhaps the second myth that deserves the most attention. Trotsky was, of course, the second best-known Soviet

leader. But his career in 1917–1920 was marked by spectacular failures. He made major mistakes in foreign policy in early 1918 and in economic policy in 1920. Even his career in the Red Army had the bitterness of the summer of 1919. Trotsky's vital step was to support the creation of a regular army against much party opposition. He also played an important agitational role, his famous headquarters train covered 65,000 miles, and all this was something that Lenin, as their comrade [Anatoly] Lunacharsky pointed out, could not have done. The fighting men needed a figurehead to rally around, and Trotsky played his part effectively.

At the same time the other important leaders of the Civil War should not be lost sight of. [Iakov] Sverdlov, who died in early 1919, helped organize the state and the party, and [Alexei] Rykov, disgraced in the 1930s, was the man in charge of the war economy. [Ivan] Smilga, another future oppositionist, was the chief political organizer of the Red Army. Something should be said for Stalin, too, who had a most active career in the Civil War; if he had been killed in 1920 he would certainly be remembered as one of the great activists of the war. And outside the party probably no one was as important as two former Tsarist colonels, Vatsetis and [S.S.] Kamenev.

The Soviet Union

The Effects of the Stalinist Terror

By Andrei Sinyavsky

Starting in 1934, Joseph Stalin began a systematic campaign of arresting and often executing anyone—including many of the most prominent heroes of the Bolshevik Revolution—that he viewed as potential threats to himself or the Soviet state. Estimates of deaths during the so-called Stalinist Terror vary (noted historian Roy Medvedev has put the toll at more than 40 million) but there is little doubt that Stalin's bloody repressions drastically changed the Soviet Union for the worse. Andrei Sinyavsky, one of the most celebrated Russian political dissidents of the second half of the twentieth century, analyzes the Terror not in the usual terms of being the insane result of Stalin's runaway paranoia, but rather as the product of the revolutionary mind-set advocated by Lenin. Sinyavsky argues that Stalin's murderous rampage was fully in keeping with Lenin's ideas—although applied in a much more harsh manner—and supports his claim by demonstrating four ways in which the Terror actually benefited Stalin directly. Sinyavsky also includes a number of anecdotes that illustrate the flimsiness of the charges on which many of those who suffered during the Terror were arrested.

The year 1937 marks [Joseph] Stalin's zenith when, having liquidated all this real and imagined adversaries, he reigned supreme. This process, of course, had begun earlier and would continue for years after, but 1937 will forever remain a mystical date in Russian history, on a par, possibly, with the also quasi-sacred year of 1917. Nineteen thirty-seven was a response to 1917, if an irrational one. One could say that to [Vladimir] Lenin's reason and exceeding rationality in 1917, Stalin responded in 1937, twenty years later, in an irrational way.

Stalin's irrationality consisted in imprisoning and assassinating the heroes of the revolution, in killing his own, the Party faith-

Andrei Sinyavsky, *Soviet Civilization: A Cultural History*, translated by Joanne Turnbull. New York: Arcade Publishing, 1990. Copyright © 1990 by Arcade Publishing. Reproduced by permission.

ful, many of whom died pledging their allegiance to him. These purges consumed virtually the entire Central Committee, countless captains of industry, and the Red Army's high command (all this on the eve of war with Hitler). Then came the mass executions of the Party's lower echelons, of the regional and district committees, and finally of the population at large, including Chekists [agents of the secret police, the Cheka] and militiamen involved in the actual purging. According to the operative slogan, "enemies of the people" had infiltrated everywhere. This seems insane. And there are those who claim that Stalin was quite simply mad to have acted as he did, against his own interests and those of the Party. In reality, Stalin was far from mad: his actions were perfectly logical from his point of view and even somewhat in keeping with Leninist policy. And if one considers that a crazy man was able to run the State for decades, unchecked and unopposed, then this means that the State created by Lenin possessed this potential.

But Stalin, as I've said, was not mad and acted, from his point of view, with perfect reason. For all their psychological dissimilarities, Stalin was Lenin's student, as he hailed himself and others later chorused. But the student surpassed his master.

Lenin, as we know, destroyed the opposition in other parties primarily, including socialist parties: the Mensheviks [non-Bolshevik Communists] and the Socialist Revolutionaries. But Stalin, once in power, immediately found himself faced with internal opposition from the Trotskyites; he liquidated them and then went on to destroy most of the Leninist guard, whom he saw as a threat. Many of these makers of the revolution were brighter, more experienced, and better educated than Stalin, in addition to having joined the Party before he did. The elimination of the Trotskyites meant there could be no more real opposition to Stalin, but he was painfully sensitive to the faintest suggestion of dissent, to the slightest show of independence. And since the old Party cadres had only recently occupied positions equal or superior to his, he wrote them all off as suspect. The only way to dislodge them was to destroy them, having accused them before the country and the people of heinous crimes, of treason. Hence the necessity of the show trials in the thirties, when preeminent leaders of Party and State confessed publicly to being secret agents in the employ of foreign services, their ostensible dream having been to resurrect capitalism in Russia. . . .

Ultimately, everything connected with Stalin is so involved and obscure that it's often impossible to know how to interpret the facts. For a long time one could only guess as to why Stalin's victims confessed and repented of the most implausible sins. We still don't know the whole truth behind Stalin's assassination of Politburo member Sergei Kirov in December 1934, which marked the beginning of the purges. Nor do we know which version of [noted Russian writer Maxim] Gorky's death to believe. Did Stalin, as [Leon] Trotsky suspected, make an attempt on Lenin's life? Was Stalin himself murdered (as some claim)? And what about the two versions of how his wife died?

In short, the figure of Stalin, given the opacity of his machinations, becomes lost in the murk.

Stalin's Actions as the Logical Outcome of Leninism

But all of this smacks of Lenin's logic, if taken to absurd lengths by Stalin. For Lenin, all opposition to bolshevism, to his power, or to his point of view was an expression of bourgeois class or political interests. As a Marxist, Lenin did not recognize any individual ideology: everything was an expression of someone's class interests. Therefore, he lumped all his political opponents in the bourgeois camp which, he said, was bent on crushing the Bolshevik party and then Soviet power. Lenin salted all his articles and speeches with terms like "agents of the bourgeoisie," "agents of international imperialism," "social traitors," "traitors to the working class," and so on. A person's subjective honesty, his sense that he was neither bourgeois agent nor traitor, changed nothing in Lenin's view. Because what a person thinks of himself is not important, rather it's whose positions he expresses *objectively,* involuntarily. History's only laws are the objective laws of class struggle.

Stalin embraced this Leninist "objectivity," but on a grand scale, applying it even to Party members and veterans of the revolution who struck him as suspect.

Lenin, of course, was speaking metaphorically when he used the term "agents of the bourgeoisie" to describe Mensheviks or Western Social Democrats; or when he accused them of "selling" the interests of the working class. Lenin didn't think that they were literally in the pay of the world bourgeoisie or acting at the behest of a foreign secret service. But Stalin took every-

NIKITA KHRUSHCHEV CONDEMNS STALIN

In the early morning hours of February 25, 1956, Stalin's successor Nikita Khrushchev gave a landmark, albeit secret, speech at the Twentieth Party Communist Congress in which he denounced the "excesses" that Stalin had committed during his regime. This was the first formal acknowledgement by the government that Stalin's Terror had unjustly persecuted the Soviet people. Khrushchev's speech began a brief period of relative liberalism in Soviet society known as "the Thaw," during which criticism of the Stalinist past was openly permitted (although criticism of the present regime was still largely forbidden). Note that Khrushchev's speech differs from Sinyavsky's opinion in stating that Stalin abandoned Lenin's ideas rather than taking them to extremes.

We have to consider seriously and analyze correctly [the crimes of the Stalin era] in order that we may preclude any possibility of a repetition in any form whatever of what took place during the life of Stalin, who absolutely did not tolerate collegiality in leadership and in work, and who practiced brutal violence, not only toward everything which opposed him, but also toward that which seemed to his capricious and despotic character, contrary to his concepts.

Stalin acted not through persuasion, explanation, and patient cooperation with people, but by imposing his concepts and demanding absolute submission to his opinion. Whoever opposed this concept or tried to prove his viewpoint, and the correctness of his position was doomed to removal from the leading collective and to subsequent moral and physical annihilation. This was especially true during the period following the 17th Party Congress [in 1934], when many prominent party leaders and rank-and-file party workers, honest and dedicated to the cause of communism, fell victim to Stalin's despotism. . . .

Stalin originated the concept enemy of the people. This term automatically rendered it unnecessary that the ideological errors of a man or men engaged in a controversy be proven; this term made possible the usage of the most cruel repression, violating all norms of revolutionary legality, against anyone who in any way disagreed with Stalin, against those who were only suspected of hostile intent, against those who had bad reputations. This concept, enemy of the people, actually eliminated the possibility of any kind of ideological fight or the making of one's views known on this or that issue, even those of a practical character. In the main, and in actuality, the only proof of guilt used, against all norms of current legal science, was the confession of the accused himself, and, as subsequent probing proved, confessions were acquired through physical pressures against the accused. . . .

Lenin used severe methods only in the most necessary cases, when the exploiting classes were still in existence and were vigorously opposing the revolution, when the struggle for survival was decidedly assuming the sharpest forms, even including a civil war.

Stalin, on the other hand, used extreme methods and mass repressions at a time when the revolution was already victorious, when the Soviet state was strengthened, when the exploiting classes were already liquidated, and Socialist relations were rooted solidly in all phases of national economy, when our party was politically consolidated and had strengthened itself both numerically and ideologically. It is clear that here Stalin showed in a whole series of cases his intolerance, his brutality, and his abuse of power. Instead of proving his political correctness and mobilizing the masses, he often chose the path of repression and physical annihilation, not only against actual enemies, but also against individuals who had not committed any crimes against the party and the Soviet Government. Here we see no wisdom but only a demonstration of the brutal force which had once so alarmed V.I Lenin.

Congressional Record: Proceedings and Debates of the 84th Congress, 2nd Session (May 22, 1956–June 11, 1956), C11, Part 7 (June 4, 1956), pp. 9389–9403.

thing literally: an "agent of the bourgeoisie" equalled an actual spy. In this sense, the trials and executions of the thirties were nothing other than literal translations of Leninist metaphors. On Stalin's orders, the Soviet Chekists and investigators began torturing people arrested as agents of the bourgeoisie so that they would confess to spying for the Japanese, the Germans, or the English. The metaphor was taken to its real-life conclusion.

And like any metaphor made real, the result was a monstrous and fantastic scene. The country was crawling with invisible "spies" and "saboteurs" constantly being caught and exposed. In the street, any passerby could turn out to be a secret enemy. So it goes with any metaphor taken at face value. For instance: "The rain is coming." Let's imagine the rain strolling across bridges, striding through puddles, then starting to run or jump. The result is a kind of live grotesque—not unlike what happened to Lenin's metaphors in the thirties.

But Lenin isn't only guilty of coining phrases like "agents of the bourgeoisie" or "capitalist lackeys," which instantly entered the State's official vocabulary and modus vivendi. He also envisaged the harshest punishments for those who, in departing from the Party line or State policy, appeared *objectively* to be "agents of the bourgeoisie." In 1922, Lenin requested [Dmitry] Kursky, people's commissar of justice, "to broaden the application of capital punishment," especially for agitation and propaganda, and "to find a formula which establishes a connection between these acts and the international bourgeoisie" for the criminal code. Note: it is precisely this "connection with the international bourgeoisie" that entitles a person to be shot. And for this, the person doesn't have to have been literally recruited by foreign services; that his statements or writings *objectively* help the international bourgeoisie is sufficient. In another letter to Kursky, Lenin found the right formula and proposed it as his personal draft of the corresponding article for the criminal code: "Propaganda or agitation objectively promoting . . . the international bourgeoisie" is punishable by death (or exile abroad).

In the early twenties, expulsion was applied to prominent professors, philosophers, and writers whom, in the face of Europe, it would have been awkward to shoot or imprison for protracted periods.

According to Lenin's formula, "propaganda or agitation objectively promoting . . . the international bourgeoisie" automatically merited the harshest sentences. But with the application of this formula under Stalin, even the mildest criticism of the State and Stalin was regarded as bourgeois agitation and propaganda. And this criticism didn't have to be uttered: the suspicion of an unorthodox thought was enough; a slip of the tongue or a misprint was ample. The widow of the poet Eduard Bagritsky, a man greatly esteemed in the 1930s in the USSR and officially recognized as one of the best revolutionary poets, landed in prison and then in camp after she went to the NKVD (a successor to the Cheka) to petition for her sister's husband, the poet Vladimir Narbut, who had just been arrested and later died in a camp. "Why," she asked the Chekists, "do you just grab everyone indiscriminately?" When they laughed at her she screamed, in a fit of rage: "Nothing gets through to you!" For this exclamation she was arrested on charges of preparing an armed assault on Soviet power. Material evidence of her terrorist intentions was discovered during a search of her apartment: an old saber, given to Bagritsky by a distinguished Red Army commander, hanging on the wall over the ottoman.

Another typical case: A man went to see his friend, an official of some kind, at his office but found that he was out. The official had promised to do something for his friend and then hadn't done it. The friend decided to leave him a note. For lack of anything better to write on, he grabbed a newspaper that was lying on the desk and scrawled: "You scum, you broke your promise!" He didn't notice Stalin's speech right next to his angry, impromptu note. But somebody else did—and called the NKVD. The poor devil was promptly arrested.

The mass arrests in the thirties mainly affected privileged people. Earlier, with collectivization and the dispossession of the kulaks, it was the peasantry that had suffered most. But in principle, anyone could be made to suffer, regardless. One simple old woman dreamed that she gave herself to Kliment Voroshilov, the commissar of defense. The next morning, in the communal kitchen, she told her dream to a neighbor, who quickly denounced her to the NKVD. The old woman was sent to camp for her "crime": "for having unethical dreams about the leaders." There are innumerable stories like this one and countless variations on the theme of "bourgeois agitation."

The repressions in the 1930s were of enormous benefit to their instigator, Stalin.

First, there was the wholesale liquidation of the Party's active ranks, deemed dangerous by Stalin given their connection to revolutionary tradition and to Lenin. Stalin loathed this elite, if only for its popularity at a time when he was still a virtual unknown. It was a bastard's envy of the revolution's legitimate children. Thus it wasn't enough to simply exterminate them, Stalin dragged them through the mud. It became dangerous for any prominent Party member or old revolutionary to keep a journal or to write his memoirs for the desk drawer. If someone found out, he would instantly suspect that the writings contained something that either conflicted or could conflict with Stalin's line. And this suspicion alone could lead to the author's death.

Having eliminated the elite, those who "knew too much," Stalin undertook his second coup, the revision of history to suit his own taste. So that under Lenin the ubiquitous top man turned out to be Stalin, while his rivals—[Leon] Trotsky, [Nikolai] Bukharin, [Grigory] Zinoviev, [Lev] Kamanev, and others— turned out to be subversives. It was no accident that the height of these repressions coincided with the publication in 1938 of *The History of the Communist Party of the Soviet Union (Bolsheviks), Short Course*, a rewrite of the Soviet past according to Stalin, edited and partly written by him. This manual on the history of the Party and Marxism-Leninism became required reading for any literate Soviet citizen, especially "ideological front" workers. It was the bible of Stalinism. . . .

The third boon for Stalin in the wake of the repressions was the replacement of cadres and the emergence of a new type of Party and State leader. The Party underwent a social and psychological sea change. The veterans who had been eliminated were generally replaced by people without a past, by the rank and file from the provinces who hadn't been in the revolution or in the underground and had joined the Party for their careers. These were simple people for the most part, with limited horizons and little education: the basis of what [Yugoslavian dissident] Milovan Djilas calls the "new class." As opposed to the old guard, these people were not burning with revolutionary enthusiasm; they thought and acted unquestioningly, dully doing as they were told to do by the higher-ups. They became the ballast of the Stalin throne.

With their rise, the entire style of life changed. The barely educated but very dutiful functionary was now in charge.

Stalin's fourth triumph was in transforming the country into a servile state, where people were treated like slaves and had a slave's pyschology. Collectivization had enslaved the countryside, depriving huge numbers of people of even the most elementary independence. But the prisons and torture, camps and executions of the 1930s extended this servile system across the board. Stalin forced society to live in a state of terror, a terror that left its permanent mark on every Soviet citizen. Before, the concept of the enemy had had a class connotation. But now the enemy could be any Soviet person, himself unsuspecting and unable to secure any advance guarantee that he wasn't an enemy. According to a then-current anecdote, three men were sitting in a prison cell when one asked another what he was in for. It turned out that the first man was in for criticizing Karl Radek, the distinguished journalist, while the second, arrested later, was in for singing Radek's praises. The third man sat slumped in silence. "What are you in for?" they asked. And he said, "I'm Karl Radek . . ."

How the Soviets Fought World War II

By Peter Kenez

In the Soviet Union, World War II was known as the "Great Patriotic War." Having initially entered into a secret nonaggression pact with Nazi Germany in 1939, the Soviet Union was caught off guard in June 1941 when the Germans violated that agreement and launched a massive invasion of the USSR. Peter Kenez, professor of history at the University of California at Santa Cruz, looks at several ways in which Soviet culture reacted to the threat that Germany presented. Kenez discusses the military response to the German invasion, including that of both the regular Soviet army and that of partisan bands caught behind enemy lines. He also analyzes how the Soviet leadership utilized various forms of propaganda—from fairly standard images of victorious soldiers to unusual tolerance for religion—to help motivate the Soviet people to defend the motherland despite the widespread repression that Stalin inflicted on the country during the 1930s.

The Second World War was the supreme test of the Soviet system. The economy passed that test: the industrial base, partially created during the great drive of the 1930s, was large enough ultimately to produce weapons in sufficient quantity and quality to match the German war materiel. It is more difficult to draw conclusions concerning the allegiance of the Soviet people to their political system. Although the Soviet Union defeated Nazi Germany, this fact alone did not demonstrate the commitment of the peoples of the Soviet Union to communism. On the basis of reports from defectors who chose to stay in the West after the war, we may draw some conclusions. Only

Peter Kenez, *A History of the Soviet Union from the Beginning to the End.* Cambridge, UK: Cambridge University Press, 1999. Copyright © 1999 by Peter Kenez. Reproduced by permission of the publisher.

a rather small minority of the peoples of the Soviet Union were devoted communists, people who fought for the maintenance of the Soviet system. Another minority, perhaps a somewhat larger one, were so hostile to Stalinism that they were willing to collaborate with the Nazis. The great majority were somewhere in between: they were willing to fight for their country and obey the communists in order to defeat a beastly enemy.

Collaboration with the Nazis

We should remember that in every country that came under Nazi occupation, without exception, the Germans found collaborators. The Soviet Union was a multinational empire in which only slightly over half of the population was Russian; and here the potential for collaboration was particularly great. In territories that had come under Stalinist rule between 1939 and 1941, the people remembered the brutal policies of Sovietization, the terror and deportations carried out by the Stalinist regime. In Ukraine, in the Baltic states, in Belorussia and in Bessarabia large segments of the population, perhaps even the majority at first, welcomed the Germans as liberators. The Germans also found allies among the indigenous people of the Caucasus and among the Cossacks, people who had felt particularly mistreated by the communist rulers. Given the potential, it is surprising how little the Nazis took advantage of the centrifugal force of the nationalisms of the non-Russians. On the basis of their racialist ideology, the Nazis made distinctions among the nationalities, and treated some better than others. Estonians and Georgians, for example, were relatively high in their scale, while Slavs and Armenians were low. They organized "national legions" from non-Russian and Cossack prisoners of war and sent most of these to the West, where they performed police duties.

The Germans also used collaborators as administrators in towns and villages and organized auxiliary detachments to carry out particularly distasteful tasks, such as shooting Jewish children. How many collaborators there were is impossible to establish and, of course, the degree and nature of collaboration varied; but it is fair to say that millions of Soviet citizens to some extent collaborated. General Andrei Vlasov, one of the heroes of the battles for Moscow, was captured by the Germans in the summer of 1942. An honest but politically inexperienced man, he was willing to have his name used by the enemies of his country, presumably because of his anti-Stalinist convictions. He became the leader of the largest Russian anti-Soviet movements; by the end of the war he commanded an army of over 50,000 formed from prisoners of war. The Germans, given their ideology, distrusted this small Russian army, never equipped it properly, and did not use it in the war.

Some joined the Vlasov movement out of hatred of the Soviet regime, and others in order to escape the dreadful fate of Soviet prisoners of war in German captivity, where approximately three million men died. It is therefore not clear to what extent the Vlasov movement can be used as an example of disaffection. At the end of the war, about five million Soviet citizens found themselves in the West as a result of having been prisoners of war or slave laborers, or voluntarily having joined the retreating Germans. [British prime minister Winston] Churchill and [U.S. president Franklin] Roosevelt, who had signed agreements guaranteeing repatriation, never considered that people might not want to return to their homeland. At the end of the war hundreds of thousands had to be forced to return to the Soviet Union. Many of them were directly sent to concentration camps on their return.

The Nazis as the Ideal Enemy

The Soviet regime was saved by the fact that it faced an enemy which made it impossible for the people of the Soviet Union to accept defeat. They had to fight whether they believed in the existing system or not, because the Germans gave them no option. German policy in the occupied territories was based on a racist ideology that considered the Slavs subhuman and treated them accordingly. According to this ideology, the Jews were not human at all, but vermin to be exterminated. The Germans followed a mad policy of destruction: they wanted to reduce Russians and Ukrainians to slavery and exploit the territories to benefit Germany. In order to bring this about, they wanted to destroy the intelligentsia physically. They wanted to create conditions in which many "natives" would die, and thereby create room for German colonization. When the Nazis exterminated villages in reprisal for partisan attacks they intended them to be repopulated by ethnic Germans. In the course of the war over four million men and women were taken to Germany to work as slave laborers.

From the very outset the Nazis had a special policy for Jews and communists who fell into their hands: they killed them. The Nazis commenced their genocide immediately after the invasion. The invading armies were accompanied by "special groups of the SS," *Einsatzgruppen*, which rounded up and shot Jews. The German army thus became an accomplice in genocide. Within the first few months of the war a half-million were so murdered, and by the end of the war over a million Soviet Jews had fallen victim to Nazi madness.

The Germans conducted very little propaganda, for offering anything to the Soviet people would have conflicted with their goals. Later, when it became clear that the war would not end quickly with a German victory, the invaders changed their approach. But even at this time German efforts were confused and contradictory. In any case, actions spoke louder than words. The population well understood what the invaders wanted and who they were. The Germans, having made little effort to appeal to the population when victorious, could not hope to do so in a period of defeat. One is tempted to pose a counterfactual question: what if Nazi policy had been more clever and the Germans had posed as liberators? The flaw in this perspective is that had the Nazis not been so brutal, had they not been devoted to a mad ideology, they would have never commenced the war in the first place. The various aspects of Nazism could not be separated: daring, conviction of superiority, amorality, will to war and destruction, determination and ruthlessness—all these had brought victory, and all ultimately brought defeat.

But in June 1941, the Soviet leadership could not possibly have known the depth of Nazi criminality and political ineptitude. In the past the Soviet people had complied because they had no alternative: terror had eliminated all real and potential enemies. But would people now continue to obey? Stalin was immobilized for ten crucial days: he did not know how to address his subjects. When he finally did so on July 3, he did it most effectively and movingly. He addressed his listeners as brothers and sisters, and thereby foreshadowed the great change that was to take place in Soviet propaganda during the war years.

Changes in Propaganda and Punishment

The might of German armies, enjoying victory after victory, was impressive. The enemy seemed unstoppable, and in the new circumstances it took some time for the Soviet propaganda machine to reorient itself and find its voice. However, decades of experience in mass mobilization and practice in various agitational methods all turned out to be useful. The themes of propaganda changed, but the instruments were already in place, ready to be used. Although the regime deemphasized ideology, the party as an institution retained its importance. It carried out a special recruitment drive during the war, making it easier for soldiers to enroll. It was assumed that identification with the regime would strengthen loyalty and raise the morale of the troops.

For the same reason, the Komsomol [Communist Youth League] was also greatly expanded during the war: between 1940 and 1945 its membership grew from approximately ten to fifteen million. The youth organization was especially useful for the regime when operating in occupied territories. The regime had greater faith in the young, those who had been educated entirely under a communist system. Indeed, Komsomol members were the most likely to join the partisan movement.

Nor should we forget another important Soviet institution, the NKVD [the secret police]. Propaganda and coercion, as before, went hand in hand. This leopard did not change its spots; terror did not abate during the war. Those who had lived under German occupation, or who had become prisoners of war and escaped, suffered the consequences of NKVD suspicion, and hundreds of thousands of them were arrested. The Soviet regime punished the families of deserters. A new phenomenon during the war was the punishment of entire nations: the Volga Germans were deported immediately at the outbreak of the war. In 1943 and 1944 it was the turn of the Crimean Tatars and Muslim minorities of the Caucasus: deported to Central Asia, they lived in the most inhuman conditions. The new element in this terror was its naked racism. Every member belonging to a certain minority group was punished, regardless of class status, past behavior, or achievements. Communist party secretaries were deported as well as artists, peasants, and workers.

Despite the arrests, the number of prisoners in camps declined during the war. This happened partly because inmates were sent to the front in punishment battalions, where they fought in the most dangerous sections. The morale and heroism of these battalions were impressive: most of the soldiers did not survive. The camps were also depopulated by the extraordinary death rates: approximately a quarter of the inmates died every year. People died because of mistreatment, overwork, and undernourishment.

The Soviet Fighting Forces on Both Sides of the Front

In wartime nothing is more important than maintaining the morale and loyalty of the armed forces. In addressing this need the Soviet Union learned from decades of experience. At first, the regime reverted to the dual command system it had developed during a previous time of crisis, the civil war. From the regimental level up, political appointees supervised regular officers. They were responsible for the loyalty of the officers and at the same time directed the political education system. The abandonment of united command, however, harmed military efficiency; once the most dangerous first year had passed, the Stalinist leadership reestablished united command. This did not mean that the political officers had no further role to play. The network of commissars, supervised by the chief political administration of the army, survived. The commissars carried out propaganda among the troops: they organized lectures, discussed the daily press with the soldiers, and participated in organizing agitational trains that brought films and theater productions to the front.

Yet another network within the army functioned to assure the loyalty of the troops—the network of security officers. Although these men wore military uniforms, they were entirely independent of the high command and reported directly to the NKVD. According to contemporary reports, these security officers were greatly disliked by regular officers.

Of course, it was much harder to control the partisan movement than the army. The German advance during the summer of 1941 was so sudden that the retreating Soviet forces did not have a chance to prepare for resistance in enemy-held territory, and the partisan movement began autonomously. One manifestation of the independence of the movement was that its propaganda, while necessarily coinciding with Soviet themes in most respects, had distinctive features. For example, Soviet propaganda never admitted past Soviet errors; but the partisans, especially in their oral approach to the population, could and did say that the errors of the past would be eliminated in a future and victorious Soviet Union.

The partisan movement had great significance: it tied down

and harassed the Germans, and it projected Soviet presence in an area not under the regime's control. It was essential for the future that the population in the occupied areas receive the Soviet point of view and live with the expectation that the previous rulers would return. The best propaganda carried out by the partisans was propaganda by example. By their very existence they showed to the Soviet population that the power of the Germans was not limitless. By their willingness to accept martyrdom, they exposed the bestial nature of the Nazi occupiers. The Soviet regime, well aware of the value of this work, did not spare scarce resources. Planes dropped pamphlets distributed by partisan propagandists; the partisans obtained small presses that enabled them to spread information they received on short-wave radio; and they carried out oral agitation. As the movement grew, the leadership set up agitational sections consisting not only of experienced agitators, but also of singers and artists who gave performances.

The Role of Propaganda in Fighting the War

In regions not under enemy occupation, every branch of art was pressed into service. Novelists described the heroism of the soldiers and civilians, musicians composed patriotic songs, and graphic artists drew posters that glorified the Red Army and the Soviet people and ridiculed the enemy. It is worthwhile to examine Soviet films made during the war, not for their artistic merit, but because these show most clearly the character of the propaganda. The leadership had a special appreciation for the role of cinema and film documentaries, and filmmaking came to be fully mobilized for the war effort. During the war Soviet directors made a total of 78 films; only a handful did not deal directly or indirectly with the war. Documentaries made a specially great impression on audiences, and documentary makers received all the support they needed. In the course of the war thousands of cameramen shot 3.5 million meters of film, thereby producing a remarkable chronicle of the war. These documentaries, unlike the German ones, did not shrink from depicting the suffering imposed on civilians.

At first the main task of Soviet propagandists was to puncture the Germans' image of invincibility in order to lessen the likelihood of collaboration. Soviet publicists overstated German losses, passed over Soviet defeats, and stressed the courageous resistance of the population. With the first important victory of the Red Army at Moscow in December 1941, the task of the propagandists became much easier. People hungered for good news. When newsreels of that important battle appeared in the theaters, people stood in line for tickets. Seeing German prisoners of war led through the streets of the capital was a wonderful experience for people who have suffered so many humiliating defeats.

The soldiers of the Red Army and the partisans went to fight for "motherland, for honor, for freedom and for Stalin." On this list, motherland was the first and most important. The heart of appeals to the people was Russian nationalism, a love for the native land and its traditions. The resurrection of Russian nationalism had preceded the war. Historians and publicists extolled the achievements of tsarist generals and statesmen, and by dwelling on the great figures of the past conveyed the message that their contemporaries had a high tradition to live up to. By showing past Russian successes they intended to convince the audience that Russia once again would prevail. . . .

The propagandists had to draw a delicate line. On the one hand it was essential not to demoralize the communist activists by repudiating the past, but on the other it was self-evident that for the great bulk of the Russian people it was the defense of the motherland, not the defense of the communist system, that mattered. Soviet propagandists handled the task with skill. They depicted the country's past and future in such a way as to allow people of different political persuasions to draw different conclusions. Soviet newspapers, novels, and films repeatedly contrasted the happy life of the people before the war with the terrible present. The writers, however, remained vague about the nature of that happy life. The soldiers fought under the Red banner; they went to battle "for Stalin"; the Soviet people continued to celebrate holidays such as the anniversary of the October revolution and May Day; they listened to unceasing glorification of the founder of the Soviet state, Lenin. And, of course, the leaders of the regime apologized for nothing.

A temporary abandonment of antireligious propaganda accompanied the deemphasis of communism. If tsars, generals, and aristocrats could be held up as examples to follow, there was no reason why churchmen should be excluded. The glorification of the Russian past helped the revival of the church. After all, the Orthodox Church was an inseparable part of Russian history.

The motives for abandoning the persecution of the church are easy to see. The Soviet leaders wanted to prevent the Germans from posing as the defenders of religion, and they wanted to gain the good will of the democratic West; but most importantly, they wanted the help of the church in the great national effort. The state allowed the printing of religious books; it reopened churches; radio Moscow started to broadcast religious hours. The church responded warmly: the Orthodox leaders visited Stalin in the Kremlin and gave their blessings to the war effort.

The leaders of the regime well understood the hostility of the Russian people to antireligious policies and the necessity for concessions. They also knew that the overwhelming majority of the peasants deeply resented the collective farms. In this matter, however, it was far more difficult to retreat. Even if the creators of the system had been willing to sacrifice the collective farms, which is questionable, such a move in the short run would have led to enormous confusion. The Soviet leaders, good politicians that they were, well understood this weakness in their position. They braced themselves for an attack, because they assumed that the enemy would exploit their weakness. But the attack never came; for the Germans, instead of identifying themselves with the aspirations of the peasants, decided to exploit the collective farms for their own purposes. They, too, found it easier to compel the collectives to provide food than to force individual peasants. Partisan propaganda took advantage of the failure of the Germans. The partisans encouraged the belief that after the victorious conclusion of the war the farms would be dissolved. It is impossible to establish to what extent this aspect of partisan propaganda was centrally planned. Most likely the partisans used their independence to tell the peasants what the peasants wanted to hear. As the war was drawing to a victorious conclusion, the Russian people expected "good things" to happen, even if such expectations were unrealistic and sometimes even mutually exclusive.

How Stalin's Actions Helped Start the Cold War

By Thomas W. Wolfe

*Forced together by circumstance, the Soviet Union, the United States,
and Great Britain cooperated during World War II to defeat their common enemies. Even before the war ended, though, the seeds of disagreement were sown among the allies and these would soon bloom into the
nearly fifty-year era of international tension known as the "Cold War."
Thomas W. Wolfe was a longtime Russian specialist with the RAND
Corporation, a prominent public policy and military strategy "think-
tank." He examines the manner in which Stalin and the leaders of the
other two wartime allies interacted in the immediate aftermath of the war
and concludes that Stalin is most responsible for creating the atmosphere
of ideological conflict that quickly resulted in the division of the world
into Communist and capitalist sides. Although he does not lay all the
blame for the Cold War on Stalin, Wolfe argues that Stalin's steadfast
desire to establish a lasting Communist sphere of influence in Eastern
Europe caused him to make decisions that inflamed an already tense situation, thereby fostering the deep distrust between the United States and
the Soviet Union that would last until the late 1980s.*

In the fullness of time, history may provide answers to all the
questions it poses, as [British historian] Max Beloff has observed, but it does not tell us much about the possible outcome of the lost opportunities with which it is strewn. One such
lost opportunity was doubtless the failure of the Soviet Union
and the West to establish a mutually acceptable set of relationships in the world which emerged from World War II. If there is
little point in speculating on what might have been, it is at least

Thomas W. Wolfe, *Soviet Power and Europe, 1945–1970.* Baltimore, MD: Johns Hop-
kins Press, 1970. Copyright © 1970 by The RAND Corporation. Reproduced by
permission.

appropriate to note that in the first years after World War II [Soviet premier Joseph] Stalin chose a policy course which not only prejudiced the possibility of postwar collaboration with the West but which also served to unite the West in opposition to his aims. That Western attitudes and statesmanship also contributed to the breakdown of wartime unity and helped to give rise to what was to become the Cold War goes without saying; however, to recognize this is not to embrace the thesis—expounded by some writers of the so-called "revisionist" school—that Stalin stands in the eyes of history as the injured party, put upon by erstwhile allies bent on humiliating the Soviet Union and depriving it of the rightful fruits of victory.

Many interpretations of Stalin's motives have been offered. They tend to fall into two categories: those stressing his desire to exploit the postwar situation in order to make positive gains for Soviet policy on the one hand; and those emphasizing his concern to ward off anticipated threats to Soviet security on the other. In the first category, for example, is the view that Stalin, sensing that the floodgates of social and political upheaval after the war would not remain open forever, decided he must make the most of a transitory period for revolutionary advance, even at the cost of alienating his wartime allies. Or, as a variant interpretation, the collapse of Germany left a power vacuum in the heart of Europe which Stalin was cynically prepared to fill, the main restriction upon his expansionist urge being what, in [longtime U.S. diplomat] George Kennan's phrase, "the amiable indulgence of the Western powers," would tolerate.

In the second category, by contrast, Stalin was said to be primarily concerned to stave off anticipated efforts by the Western powers to undo his wartime gains, and he therefore sought to forestall them by militant consolidation of Soviet control over territories occupied by the Red Army. A variant explanation, which contrives to fit into both categories, holds that Stalin was prone to disguise his expansionist aims as security guarantees, and that, in fact, as he understood it, there was little difference between the extension of Communist rule and the enhancement of Soviet security. There is also, of course, the revisionist argument that Stalin wished to preserve the wartime alliance and cooperation with the West and that he adopted a tough line in East Europe only after being confronted with Western demands that the Soviet Union give up its "hard-won military positions" under the "clear threat of preventive war."

Perhaps many of these elements entered in one degree or another into Stalin's perception of the international scene in the early postwar years when, as [U.S. statesman] McGeorge Bundy has described it, Stalin seemed bent upon squandering the "reservoir of good will" he had inherited from the wartime years of partnership with the West. In any event, without trying to exhaust the sources of Stalin's motivation, one may identify several factors that seem to have had a particular bearing upon his military policy decisions at this period.

Some Reasons for Stalin's Actions After World War II

The frame of mind which led Stalin to interpret the postwar diplomacy of the Western powers as confirmation of ingrained hostility to the Soviet Union was probably one of the chief factors that underlay his decision to maintain large military forces. A desire to stake out a protective belt of territory to cover the Soviet Union's traditionally vulnerable frontier with Europe was probably another factor that led Stalin to keep substantial Soviet forces deployed in Central and Eastern Europe. Stalin's reluctance to remove these forces from their wartime lodgement in Eastern Europe may also have been due to the belief that local resistance to satellization of the area would otherwise present serious problems. His awareness that the postwar presence of military forces in Europe would help determine its future political boundaries may also have stayed him from a hasty decision to bring his troops home. Another key element in Stalin's perception of the postwar scene—and perhaps one which weighed most heavily of all in his military policy decisions—was the possibility that American involvement in Europe might threaten not only the Soviet Union's wartime gains but also its prospects for future political advance.

Initially, Stalin may have hoped, or even expected, that the United States would in fact disengage itself from postwar Europe, as suggested by President [Franklin] Roosevelt's comment at [the meeting of Allied leaders in] Yalta in 1945 that he "did not believe that American troops would stay in Europe much more than two years." For many reasons, including the prospect of gaining a free hand to deal with the question of postwar Germany's political future, an American withdrawal from Europe would certainly have seemed to be in the Soviet interest. In connection with the German question, the Soviet Union in the spring of 1946 rejected a US proposal for what would have amounted to a twenty-five-year alliance to insure the disarmament of Germany.

Presumably, Soviet objections rested on the fact that such an agreement would have given the United States a lasting foothold in Europe and a continuing voice in German affairs, whereas an American return to isolationism would have left Germany little choice but to accept the Soviet alternative for its future. Indeed, the latter expectation probably lent support to an initial Soviet policy favoring German unity, on the grounds that political capture of a reunified Germany was possible. As long as there was a prospect that the political forces in Germany opposing dismemberment of the country could be mobilized to support a Soviet alternative, the Soviet Union was willing to consider the idea of reunification; when this prospect evaporated with the inability of the Socialist Unity Party (SED) to capitalize on reunification sentiment, so did Soviet interest in ending the de facto division of Germany. However, up to the time of Stalin's death, at least, the idea that a reunified Germany would tend to disrupt Western unity and thus serve Soviet policy ends was kept alive by Stalin himself. . . .

Despite the fact that American disengagement from Europe must have been a desideratum [something wanted or needed] high on Stalin's priority list, his maneuvering for position toward the end of the war and in the early postwar period was scarcely calculated to encourage it. Of course, it is only fair to recognize that Stalin's policies evolved in the context of a mutual decay of confidence on both sides, a process fed by conflicting Western and Soviet conceptions of what was necessary to insure postwar security and a sound peace. However, one can but remark that Stalin helped to defeat his own purposes. Skeptical that the Soviet Union might find security through the international machinery of a United Nations, suspicious of US advocacy of self-determination for East Europe, Stalin set out to work his will there unilaterally, above all in the test case of Poland, and thereby stirred forebodings in the West about Soviet intentions which virtually precluded the possibility of a prompt American exodus from the postwar European scene.

Although Stalin's moves—from those involving East Europe and Germany to his demands for revision of the Montreux Convention [a prewar agreement on use of the Black Sea straits] and his territorial claims on Turkey—certainly had the effect of blighting the Big Three [that is, the three major WWII Allies—the United States, Great Britain, and the Soviet Union] spirit of co-operation, they did not necessarily mean that Stalin was indifferent to the need for allaying the growing suspicions of his wartime allies. Indeed, he demonstrated more than once that he was anxious not to provoke a Western reaction that might jeopardize his plans for setting up a system of Soviet-controlled states in East Europe. One such instance was the withdrawal of Soviet troops from northern Iran in the spring of 1946, in response to President [Harry] Truman's warning, a gesture suggesting that Stalin was neither prepared for nor wished to invite a showdown with the United States which could arrest the latter's hoped-for return to isolationism.

Another instance was Stalin's quiet advice to Communist leaders in France and Italy to refrain from trying to seize power immediately after the war, though his caution in this regard may have stemmed no less from wanting to lull US apprehensions than from his appreciation, as expressed later to the Belgrade Politburo, that the way the war ended—i.e., without Soviet forces reaching France and Italy—had "unfortunately" made it impossible for the Soviet Union to establish "people's democracies" in those countries. A third example of Stalin's desire to avoid giving the West an excuse for action which might jeopardize the Soviet foothold in southeastern Europe came in connection with Greece, following the proclamation of the Truman Doctrine in March 1947. As [Yugoslavian dissident] Milovan Djilas has disclosed, Stalin grew alarmed lest the guerrilla uprising in Greece "endanger his already-won positions," leading him to insist in early 1948 that it be called off.

Precisely when the possibility of maintaining Big Three unity and a collective approach to the problems of the peace was lost, if indeed it was ever in the cards, no one can say with certainty. Perhaps it was in Poland in the troubled year of 1944, or perhaps it was sometime in the period between [meetings of Allied leaders at] Yalta in February 1945 and Potsdam six months later, when the military deployments at war's end began to congeal into what was to become, in Walter Lippmann's words, "the political boundary of two hostile coalitions." By the end of 1946, certainly, the prospects for postwar co-operation no longer appeared very encouraging. Early in the year—a month before [former British prime minister Winston] Churchill's Iron Curtain speech in Fulton, Missouri—Stalin had delivered his celebrated February 9 election speech in Moscow, which, along with similar ominous statements made later by Andrei Zhdanov, publicly reintroduced the assumption of deep-rooted conflict with the West and foreshadowed a return to the doctrine of a world divided into two hostile camps. Throughout the remainder of 1946, increasing Soviet truculence in the series of futile negotiations aimed at drafting peace treaties with Germany and Austria did not augur well for the future.

Even so, the situation might have been salvaged in the early months of 1947, for the United States was still seeking conceptual moorings for its postwar policy toward the Soviet Union, and the door was kept at least partly open for co-operation with the Russians in Europe. According to some observers, the conclusive turning point in postwar Soviet-US relations probably came with failure of the March 1947 Conference of Foreign Ministers in Moscow to reach a settlement on Europe, a failure which coincided with and, in the opinion of some critics, could be blamed upon the Truman Doctrine speech of March 12 [in which Truman put forth a clear signal that the United States would oppose Communist expansion]. Or, it might be argued that the Marshall Plan initiative of June 1947 represented still one more chance to find a way out of the impasse in which the World War II victors found themselves. The Soviet Union had been invited to participate in this general program for the reconstruction of all Europe and had even sent [foreign minister Vyacheslav] Molotov to Paris on June 28, 1947, with a bevy of advisors to look the plan over. However, after two days, the Soviet delegation pulled out, and Stalin also forbade the governments of Poland and Czechoslovakia to take part in the European Recovery Program (ERP). To many observers, this was the irreversible turning point which marked the postwar division of Europe and the beginning of the Cold War.

Perestroika, Glasnost, and Soviet Reform

By Mikhail Gorbachev

Mikhail Gorbachev is often viewed as the man who brought about the collapse of the Soviet Union, but such an assessment is not entirely accurate. During his tenure as General Secretary of the Communist Party (1985–1991), Gorbachev oversaw the attempted reform of the socially repressive and economically stagnant Soviet Union that had developed for twenty years under Leonid Brezhnev and his two short-lived successors, Yuri Andropov and Konstantin Chernenko. As can be seen in this excerpt from his 1987 book Perestroika, *Gorbachev was a committed Communist, having been a Party member since 1952, and intended to reform, not destroy, the Soviet Union. He hoped that his policies of perestroika (restructuring) and glasnost (openness) would fundamentally change the fabric of Soviet society by allowing for greater economic and social freedom, respectively. However, much as had been the case after Nicholas II's concessions of 1905, Gorbachev's reforms only temporarily satisfied the dissident elements in the country. The taste of limited freedoms offered by perestroika and glasnost quickly convinced many Russians that Communist rule and democratizing reforms were incompatible.*

The new atmosphere is, perhaps, most vividly manifest in glasnost. We want more openness about public affairs in every sphere of life. People should know what is good, and what is bad, too, in order to multiply the good and to combat the bad. That is how things should be under socialism.

It is important to be aware of all that is positive and constructive, to use it, to make it an asset of all the people, the entire Party, so that the shoots of new attitudes can be used in the conditions of perestroika.

Truth is the main thing. [Bolshevik revolutionary leader Vladimir] Lenin said: More light! Let the Party know everything! As never before, we need no dark corners where mold can reappear and where everything against which we have started a resolute struggle could start accumulating. That's why there must be more light.

Today, glasnost is a vivid example of a normal and favorable spiritual and moral atmosphere in society, which makes it possible for people to understand better what happened to us in the past, what is taking place now, what we are striving for and what our plans are, and, on the basis of this understanding, to participate in the restructuring effort consciously.

Democratization of the atmosphere in society and social and economic changes are gaining momentum largely thanks to the development of glasnost. It goes without saying that the policy of the Party is the basis of this process. Things will not start changing, however, if the political course is not pursued in a way understandable to the masses. The people should know life with all its contradictions and complexities. Working people must have complete and truthful information on achievements and impediments, on what stands in the way of progress and thwarts it.

People might be said to have developed a taste for glasnost. And not only because of their natural desire to know what is taking place, and who is working how. People are becoming increasingly convinced that glasnost is an effective form of public control over the activities of all government bodies, without exception, and a powerful lever in correcting shortcomings. As a result, the moral potential of our society has been set in motion. Reason and conscience are beginning to win back ground from the passiveness and indifference that were eroding hearts. Naturally, it is not enough to know and to tell the truth. Acting on the knowledge of the truth and of understanding it is the main thing.

We have come to realize the necessity of learning to overcome the inveterate discrepancy between the reality and the proclaimed policy. It is this major shift in the moral sphere that makes up the emotional content and the essence of the present socialist revolutionism in our society.

We have begun drafting bills that should guarantee glasnost. These bills are designed to ensure the greatest possible openness in the work of government and mass organizations and to enable working people to express their opinion on any issue of social life and government activity without fear.

The Importance of the Media in Reform

When beginning the restructuring process, the CPSU [Communist Party of the Soviet Union] Central Committee relied on two powerful real forces—the Party committees and the mass media. I can even say that the Party might not have reached the present level of discussion about the entire package of perestroika issues—and the process of perestroika is very vast, diversified and contradictory—if the mass media had not joined it actively, and in an appropriate manner, immediately after the April 1985 Plenary Meeting of the CPSU Central Committee.

The Central Committee highly appreciates the contribution the media have been making to perestroika. Why so? Because everything depends on the people. People are in the vanguard of the struggle, and perestroika develops through them. That is why the way people think, the level of their civic awareness and their civic stand are of decisive importance.

Our socialist society, which has resolutely embarked on the road of democratic renewal, has a vital stake in active participation by every citizen—every worker, every collective farmer, every scientist and every professional—in both the discussion of our plans and their implementation. And the mass media are playing and will continue to play a tremendous role in this. Naturally, they are not the only channel for expressing the people's will, for reflecting their views and moods. But they are the most representative and massive rostrum of glasnost. The Party wants every citizen to voice his opinion confidently from that rostrum; the voice of citizens should not only make known the discussions that are taking place in the country but also be a guarantor of democratic control over the correctness of decisions and their conformity with the interests and requirements of the masses and, at the next stage, over the fulfilment of the decisions.

The current democratization process is reflected not only in publications, it is increasingly influencing the activities of the mass media. Gradually, as though thawing, our newspapers, magazines, radio and television are uncovering and handling new topics. One of the signs of the general revitalization is that our press is increasingly preferring dialogue to monologue. Formal reports are giving way to interviews, conversations, "round-table" discussions, and discussions about letters from readers. True, there is a tendency sometimes to limit the number of contributing writers to three to five people. This is nothing but professional arrogance. It is much more useful to diversify the authorship so that all citizens have a say, so that socialist pluralism, as it were, is represented in each publication in its entirety. It is certainly a good thing when a professional writer defines his position. It is much more interesting, however, to read conversations and interviews with workers, secretaries of district Party committees, chairmen of collective farms, scientists and cultural personalities. They are the carriers of live ideas. Or take the letters—what wonderful documents they are! They are truly moving.

Not everyone, however, likes the new style. This is especially true of those who are not used to living and working in the conditions of glasnost and broad criticism, who cannot and do not want to do this. It is they who voice discontent with our mass media and sometimes even demand that glasnost be constrained, curbed.

We do not regard it as negative that there are debates on whether there is not too much criticism, whether we need such broad openness, and whether democratization will have undesirable consequences. These debates, in a way, demonstrate concern for the stability of our society. Democracy and glasnost may be drowned in rhetoric and their meaning distorted. There are people who are seemingly all for the innovations, but when it comes to action they attach all sorts of conditions and reservations to the development of democracy, criticism and glasnost.

It is no longer a question of whether the CPSU Central Committee will continue the policy of glasnost through the press and the other mass media and with the active participation of citizens. We need glasnost as we need the air.

I would like to stress once again that the policy of broadening glasnost and developing criticism and self-criticism, rather than playing at democracy, is a matter of principle for our Party. We regard the development of glasnost as a way of accumulating the various diverse views and ideas which reflect the interests of all strata, of all trades and professions in Soviet society. We won't be able to advance if we don't check how our policy responds to criticism, especially criticism from below, if we don't fight negative developments, don't prevent them and don't react to information from below. I cannot imagine democracy without all this.

On the other hand, the criteria and character of criticism are also changing in the conditions of restructuring and democratization. Criticism is, first and foremost, responsibility, and the sharper the criticism, the more responsible it should be, for each article on a social topic is not only a self-expression by a certain person or a reflection of somebody's complexes or ambitions, but a matter of public importance. Democratization is introducing substantial corrections into the relationships between those who criticize and those who are criticized. These should be relations of partnership built on mutual interest. A dialogue is more appropriate in such instances, while all sorts of condescending lecturing and didactics and especially courtroom tones are absolutely inadmissible. And the latter can be found even in articles written by good and respected authors. No one has the right to a final judgment.

One thing is obvious: criticism should always be based on the truth, and this depends on the conscience of the author and the editor, on their sense of responsibility to the people.

The press must become even more effective. It should not leave in peace loafers, profit-seekers, time-servers, suppressors of criticism, and demagogues; it should more actively help those who are selflessly working for perestroika. A lot here depends on the local Party committees. If the Party committee reorganizes its work, the press does so, too.

I want to emphasize that the press should unite and mobilize people rather than disuniting them and generating offence and a lack of confidence. Renewal of society also means striving to assert the dignity of man, his elevation and his honor. Criticism can be an effective instrument of perestroika only if it is based on absolute truth and scrupulous concern for justice.

To uphold the fundamental values of socialism is a tradition of our press. Any fact, whether it is the burning issue of today or some unfortunate event of the past, may become the subject of analysis by the press. What values you defend, whether the people's destiny and future are of concern to you is what matters the most. It so happens, sometimes, that an author brings a sensational fact, a topical fact, out in a newspaper and begins to dance around it, imposing on others his own ideas and likes. In my opinion, any honest, open talk, even if it arouses doubts, should be welcomed. But if you try to fit somebody else's suit on us, beware! Glasnost is aimed at strengthening our society. And we have a lot to assert. Only those whom socialist democracy and our demands for responsibility prevent from satisfying their personal ambitions, which are, anyway, far removed from the people's interests, can doubt this.

Of course, this is not a call to put a ban on criticism or to switch to half-truths and give up critical analysis. The interests of deepening socialist democracy and enhancing the political maturity of the people require fuller use of the mass media for discussing public and state issues, broadening control by the public, active striving for greater responsibility, for stronger discipline at work, for observance of socialist law and order, and against violations of the social principles and ethical standards of the Soviet way of life. We seek to organize this work in such a way that the mass media can act as a free, integral and flexible force nationwide, a force capable of promptly tackling the more topical events and problems.

Glasnost, criticism and self-criticism are not just a new campaign. They have been proclaimed and must become a norm in the Soviet way of life. No radical change is possible without it. There is no democracy, nor can there be, without glasnost. And there is no present-day socialism, nor can there be, without democracy.

There are still quite a few officials who continue to react painfully to criticism in the media and assess articles or broadcasts from the angle of personal taste, past experience, wrong interpretation of the interests of society, or simply do not understand the role of the press in the socialist society of today. Sometimes, they try to scare the critics by warning of the possible reaction to a critical article on the part of the West. The West, they claim, is eager to hear our self-criticism in order to turn it against us, to discredit the socialist way of life. I cannot say anything definite about others, but I myself do not fear criticism. A critical review of our own experience is a sign of strength, not weakness. Such an approach accords with the principles of socialist ideology.

But there exists, also, another, "quiet" method of suppressing or avoiding criticism, when officials agree in public with it, and even applaud it and promise to take effective measures, but in actual fact are in no hurry to draw practical conclusions. They hope that everything will end in talk, "sink into the sand," and their sins will not be recalled any longer. For such people the important thing is to repent in proper time. . . .

We will do all in our power to prevent anyone from either suppressing criticism or sidestepping it. Criticism is a bitter medicine, but the ills that plague society make it a necessity. You make a wry face, but you swallow it. And those who think that criticism need only be dosed out at intervals are wrong. People who are inclined to believe that stagnation has fully been overcome and it's time to take it easy are just as wrong. A slackening of criticism will inevitably harm perestroika.

The Final Years of the Soviet Union

By Martin McCauley

Soon after implementing his dual reforms of glasnost and perestroika, Mikhail Gorbachev realized that more vigorous measures would be needed to force the more reluctant "old guard" of the Soviet leadership to participate in the process of reforming the country. Martin McCauley, a scholar of twentieth-century Russia, examines the unprecedented steps that Gorbachev took in trying to remake the Soviet Union in what proved to be its final years. McCauley begins by looking at the steps that diminished the unquestioned dominance of the Communist Party over the affairs of state, such as the replacement of the Supreme Soviet by the Congress of People's Deputies, a nominally more democratic legislative body, and the legalization of non-Communist political parties. McCauley discusses the strong negative reaction that Gorbachev's efforts at reform caused among hard-line Communists and places the attempted coup of August 1991 into this context. The failure of the reactionaries to reassert their control showed the powerlessness of the Soviet leaders—both the reformers and their hard-line opponents—and the country ceased to exist by the end of the year.

The perceived need for political reform, coupled with the unwillingness of many in the party apparatus to agree on an agenda, led [Soviet premier Mikhail] Gorbachev to convene a party conference in June 1988. Its proceedings were conducted with a freedom of speech and criticism that had not been seen since the early days of the revolution. Gorbachev's overriding achievement was to emasculate the party Secretariat: it lost its power to vet all key nominations to government and soviet posts, to interfere in the economy and to dominate local party bodies. In effect, Gorbachev had stripped the party 'centre' of its power over the state, economy, and even lower-ranking

Martin McCauley, "From Perestroika Towards a New World Order, 1985–1995," *Russia: A History*, edited by Gregory L. Freeze. Oxford: Oxford University Press, 1997. Copyright © 1997 by Oxford University Press. Reproduced by permission.

bodies. All this accelerated the centrifugal flow of power to the periphery, a process that indeed had already gathered momentum in the late [Leonid] Brezhnev era. The conference further agreed to establish an executive-style presidency (Gorbachev being the President-in-waiting) and restricted party executives to five-year terms of office, renewable only once. They were also to be appointed after contested elections. Other resolutions welcomed the formation of new social groups in favour of perestroika but condemned 'any action aimed at destroying the socialist basis of society, inciting nationalism or racism, or advocating war, violence, or immorality'. Freedom of conscience and the right to take part in decision-making were listed as basic human rights. What was needed was an 'effective mechanism for free dialogue, criticism, self-criticism and self-control'. Gorbachev proposed to restore power to popularly elected soviets, but still within the framework of a one-party communist system. In order to win over party officials, he proposed that the local party secretaries chair the local soviets 'in order to confer legitimacy on them'. As some were quick to point out, however, this proposal was contradictory to Gorbachev's declared goal of transferring power to local soviets.

A New Legislature Is Created

According to the Brezhnev constitution of 1977, the USSR Supreme Soviet was the supreme legislative body, but in reality of course it ceded precedence to the Politburo and Central Committee. Its ceremonial function was evidenced by the fact that it normally adopted all resolutions unanimously. By October 1988, however, glasnost led to dissent appearing in the Supreme Soviet. At issue was the right of Ministry of Interior troops to enter private homes without a warrant, and the right to control demonstrations without reference to local authorities. On the first issue thirty-one deputies voted against, and on the second thirteen opposed the adoption of the decree.

On 29 November 1988 the Supreme Soviet adopted a law that was tantamount to its own dissolution when it established a new institution, the Congress of People's Deputies (CPD) with 2,250 members. Two-thirds were to be elected under the old system: 750 members were to represent nationalities, another 750 were to be chosen by electoral constituencies of the same approximate size. The remaining 750 were to be nominated directly by the CPSU [Communist Party of the Soviet Union], Komsomol [the Communist Youth League], trade unions, the Academy of Sciences, and Churches. This CPD was then to elect a new USSR Supreme Soviet; comprised of two chambers (with 271 members in each), which were to function as a real parliament and to meet for three- to four-month periods in spring and autumn. Those nominated did not have to be party members, but electoral meetings normally favoured party candidates. To be elected, a candidate had to obtain over 50 per cent of the vote, even if he or she were the only candidate. If no one was elected in the first round, a second round had to take place not more than two months later. On this occasion the candidate with most votes was declared the winner. Candidates could put forward their own political programme and debate with one another.

When the CPD elections were held in March 1989, approximately a quarter of the 1,500 directly elected deputies faced no opposition in their constituencies. Over 80 per cent of the candidates were CPSU members; one-fifth were women. Some prominent party officials were defeated, including five members of the Central Committee. The most prominent casualty was Iurii Solovev, first party secretary of Leningrad *oblast* [a political unit between city and state]. Prominent radicals, such as Andrei Sakharov and Roy Medvedev, were elected. Boris Yeltsin won a landslide victory in Moscow; voters took his side after the minutes of the Central Committee meeting of 21 October 1987, when he was humiliated and sacked as a member of the Politburo and the party secretary for Moscow, were published in an effort to undermine his popularity. Yeltsin, ever the populist, promised to 'free Moscow from the mafia of bureaucrats'. Gorbachev's failure to support Yeltsin in his conflict with [Politburo member Egor] Ligachev and the conservative Party élite led to the two falling out and the beginning of the titanic struggle that was to end in the Soviet leader's political destruction. Yeltsin was elected to the USSR Supreme Soviet after a Siberian deputy stood down and offered Yeltsin his mandate. This afforded Yeltsin a national platform for the first time, which he used to promote the interests of the Russian Federation and to attack party privilege, the failings of perestroika, the need for market-oriented reforms, and Gorbachev himself.

In republican and local elections in March 1990 radical electoral groups won in the major cities and many prominent party officials were defeated. In Moscow 'Democratic Russia' won 85 per cent of the capital's seats in the CPD of the Russian Federation and 56 per cent of the seats in the city soviet. In Leningrad, the group 'Democratic Elections 90' took 80 per cent of the mandates to the CPD and 54 per cent of the seats in the city soviet. . . .

The Erosion of Communist Control

The emergence of informal groups and movements brought into question Article 6 of the 1977 constitution, which explicitly guaranteed the [Communist] party's leading role in society. But many reformers still believed that the party, the only organization with a nation-wide organization, was the most effective vehicle for change. Elections to the CPD in March 1989 stirred debate within the party, and Gorbachev appeared to have a solid constituency for change. Nevertheless, both radicals and conservatives were suspicious about his motives, the former because he moved too slowly, the latter because he was undermining the existing power structure. In April 1989 he persuaded about a quarter of the Central Committee members to retire; most, in fact, no longer occupied the positions that had ensured their election in the first place. Twenty-four new members were added. Gorbachev spoke enthusiastically about a 'new type of working person' who would 'feel like a human being' as a result of participating in the whole range of economic and social development.

In December 1989 Gorbachev underlined the party's role as a 'consolidating and uniting force' and defended article 6 that had legitimized this role. He was under pressure from Lithuania: the Communist Party of Lithuania had just removed a similar article from the Lithuanian constitution and, still more ominously, was preparing to break from the CPSU and form a separate national Communist Party. Gorbachev warned the Lithuanians 'not to cross the line' that threatened to destroy the CPSU 'as a single political organization and the vital consolidating force of the Soviet Union'.

As an inter-regional group (led by such radicals as Sakharov and Yeltsin) emerged in the Supreme Soviet, some party members began to break ranks and urge the formation of an opposition party. Gorbachev's decision to retain the leading role of the party may have been a tactical blunder; with hindsight it seems that he might have achieved more by splitting the party and assuming leadership of its radical wing.

The date for the Twenty-Eighth Party Congress was moved up to July 1990. Gorbachev's programme remained fundamentally contradictory: on the one hand, he called for the reform and renewal of the party, but on the other he revived Lenin's slogan of 'all power to the soviets'. He could not have it both ways, however: either the renewed party or the soviets were to exercise power, not both. The draft proposal, 'Towards Humane Democratic Socialism' (prepared for the Central Committee plenum in February 1990), was perhaps indicative of his thinking. The party would no longer exercise any state or government functions; hence it was to renounce its monopoly of power, enshrined in the Brezhnev constitution, and permit the emergence of multi-party politics. If the party wanted a leading role, it must first acquire it by popular mandate; it was to participate in the political process, but without special privileges or advantages. The document noted that the democratization was already under way and leading towards greater 'political pluralism'; the emerging political organizations and movements might coalesce to form regular political parties. The CPSU was prepared to 'co-operate' and enter into a 'dialogue' with all organizations committed to the Soviet constitution and the social system that it prescribed. It also proposed to water down the democratic centralism that had concentrated decision-making at the top and stifled debate and grass-roots initiative. Party branches, for example, were to play the 'decisive role' in electing delegates to the Congress.

Gorbachev's proposals ignited a fierce debate in the party and provoked growing criticism of his leadership. And as the Central Committee met in plenary session, a huge pro-reform demonstration gathered outside the walls of the Kremlin. In any event it agreed to deprive the Politburo of its dominant role in the state; henceforth it was to deal solely with internal party matters. Article 6 of the constitution was thus modified; the new text declared that the party merely 'participates' in running the country and vowed that it 'does not lay claim to full governmental authority. It seeks to be the political leader but without any claim to any special position laid down in the constitution'.

The programme elicited strong opposition from both conservatives and radicals. The fiercest radical critics of the plenum were Boris Yeltsin and the younger generation, who regarded the resolutions as a vain attempt to conciliate right and left. Egor Ligachev, expressing the fears of the conservative bureaucracy, called for party and national unity. In his view, the greatest danger to perestroika emanated from the 'powerful forces of a nationalist, separatist and anti-socialist tendency'.

Pravda, the party's own voice, had been lukewarm towards reform, but Gorbachev managed to install Ivan Frolov as editor. He duly praised Gorbachev as the 'leader of the progressive forces in the party'. That very statement, in effect, conceded that the 'monolithic Party' was a thing of the past, that it was riven with dissent. In March 1990 *Pravda* published the programme of the 'Democratic Platform', a radical faction in the party, which demanded the outright abandonment of a single ideology and the rejection of communism as the party's goal. The programme further urged the party to renounce democratic centralism and cells based on production units, and instead to build a democratic society and become one of several political parties based on freedom, justice, and solidarity. The programme, understandably, sent shock waves through the party.

The Politburo and Central Committee reacted in high dudgeon in an open letter to all members. They called for an end to factionalism, enjoined those involved to resign, expressly denounced the Democratic Platform, and expelled its leaders from the party. This caused Yeltsin and others to sign an open letter, which accused conservatives of 'making furious efforts on the eve of the Congress to effect a coup against perestroika in the party'. They did not recognize the 'right of party officials to impose their will on the rank and file'. Advocates of the Democratic Platform debated whether they should leave the party before the Congress or wait to see if it could regenerate itself. Although some supporters had already left the party, most opted to wait and see. . . .

[By summer 1991] the odds were certainly in favour of a successful coup by the eight-man 'Emergency Committee' comprised of the heads of the military, police, KGB, and government. Although the nominal head was Gennadii Ianaev (Gorbachev's Vice-President, who was to assume the top position), the real mastermind was Vladimir Kriuchkov, the KGB chief. The announcement that the treaty to establish a union of sovereign states was to be signed on 20 August 1991 triggered the move. The plotters also believed that Gorbachev would accede to their demand that he resign in favour of Ianaev; they laid no contingency plan when, in a meeting at his dacha at Foros, Crimea, on the

evening of 18 August, he flatly refused. At 6 A.M. the following day Moscow radio broadcast an 'appeal to the Soviet people', claiming that Gorbachev's policies had failed and left the country ungovernable and on the verge of collapse. The plotters sent tanks into Moscow but failed to arrest Yeltsin, who boldly made his way to the Russian White House, passing through the lines of tanks and daring anyone to arrest him. His refusal to acquiesce proved the turning-point: standing on a tank (reminiscent of Lenin's arrival at Finland Station in April 1917), Yeltsin demanded the restoration of Gorbachev as President, called for a general strike, declared the Russian Federation sovereign, and ordered all authorities to obey him. He called the *putsch* [German word for an attempted overthrow of a government] an attempt to crush Russia. Eventually, the military itself split, with some tanks and units changing sides and coming to defend the White House. The plotters had to abandon their plan to storm the White House and by 21 August had obviously suffered a complete rout, the entire *putsch* exacting just three fatalities. Gorbachev now returned to Moscow, but the capital in fact already belonged to Yeltsin.

The organization of the *putsch* itself had been astonishingly inept, but its most critical error had been the failure to identify and deploy loyal troops. The plotters had simply assumed that the military would obey. They had failed to grasp the political and social transformation that perestroika had wrought, that it was no longer possible to seize power by simply declaring that the President had retired on 'grounds of health'.

The attempted coup none the less had important consequences: above all, it destroyed prospects for a new union. As republics rushed to declare independence before another coup could succeed, Gorbachev tried desperately to salvage something from the wreckage. But when Ukraine voted for independence on 1 December 1991, it dealt the Soviet Union a final mortal blow. One week later the three Slav republics—Russia, Ukraine, and Belorussia (renamed Belarus)—issued the 'Minsk Declaration' stating that the Soviet Union had been superseded by the Commonwealth of Independent States (CIS). On 21 December, in Alma-Ata (Kazakhstan), eleven states signed a protocol formally establishing the CIS. The other four republics of the former Soviet Union (Estonia, Latvia, Lithuania, and Georgia) refused to sign. Gorbachev waited until Christmas Day to resign and laid the Soviet Union to rest on 31 December, 1991.

The principal legal successor state to the Soviet Union was the Russian Federation. Thus it formally assumed the Soviet seat on the UN Security Council, took control of all the Soviet embassies and property around the world, and accepted responsibility for outstanding Soviet debts (approximately 60 billion dollars). Russia was by far the predominant power, accounting for 60 per cent of the GDP and occupying 76 per cent of the territory of the former USSR. Although its population (148 million) was now far smaller, Russia was the largest country in the CIS, with 51 per cent of the former Soviet population. It still occupied more than one-eighth of the globe's territory, wielded a vast arsenal of nuclear weapons, and could draw upon a rich wealth of natural and human resources.

The History of Nations
Chapter 5

Current Challenges

Putin's Efforts to Eliminate Corruption

BY LILIA SHEVTSOVA

Many observers were surprised in August 1999 when Russian president Boris Yeltsin named a relatively unknown politician named Vladimir Putin to be prime minister. When Yelstin announced that he would not run for reelection in March 2000, it became clear that Putin had become Yeltsin's choice to succeed him. Putin was elected with 52 percent of the vote (defeating his nearest rival by more than 20 percent) and quickly began making changes in the government's policies. Lilia Shevtsova, senior associate at the Carnegie Endowment for International Peace and a noted scholar of post-Soviet Russia, examines the challenges that faced Putin when he took office—most notably the rampant corruption and favoritism that had crippled the Russian economy and political system after the Soviet Union's collapse. Shevtsova presents several hypotheses about the potential effects that Putin's responses to these challenges could have on the development of Russia in the near future. She argues that Putin is likely to revert to a more autocratic form of government as a solution to the corruption of the Yelstin era.

At the start of 2001, [Russian president Vladimir] Putin was faced with a dilemma: introducing innovative models for transforming the economy, that is, decisive structural reforms, which [Putin's predecessor Boris] Yeltsin was incapable of accomplishing, would mean destroying the basis for the relative stability in society—patron–client relations. But if this were to happen, the president would face losing the support of many groups that exist because of shadowy relations and that see

Lilia Shevtsova, "From Yeltsin to Putin: The Evolution of Presidential Power," *Gorbachev, Yeltsin, and Putin: Political Leadership in Russia's Transition*, edited by Archie Brown and Lilia Shevtsova. Washington, DC: Carnegie Endowment for International Peace, 2001. Copyright © 2001 by Carnegie Endowment for International Peace. Reproduced by permission.

him as a guarantor of their well-being. The result would shatter stability in society. Is Putin ready to do this? At this particular stage, it was not clear. Furthermore, he was not even able during this time to consolidate his base of support to effect decisive structural reforms.

Putin's policies still leave the impression that he is trying to base his power and economic measures on the principle of personal loyalty. This is reflected in his allowing separate groups of influence to operate in a "gray zone," permitting them to circumvent the law if they are personally loyal to him. This selective approach is unlikely to help him make effective reforms, one of the goals of which is to eliminate the union between political power and business. For now at least, Putin himself is trying to change the nature of this union and make business dependent on the state and the leader. But the patron-client relations that have developed remain unchanged and could undermine the future course of reform.

Will Putin Become an Autocratic Leader?

Theoretically, it cannot be ruled out that Putin will pursue more vigorously the idea of a "transmission belt" system [a political system in which authority is passed down from the top of the leadership hierarchy, rather than distributed and shared horizontally], will overcome his hesitation, and will take more decisive steps toward making his regime more authoritarian—first by neutralizing independent political actors and curbing political freedoms. As Putin said in an interview with French journalists before his visit to Paris in October 2000: "The state has in its hands a cudgel that strikes only once. But on the head. We have not yet resorted to this cudgel. We have simply laid our hands on it, and this turned out to be enough to attract attention. But if we are angered, we won't hesitate to put it to use." This statement can be considered a manifesto of the new post-Yeltsin authorities. It points to the direction in which Putin still is trying to move, emphasizing the bureaucratic-coercive component of his regime. But the question remains: Will simple solutions help unravel the very complex knot of Russian development?

There is much more evidence that Putin's leadership is most likely to evolve with attempts to consolidate his regime through a mixture of semi-authoritarian steps and political bargaining. What does this entail? It means the tactic of "one step forward, one step back." The president will continue to increase control over all institutions, influence the formation of parties friendly to the Kremlin, strengthen control over the news media, and create his own loyal oligarchs [individual desiring power for a select few, usually for corrupt purposes]. But if this policy of building a manageable political field meets resistance, he will most likely temporarily yield and even step back. Such a "policy of impulses" could include the wide use of means of fear and manipulation. But the fact is that the politics of fear can only be partially effective, since the failure to strike a coercive blow—that is, apply force—could create the impression that the authorities are powerless. Manipulative politics also have their limits. As the experience of Putin's rise has shown, the manipulative use of technology to exclude opponents and boost the president's ratings can only be successful during elections. But in the process of real governing, virtual means of supporting the president gradually lose their significance. What is needed are concrete and palpable results from his actions. In the end, the policy of "one step forward, one step back" will most likely produce only the imitation of a strong state and effective leadership. As a result of the evolution of Yeltsin's political legacy under Putin, we can ascertain the formation in Russia of a hybrid bureaucratic quasi-authoritarian regime which at the moment is not stable or consolidated and can develop in different directions. This regime, less patrimonial and seemingly more rational and pragmatic than Yeltsin's, fully fits within the framework of Yeltsin's "elected monarchy." That is, the very formal and constitutional basis for the structure of the Yeltsin regime remains as before, comprising a personal style of governing and a concentration of all the levers of power and administration in the hands of the president, with a weak role reserved for other institutions and the same merger of power and capital. Still, because the other sources of legitimacy of power in present-day Russia—the armed forces, parties, ideology, hereditary monarchy—have become exhausted, the need for exercising democratic institutions, above all elections, to legitimize this power most likely will be preserved, but their democratic substance will become thin.

As for possible steps Putin will take regarding the economy, it is clear that if he does not use his high ratings and the favorable economic conditions for conducting more decisive reforms (such as adopting the second part of the tax code, land reform, judicial reform, bank reform, and guarantees of private property), then it is possible he will not be able to accomplish them by the end of his term.

Putin Begins His Reform Program

In spring 2001, Putin pushed forward the implementation of long-delayed judicial, pension, housing, and utility reforms. He initiated the change of leadership in Gazprom [Russia's major producer of natural gas and a notably corrupt corporation under Yeltsin]. The office of General Prosecutor reopened investigation into the activity of some influential members of Yeltsin's "family" [his circle of close advisers], including notorious oligarch Roman Abramovich, which could not happen without the consent of the Kremlin. These steps gave rise to hopes that Putin had finally begun his liberal breakthrough. But so far, a lot of questions remain. It is unclear whether the ruling team will succeed with painful reforms that exclude the public from dialogue on their substance. It is also not clear if Putin's reshuffles and distancing from the previous entourage demonstrate readiness to change the interdependence between political power and business or if it simply means a changing of the guard and an attempt to expand his own constituency. So far there are no answers. As long as the Russian president continues to rely upon personal networks and the loyalty of his own cadres, and until he is willing to go beyond making governance *look* more rational and pragmatic and actually changes its substance, he hardly can change the previous logic of development. In the final analysis, he might only become a hostage of the surrogate, imitation democracy that has emerged in Russia.

If Putin fails to break the logic of personal networking, it cannot be ruled out that he will be forced to return to a policy of connivance and pay for his survival with concessions to interest groups. But no one would be able to guarantee his survival, for the political elite, which is accustomed to changing its allegiance at will, can at any moment support a new pretender to the role of master of the Kremlin, if this claimant offers a more advantageous deal.

[Russian media mogul and close confidant of Yeltsin] Boris Berezovsky, who bears much responsibility for the degradation of power in Russia and for the changes now occurring in the country, should be quoted in this regard. Having been thrown out of the circle of power, the observant Berezovsky was able to give a good diagnosis of the policies that the Kremlin is now trying to carry out. "Putin," he says, "does not believe that Russia is ready to become a liberal, free country. He does believe that the president or other bosses should still take care of people."

This paternalism and attempt of the new team to make the people happy and punish heterodox thinkers—although for the time being not yet severely, but simply by scolding and threatening with the finger—have already begun to bear fruit. Some Russian citizens have preserved the remnants of slavery, and some have even taken refuge in the Soviet past with pleasure. Some have begun to glorify Putin enthusiastically, others have started to write textbooks about him, yet others have created for him political parties and youth organizations. Part of the country has begun to return to a seemingly forgotten time. There are some signs, however, of a degree of optimism, largely among thinking people who are accustomed to analyzing events independently and for whom a return to lack of freedom would be very difficult, if not impossible. According to opinion polls, such thinking people in Russian society make up between 44 and 47 percent of the population including about 15 percent of Westernizers, those who consider liberal democracy and moving Russia toward Europe the optimal scenario. For the moment, a good number of them are still biding their time, giving Putin a chance, and even agreeing to some limits on their freedom for the sake of market reform. But this part of the population clearly does not wish to live in a society that operates on the principle of a "transmission belt," and sooner or later it will present a serious problem for the new team if that team continues on its course of turning society into a marching colony.

The Challenges Facing Putin

Putin will apparently have to dispel several illusions linked to reform of Yeltsin's government. First is the illusion of a relatively painless construction of a presidential "pyramid" [i.e., a system in which the president's power is established on a democratic base] in a pluralistic society accustomed to freedom. He will have to think about how to make his authority legitimate, given the lack of independent institutions in the country other than the presidency, and how under such conditions he can avoid responsibility for the failures of those at every level of power who become appendages of the presidency.

The hope that the president's strength will help to continue economic reform could also turn out to be an illusion. Few remember that, in 1991, Yeltsin tried to introduce liberal authoritarianism in Russia, but nothing came of it. [In 2001] apologists of the new "firm hand" in Russia try to show that Yeltsin was unable to accomplish anything because of his weakness and inconsistency. Putin, they argue, will have more luck because he is a disciplined person and knows how to apply coercive methods. As for the many cases in world history of failed attempts to make authoritarian and totalitarian regimes economically effective, the Russian ruling team is not so far interested in drawing analogies. Yet again, there are powerful groups in Russia who try to force society to start a new experiment on its own only to convince itself of its more than likely failure.

An "elected monarchy" based on the loyalty of cadres to a single figure and their servility—a mere imitation of democratic institutions—could turn out to be a form of strengthening shadowy relations and corruption. In any case, the regime's reliance on the bureaucracy, which in Russia has long been the coffin maker of any reform, will hardly promote economic transformations. It is rather more likely that something else will occur: given the lack of counterbalances, the bureaucracy could make the president its hostage. In addition, by bringing representatives of the security structures and especially the secret service into the government, its closed nature and opaque decision making process will only be exacerbated, which will make dominating the narrow interests groups within it easier.

Thus there are serious doubts about whether the attempt of Vladimir Putin to unite mobilizing and innovative types of development as well as find a formula for a dynamic leadership based on the subordination and loyalty of cadres can be effective. Moreover, there are doubts about whether such an attempt can be carried out at all. It is rather likely that Putin's idea of a vertical and coordinated pyramidal structure of power will fail in the end. [As of summer 2001], Putin has discovered increased uneasiness to make decisions and tried to escape taking responsibility, demonstrating a lack of sense of direction, thus proving that he most probably is not a candidate for the role of a Russian [version of Chilean dictator Augusto] Pinochet. But it is still unclear what Putin will do, when he fails to create a "transmission belt" in contemporary Russia: will he allow independent institutions to operate and grow and renounce autocracy and personified rule; or, out of frustration, will he try to establish a regime with a firm rule; or will he continue his policy of avoiding the final choice? Only time will provide answers to these questions.

What Direction Will Russia Take?

The future of Putin's leadership will depend a lot on his capacity for evolution—for acquiring the skills of a politician, for understanding the many directions in which society will develop, and for recognizing the need for social consensus on the basic questions of Russia's development. The dynamism and pragmatism of Putin and his striving to understand complex phenomena give some hope for his ability to expand on his political experience. It seems that the international community still has many opportunities for influencing him.

At the same time the character of the negative circumstances, from a liberal-democratic perspective, that in the near future will influence the Russian president should be taken into account. Among them is the lack of powerful democratic forces that would attempt to reform the elected autocracy. But even more serious is that all the main participants in the political process are accustomed to stability through shadowy relations, which form a systemic element that has saturated not only the economy but also Russian politics, and into which society itself has been drawn. It appears that Putin is hoping that, having accumulated all the resources of power and eliminated all the centers of influence, he will be able to take steps toward more decisive market reform. But it should be recalled that, when Yeltsin was formulating his leadership, he tried to do the same and ended up trading away his power for the sake of self-preservation as well as causing the degradation and decay of his regime.

Putin has, albeit theoretically, the chance to make a breakthrough. But he is left with little time to do so, and the steps he has already taken are leading Russia to new disappointments, for which some price will have to be paid. Thus, the result of the latest experiment of trying to prolong the life of autocracy in the 21st century is almost clear. What is uncertain is in which direction Russia will go when it becomes clear that the resources of autocratic forms of leadership have been exhausted.

The Orthodox Church in Post-Soviet Russia

BY JERRY G. PANKHURST

In keeping with Karl Marx's hostility toward religion—he famously called it the "opiate of the masses"—the Soviet Union was a society in which the influence of the Russian Orthodox Church was heavily suppressed. Jerry G. Pankhurst, professor of sociology at Wittenberg University in Springfield, Ohio, examines the slow resurgence of the church in the post-Soviet period. Pankhurst notes that Russian Orthodoxy remains the dominant faith in Russia today but faces a number of challenges in regaining its traditionally central place in Russian culture. Not only does the church face a chronic shortage of priests because of the closure of seminaries during the Soviet period, but it also suffers from theological stagnation in that many of its teachings are still geared toward the believers of the late nineteenth century. Pankhurst concludes by asking a number of as-yet unanswered questions that face the church as it moves into the twenty-first century.

The atheist upbringing in Soviet society was fraught with many problems and, as time revealed, had little resonance among the general population. However, it had been undertaken in the context of the Russian religious culture and, as such, was bound to have reverberated throughout society. We recall that *pravoslavie*, or Orthodoxy, was imposed upon the pagan population from above [by Vladimir in 988] and never fully replaced ancient religious customs with the new forms of spirituality and spiritual discipline. Cultural development nearly stopped at the point where Christian rituals were implanted in everyday consciousness without transforming its spiritual content. The Or-

Jerry G. Pankhurst, "Religious Culture," *Russian Culture at the Crossroads: Paradoxes of Postcommunist Consciousness,* edited by Dmitri N. Shalin. Boulder, CO: Westview Press, 1996. Copyright © 1996 by Westview Press. Reproduced by permission.

thodox Church tended to equate religiosity with ritual. The Church never made any attempt to foster a religiously literate population. In fact, for a long time Russian Orthodoxy eschewed general literacy as a worthy goal. Even less was the religious establishment in Russia committed to critical inquiry into its spiritual moorings, to instilling an open-minded attitude toward religious practices among its participants. The religious renaissance that the intellectual elite experienced before the revolution of 1917 came to a grinding halt after the Bolsheviks came to power and made it all but impossible to convert this movement into a popular religious renaissance. The communists' attack on the Church exhausted its leadership and sealed its subservient status in a relationship that harkened back to the Byzantine principle of symphonia [harmony between religion and government, which was accomplished by making religious leaders subservient to political leaders]. Dogmatism, religious formalism, intolerance of dissent—some of the salient features of the Russian religious culture—were further reinforced by autocratic communist practices. With religious leaders and intellectuals effectively silenced, the common faithful had few means of preserving anything more than a flawed memory of Orthodoxy along with the sentimental attachment to the beauty of the Russian Orthodox liturgy. By the end of the Soviet era, Russians were a religiously malformed people who had sustained heavy damage, both individually and institutionally, from the decades of party-sponsored atheism overlain upon centuries of religious submission to autocracy.

The Resurgence of the Russian Orthodox Church

Orthodoxy is prone to celebrate its martyrs above all saints, but nobody is denying the blessings that religious freedom gave to the believers in the mid-1980s. Religious freedom arrived, first surreptitiously, as the state lapsed in its efforts to enforce antireligious laws, then more openly, beginning with the decision to release religious prisoners of conscience in the period 1986–87. From that point on, believers faced fewer problems registering their congregations. Liberalization gained momentum after the 1988 festivities surrounding the millennium of Russian Orthodoxy. This glorious event opened auspiciously with General Secretary [Mikhail] Gorbachev granting an audience to the patriarch and chief bishops. About the same time, drafts of new laws on "freedom of conscience and religious organizations" reached the public. After extended public discussion, final versions thereof were adopted by both the Soviet Union and the Russian Republic in October 1990. These laws eliminated the primary means by which the Soviet government had waged its war on religion since the end of the 1920s and finally permitted—for the first time in over fifty years—what most people elsewhere in the world would consider normal religious worship. Orthodox and other religious believers in the Soviet Union were just getting adapted to the new circumstances when the whole structure of the Soviet state collapsed in late 1991.

Seldom does a religious institution find itself in such a truly historic circumstance as the Russian Church does in the post-Soviet era. The changes engulfing Russia have portents not only for its citizens but for the whole world. A vigorous, decisive, democratic church might wield great influence on the direction those important changes take. Such a church would possess a social ethic conducive to democratic ideology and free market entrepreneurship. It would spearhead a debate about society's values and goals, as well as spell out its own agenda in the various arenas of policy planning. It would exercise its spiritual influence on the population and shape the spiritual identity of the newly emerging autonomous nation. To paraphrase Richard John Neuhaus, a Protestant theologian, such a church should be a visible presence in the public square. Has the Russian Orthodox Church established a permanent residence there?

Physically, the Russian Orthodox Church is quickly reestablishing itself on the town square. Since 1988, when Gorbachev and the leaders of the Russian Orthodox Church met for the first time, the number of congregations and operating churches has burgeoned. According to one source, this number nearly doubled between 1985 and 1991, from 6,806 to approximately 12,000. However, the costs of this expansion have been extremely high. Without many outlets for its resources, the Russian Church had grown used to being relatively well off under the Soviets. Now, the Church has been essentially bankrupted by its rapid expansion. We should bear in mind that institutions are real and organized societal beings, that they are in conflict and competition for the hearts of the people. So far, the state has been a big winner in its competition with the Russian Church. The question now is whether the religious institution has the means to mount a new drive to better counterbalance statism in society. The Church's bankruptcy is apparent not only in monetary terms. The Church's spiritual and theological resources are stretched to the limit as well. First, there are not enough clergy to serve all the new parishes. Second, the Church does not have the ability to compensate adequately those who are serving. Third, to satisfy the growing demand for clergy, priests work excessive hours, with very little time left for new initiatives or even simple reflection. Furthermore, the Church has yet to address fully and effectively the serious issue of theological preparation for the clergy. As in the past, the Church has stressed the liturgical preparation of its clerics over their intellectual or spiritual preparations. Recognizing that the people of the parishes want someone to provide the sacraments, to baptize, marry, and bury them, the Church has responded by enlarging seminary classes without the requisite increase in faculty and staff. New teaching resources are sorely lacking; there is a tendency to fall back on the nineteenth century and earlier precedents. Very little constructive energy has been expended to find the meeting ground between *pravoslavie* and twentieth-century religious experience. In other words, while the Church may be reoccupying the public square physically—by breaking into the open, reaching out to the public, reclaiming property once confiscated by the state—it has yet to occupy the square spiritually, as a social force to reckon with in the giant reconstruction now facing the nation.

Finding a Place for Religion in Post-Soviet Russia

We cannot be too harsh in our judgment, though, for the problems facing the Russian Orthodox Church are enormous, indeed. The devout Russian Orthodox believer needs first and foremost a "spiritual father"; he needs to restore the historical bond with a priest or monk with whom he has a special relationship of trust and confidence. Unfortunately, the clergy today are overburdened with the ritual services to provide inspiration, spiritual guidance, and a clear vision of the future to everyone. . . . Moreover, we have to be concerned about the abuse of religious rhetoric by the leaders of nativist, ultraconservative movements. Numerous right-wing political and nationalist groups have risen up in Russia since the onset of perestroika, some of them tracing their roots back to prerevolutionary movements. Some of the leaders of such groups have begun utilizing religious language in their calls for Russia's return to her "greater destiny," and there are noteworthy proponents among the clergy and hierarchs of the Russian Orthodox Church who appear to be supporters. Traditional Russian Orthodox anti-Semitism has not been bridled on the extreme fringes, and it supports the reappearance in bookstalls of the scurrilous *Protocols of the Elders of Zion* [a famous anti-Semitic book from pre-Revolutionary times] and other hate literature. Although Patriarch Aleksii II has denied anti-Semitism in Church affairs, his administration has not mounted a direct attack on this problem. Without Church leadership in this regard, Pamyat ["Memory," a strongly nationalist organization] and similar nationalist-patriotic groupings have pursued their dark agendas with the support of extremist churchmen who experience no censure from their spiritual authorities.

In the legal arena itself, the Church has decided to keep silent. Several major churchmen were elected to the Gorbachev and then Russian Federation Parliament, including the patriarch, the most powerful bishops, and a number of priests. Yet, in the early 1990s the patriarch ruled that clergy were no longer permitted to run for such offices. When Father Gleb Yakunin defied the decree, he was defrocked and publicly humiliated by the patriarch. Ironically, Yakunin had been at odds with the Church hierarchy for nearly all his adult life. In 1991, he revealed some KGB records (since sealed) that indicated the close cooperation between several key bishops and the Soviet secret police. In 1993, from his seat in the Russian Parliament, Father Yakunin vigorously opposed the legislation on religious affairs sponsored by the Russian Orthodox Church. The law would have reinstated registration for all religious groups and organizations, limited the activities of foreign missionaries in Russia, and restored the Russian Orthodox Church's privileged position in the land. The manner in which the Patriarchate treated Father Yakunin indicates its unwillingness to engage in debate over its own position in Russian society, its freedom to stamp out dissent among its ranks, and its right to limit alternative forms of religious expression. This stance showed no tolerance for diversity, nor did it encourage constructive debate with its opponents inside and outside the Church. Dissenting views were handled in sadly familiar ways: exclusion, condemnation, excommunication.

Only in areas of direct interest has the Church taken an active role in the political process. Otherwise, as the run-up to the December 1993 elections demonstrated, Church authorities failed to connect their faith and their politics. No sense of moral obligation seemed to inform the clergy's politics, which are conspicuous for their absence in the seminaries, where no attempt is currently under way to initiate a coherent political discussion. This public square was naked indeed. The predominant impulse was to escape from the tough political fray into the comforting spiritual ether of the liturgy. Perhaps these developments will take time to unfold, but a religious culture that could sustain them is yet to take root. The cultural history I have sketched above does not bode well for the Church's action in the public arena, certainly not in the immediate future. Still, there is room for hope. . . .

What Lies Ahead for Russian Orthodoxy?

The path ahead is a tortuous one. Old elements must be purged, to be sure, but the bedrock of the tradition cannot be abandoned. The cultural transformation required is vast; it may be excruciatingly painful, given that *pravoslavie* faces its reconstruction exhausted by the communist era, and now further drained by the huge costs of energy, time, and money required for rebuilding its crumbling infrastructure. Although thousands of church buildings have been returned to the Church, most of them are in need of extensive and costly repair; many are, in the words of one bishop, "simply ruins," which must be totally reconstructed. There is an acute shortage of clergy, so the Church has to focus on the quick training of ritual specialists. Yet, somehow, the Church must develop the broader pastoral, theological, and philosophical concerns that could fill the public's needs the most. Can the Church find the resources to serve the great spiritual needs of the liberated population? Or will other aspirants to the status of religious supplier to Russia become more successful in fulfilling these yearnings, thus leading the transformation of Russian religious culture away from its historical Orthodox roots?

Experience in other countries suggests that, if general religious freedom persists, Russia is likely to become a great deal more diverse in its religious culture. While Orthodoxy recuperates its strength, other "religious entrepreneurs" will win a significant share of the religious market in Russia. Still, the daunting question persists: Will the Orthodox Church continue to stress the form, encourage nativistic elements in the government, and deny newer groups access to the population? Stated differently, will the Church put nationalistic goals and Church-state unity above service to the spiritual needs of the population?

One element that is affecting the Russian religious scene these days as never before is international religious culture. Historically, Russia was insulated from outside religious currents. Now, it cannot afford to be completely isolated. Although the Russian Orthodox Church has grown weary of ecumenical efforts, this international element gives one hope that the Church will continue to evolve in order to serve better its members' spiritual needs. Global culture may provide some of the innovations that will stimulate the broader revival of religion in Russia. The mature postcommunist Russia that one day will emerge after this present period of massive reconstruction will not simply ape Western society, as so many outsiders who put their entire stock in capitalist economics insist. We cannot say what shape the Russian civilization will take in the future, but we can venture a guess that it will reflect both the nation's historical religious afterimages and its present religious experience, which whittles away at the old religious culture and broadens the horizons of Russian Orthodoxy.

Russia's Economic and Political Future: Three Scenarios

BY VLADIMIR VOTAPEK

Since the fall of the Soviet Union, Russia has struggled to regain a stable economy. Rampant corruption and a lack of coordinated financial policy during Boris Yeltsin's tenure as president have made that process more difficult. Vladimir Votapek, a former Czech ambassador to Russia and current principal researcher at the Czech Institute for International Relations, analyzes the growing political and economic stability that accompanied the first two years of Vladimir Putin's presidency and uses them to predict three possible paths of development that Russia might take in the near future. Labeling these as "the miracle," "the stumble," and "the crisis," Votapek briefly discusses how each of these possible scenarios could come to pass. He also explains why the West needs to regard Russia's progress with a different perspective than it applies to itself, since the political traditions of the country are vastly different than those of the United States or Western Europe. Votapek argues that a clear understanding of which of his three hypothetical paths Russia ends up taking is impossible without such a perspective.

From the outside it looks as though Russia has, after ten years of muddle-headed economic and political reforms, reached a phase of relative stabilization [as of early 2002]. Due to the interaction of a number of favorable circumstances, Russia's economic decline has come to a halt, and during the last two years [2000–2001] it has even registered some economic growth. The political situation has also calmed down.

Vladimir Votapek, "Russia and the United States," *Toward an Understanding of Russia: New European Perspectives*, edited by Janusz Bugajski. New York: Council on Foreign Relations, 2002. Copyright © 2002 by Council on Foreign Relations, Inc. Reproduced by permission.

Among commentators and policymakers, opinion is divided on whether the above-mentioned stabilization reflects fundamental (qualitative) changes in Russian society and thus lays a foundation for undisturbed future development, or whether it is the result of a combination of factors that will expire over time and open up room for a new crisis. The analysis presented [here] tends toward the latter point of view, and holds that the stabilization of Russian society is only temporary.

Russia limps behind the developed world both in absolute figures and, more importantly, in the rate of development. Russia is grievously behind in the quality of production, services, and quality of life. Even if the Russian government were successful in combating the day-to-day problems, it would be difficult to imagine how they would cope with the challenges of the future. The Russian social system is inadequate and thus unable to meet the demands of the beginning of the third millennium. Russian society is mismanaged, and its wealth and human potential are wasted without sufficient returns.

To lead a society successfully today requires that it be managed in a systematic and transparent way. Success can result from the implementation of a management system that is designed to continually improve performance by addressing the needs of all interested parties. However, this is not the case for Russia. The pseudo-democratic and pseudo-market nature of the Russian administration is not up to dealing effectively with today's problems and is even less prepared to face the challenges of the future. The most probable scenario is that the country will continue to suffer from internal disorder, and sooner or later Russia will find itself up against a profound and multifaceted crisis.

The State of the Russian Economy

Russia's economy is growing for the third consecutive year. Industrial production and wages are up, while inflation is down. Russia's trade surplus is huge and Central Bank reserves exceeded U.S.$36 billion. The government's legislative agenda is impressive. The Duma [the Russian legislative body] adopted the second part of the Tax Code, a very important step that may become a landmark in the process of the economic transformation. The strong limitations placed on the number and type of taxes imposed on the various levels of government should clear the Russian tax system, which is still plagued by an excessive number of continually changing tax rates, regulations, exemptions, and local interpretations.

Alongside these positive factors, many negative factors that weakened the Russian economy throughout the 1990s remain in force. Price distortion supporting energy-intensive manufacturing persists. Although investment activity has increased to some extent, it has still not reached a level reflecting the simple reproduction of industrial capacity. The reconstruction of Russia's commercial banking sector remains a major challenge for the Central Bank and the government. Corruption and capital flight, along with the close connection between the economy and politics, have crippled the entire Russian economy.

Stabilization is based mainly on two factors. The first and less significant factor has been imports substituting for industrial growth, which is induced by the weak (undervalued) ruble. The second and decisive factor is export revenue caused by historically high prices that are unprecedented on the whole spectrum of energy and raw materials exported from Russia. It is hard to deny that both factors will sooner or later fade away. In fact, recent statistics have suggested that Russian economic growth is slowing, partly because inflation has begun biting into the competitiveness of industry.

Putin's Changes to the Power of the Russian Presidency

There is no need to dispute that the Russian political system under President Boris Yeltsin was ineffective and contributed to the paralysis of the country. However, the new president dramatically reshaped the power structure in Russia and created a top-down model of governance. He has not broken the constitutional framework, but his changes are enormous—executive power dominates absolutely; the Council of Federation (upper chamber of the Russian parliament) was dissolved; the Duma (lower chamber) works as a rubber stamp; the independence of the courts is restricted; local authorities are more submissive; and freedom of the press is far more limited than it was three years ago.

The authoritarian policies of President Vladimir Putin respond to the desire of many Russians for a stronger state, order, and cohesiveness in public life. His durable popularity stems from this "authoritarianism" buttressed by his very effective public relations. The electorate is disappointed both with the ideas of democratic reform and the tenets of socialism (communism). This ideological stalemate opens the door for the accession of a nonideological state authoritarianism. The top leaders of the political and economic elite have taken advantage of their de facto control over the electronic media and actively manipulate the mood of the majority of the electorate. Although elections are supposed to adhere to a series of democratic rules, unequal access to the media, finance, and different forms of state support create a de facto inequality of opportunity. It fictionalizes the results of the contest and deforms the nominally democratic process into a mere caricature.

Image makers, sociologists, and media advisers are working strenuously in Russia and are effectively manipulating the average Russian voter as a result. The last two presidential campaigns provide excellent examples of this effectiveness. In 1996, Boris Yeltsin won despite a dismal approval rating of around 5 percent only five months before the election. In the year 2000, Vladimir Putin was the victor, even though only one year earlier he was unknown to the population.

This situation completely conforms to the Russian tradition of a strong state holding the masses in passivity and provides the political and administrative elites with a secure career and a privileged position. For a large part of the Russian elite, it is thus very attractive to try to limit reforms in a way that would not threaten their comfortable status quo.

The development of both of the basic parameters—the economic situation and the internal political developments—can move within a relatively wide spectrum. Thus, the political and economic outlook ranges from Russia dealing with its problems and becoming a democratic country with a developed market economy, all the way to an economically devastated Russia breaking apart into several smaller entities based on territorial or cultural (religious) proximity. The following are three possible scenarios.

The Three Paths That Russia Might Take

The Miracle. Pursuing democratic and economic reforms, launching sustainable growth, and gradually catching up to the pace of development of the advanced world will all lead to the creation of an advanced and democratic Russia. Such a Russia will gradually reconcile itself with its post-imperial legacy and step-by-step will become an integrative core for the former Soviet republics. The probability of further territorial divisions in Russia is very slight, the armed forces are under reliable civilian control, and foreign policy is founded upon broad social consensus. Thus, Russia will stop being a source of instability.

The Stumble. An authoritative regime and an ineffective economy nevertheless ensure the ruling elite a sufficiently comfortable lifestyle. This phase is the transition variant between the Miracle and the Crisis. Depending on the favorability of external conditions and other random factors, Russia could swing between the two following variants: 1) an economically stabilized Russia with an authoritative government taking advantage of democratic attributes; or 2) an economically weak Russia with a weak central government. The first choice, an economically stabilized Russia with an authoritative government taking advantage of democratic attributes, is most likely the aim of the present ruling elite in Russia. The economy widely exploits Russia's potential in the realm of raw materials. The foreign trade balance is heavily dependent on price fluctuations in the global commodity markets. The standard of living of the population falls ever farther behind the advanced world. The social division follows the model of a very exclusive and wealthy elite and a relatively small middle class, from which new members of the elite are occasionally recruited. The vast majority of the population has a very low standard of living and negligible influence in public life. The results of elections are decided by the degree of influence of the state-controlled electronic media and financial groups linked with the government. Government retains the capability to falsify results of elections. The influence of the regions is marginal as power is concentrated in Moscow and in a few other cities.

The second choice is an economically weak Russia with a weak central government. Decisive influence is in the hands of political-financial groups and regional elites, which is the model of the 1990s. The stability of Russia, as a united state, is threatened by the greed of interest groups. Regional elites capitalize on their own interests under the political banner of regionalism and resistance against "parasitic" Moscow. Political-financial groups living as parasites off of the central power often use the rhetoric of Greater Russian chauvinism and anti-Westernism. Such a model could likely take effect if the present government's economic model proves ineffective (i.e., after the fall of the presently high prices for commodities on the world markets).

The Crisis. The increasing regression of Russia behind the advanced world raises tension both inside Russian society and in external relations. A fall in the global prices of commodities, a military defeat in the Caucasus, an extensive technological catastrophe, the effect of an external economic crisis, or any other more or less random occurrence could cause a breakdown in the unstable system, which could result in a chain-reaction crisis. If the government is not capable of stabilizing the situation, Russia will first economically, and then formally, disintegrate into several different parts.

The West has to reconcile itself with the unpleasant fact that, after ten years of reform, one-seventh of the world is still very far from the model of democracy and market economics achieved in the advanced countries. But does this mean that the West has lost Russia? Definitely not. The West has not lost Russia, because it never had Russia. The beautiful vision of Russia throwing off its totalitarian ways and integrating among the democratic and advanced countries was simply a mistake, an illusion, a fata morgana.

All of the Western countries, including the United States, have looked upon Russia with a good bit of naiveté and an unwillingness to be rational. The developed world has shown an ability to see what it wants to see in Russia and to overlook anything that would ruin its beautiful picture of a country transforming itself. The West was prepared to accept President Yeltsin in the role of fervent defender of democracy even though he had dissolved the legitimate parliament and carried out genocide upon one of the nations of his own country. The case of President Putin is quite similar. Once again we override embarrassing facts. For example, it was Putin who returned Russia to the path of Chechen war. It is Putin who is backing the return of the FSB (the former KGB) and who is limiting freedom of the press.

Time and time again, plans and intentions have diverged from reality. However, the world has demonstrated an extraordinary ability to believe Russian announcements and ignore the Russian reality. The Russian leadership has been granted undeserved trust repeatedly. It can fulfill the West's expectations to about the same extent that it can pay back all of its previous financial loans.

The United States should realize the fundamental cultural disparity between itself and Russia. Russia is in another period of modernization. Russia is under pressure to accept core Western institutions, values, habits, and attitudes. Naturally, these institutions are modified by the society in which they are placed, as they are influenced by modern and traditional elements. Nominally, they are the same as in the core countries, but in fact their functioning is different. This is why the internal logic of social, political, and economic life in Russia and in the West is dissimilar. Many observers emphasize the "strange" behavior of Russia's masses and their attitude toward the government. They reject the Western model of life, but do not want to lose political and economic freedoms. They accept the idea of a market economy but are in favor of regulations on prices and income levels. They see the United States as an enemy, yet they like Americans. They look to the communist past as a Golden Age, but do not advocate its return. Almost all Russians despise Yeltsin, yet they support Putin, who is Yeltsin's chosen successor. These contradictions are hardly explained by classical sociological models. Sociologist Vladimir Shlapentokh uses three different models for describing the Russian masses. The first model suggests that post-Soviet Russians have extremely eclectic minds that border on schizophrenia. The second model describes Russians as uncivilized people who are unable to live under democracy and whose opinions have no value for those who are trying to build a normal society. Though the basic data used to support these models cannot be disputed, both models are problematic. It is not possible to work with a model that describes some nations as schizophrenic or lazy drunkards and thieves. This is why the third model, working with the rational behavior of the masses in a concrete historical context, is needed.

Understanding the historical context and cultural disparity enables us to comprehend the differences in the social contract between the government and people in Russia and in the West. Western governments are supposed to do something positive for their citizens. The Russian citizen fears that his government will harm his life or well-being and is quite content to have his government leave him alone. This is why Russians are so patient with their irresponsible elites and governments.

As was discussed above, Russian institutions may have a different content and words may have different meanings than in the Anglo-Saxon world. When dealing with Russia one should constantly compare every piece of information and confirm every word. Otherwise, even an astute analyst will be probably misled.

The Changing Nature of U.S.- Russian Relations

By Igor S. Ivanov

The end of the Cold War also ended the ideological rivalry between Russia and the United States. Despite this, the two countries did not naturally become allies with identical perspectives on world events, as their disagreement about military intervention in Bosnia in 1998 or their differing viewpoints on the insurrection in Chechnya demonstrate. Igor S. Ivanov, foreign minister in the administration of Russian president Vladimir Putin, argues that the prospects for continued improvements in U.S.-Russian relations in the first decade of the twenty-first century are good, especially as the foreign policy goals of the two countries coincide more frequently. Ivanov singles out nuclear weapons reductions as an area in which lingering Cold War distrust has hindered relations between the two countries, but which is also steadily improving. While he does not shy away from sharply criticizing the United States in regard to some of its policies, Ivanov also repeatedly notes that cooperation rather than competition is the desired goal of Russian relations with its former archrival.

F undamental changes in the international arena during the 1990s put the United States in the position of a power that had pulled far ahead of its peers in many basic ways: militarily, financially, and economically, and in science and technology. French foreign minister Hubert Védrine coined the term "hyperpower" to describe the contemporary United States.

However, as world events show, even this seemingly enormous advantage does not equate to unconditional leadership in the world. The fabric of modern international relations is too complex and finely woven to be controlled by a single tailor. Today

Igor S. Ivanov, *The New Russian Diplomacy.* Washington, DC: The Nixon Center and Brookings Institution Press, 2002. Copyright © 2002 by Igor S. Ivanov. Reproduced by permission of Brookings Institution Press.

[in 2002], no one country has the ability to single-handedly contain a regional conflict. This is clear from events in the Middle East over the past few years.

It is also a generally accepted fact that Russian-American relations continue to have a substantial influence on the world's political climate. Russia and the United States, as permanent members of the UN Security Council and the two largest nuclear powers, bear particular responsibility for upholding international peace and security. Both states have global interests, conduct foreign policy along multiple alignments, work to limit and reduce weapons of mass destruction, and actively strive to bring conflict situations under control all over the world. Today, there is scarcely a single important global problem that can be solved without involving both Moscow and Washington.

Nevertheless, the character and content of Russian-American relations have changed radically. Relations between Russia and the United States no longer follow the logic of confrontation leading to hard-line military and political clashes. Our nations no longer see each other as adversaries, and the combined potential of Russia and the United States is great enough to be the deciding factor in the quest for global security and strategic stability.

Of course, this potential can only be realized through equal partnership and by taking each other's interests into account, and only within the context of broad international cooperation. It is fundamentally important that this approach was reflected in the Joint Statement on Common Security Challenges at the Threshold of the Twenty-First Century signed by Presidents Boris Yeltsin and Bill Clinton on September 2, 1998, in Moscow. The statement clearly states that "the common security challenges on the threshold of the twenty-first century can be met only by consistently mobilizing the efforts of the entire international community." This joint communiqué also emphasizes that "the United States of America and the Russian Federation are natural partners in advancing international peace and stability." It stresses that Russia and the United States will continue to play leadership roles "in both bilateral and multilateral settings" to reach our common security goals.

World events over the past decade have created a situation in which the global interests of Russia and the United States have not always coincided, and in fact, sometimes have been in opposition. This has generally been the case in instances when Washington was inclined to act unilaterally, not only by dictating its will to sovereign states, but by sidestepping international standards in order to use force against them.

Moscow's and Washington's divergent understandings of the world following the cold war have, to a certain extent, affected the quality of bilateral relations between them. Russia, having undergone a deep internal political and social transformation, has made a decisive break from the stereotypes of confrontation. We have begun to chart our course in international affairs with a steady eye on the creation of a new democratic world order. Moscow has sincerely sought an equal partnership with the United States; this is in our national interest. After all, it is obvious that long-term confrontation with the United States, especially a military or technical confrontation, would seriously complicate Russia's development. Moreover it would hinder our progress toward achieving a stable economy. The development of U.S. policy, however, has largely been influenced by the mentality of a "victor" in the cold war. This view clearly denigrates the role of the UN and is reflected by a strong urge to act outside the bounds of commonly recognized international law. It belies a tendency toward coercion, up to and including the use of force, particularly in the Persian Gulf and in the Balkans. A new irritant in Russian-U.S. relations has been the U.S. attempt to force Russia out of territories that formed part of the Soviet Union (such as the Caspian Sea basin), claiming that such areas now form zones of "vital American interest," even to the point of bringing in military infrastructure. This is a clear case of Washington's overestimation of its own abilities and its disinclination to take into account the new, objective imperative that is taking shape in contemporary international affairs.

All of this engendered the familiar zigzags in Russian-American relations during the 1990s. However, in moments of truth, realism took the upper hand. When something vital was at stake, both sides understood that the sphere of their mutual interests in today's world was greater than that of their differences, and that in the larger strategic issues of peace and stability, they were partners rather than adversaries. Moscow and Washington gradually developed a new style of interaction that acknowledged each other's interests and mutual desire to overcome these hurdles, and so preserve a positive outlook in Russian-American relations. This understanding allowed Moscow and Washington to begin an intense, summit-level dialogue during the 1990s. In 2000 alone, President Putin met President Bill Clinton four times. And President Putin has met with President George W. Bush four times during the new administration's first year.

Nuclear Weapons and U.S.-Russian Relations

The central theme for U.S.-Russian relations remains the reduction of nuclear weapons. After all, our two countries entered the 1990s each with arsenals of between 11,000 and 12,000 strategic nuclear warheads. After the cold war had lost its logic and the nature of the relationship between Russia and the United States began to change fundamentally, such large arsenals were an anachronism. Therefore, the Strategic Arms Reduction Treaty (START I) was a product of its time. This treaty was signed in Moscow on July 31, 1991, went into effect December 5, 1994, and stipulated that over the following seven years, each side would reduce the number of its strategic launch vehicles to 1,600 and the number of its nuclear warheads to 6,000. Overall, START I reduced the combined nuclear capability of Russia and the United States by 40 percent. Moscow has fully complied with the reductions stipulated in the treaty and expects that Washington will do the same.

The next significant step for Moscow and Washington in nuclear disarmament was START II, signed on January 3, 1993, which stipulated further reductions in strategic arms to a total of between 3,000 and 3,500 warheads for each side. In addition, because of delays in ratification, the two parties decided in 1997 to extend the period for achieving the reductions to December 31, 2007. Unfortunately, because of Washington's current position, START II and the 1997 protocol have not gone into effect. Russia, on the other hand, ratified these documents in April 2000.

In accordance with agreements between the Russian and U.S. presidents made in August 1999, reviews have been conducted on implementation details for START III, which should lead to further strategic offensive weapons reductions on both sides. At first, in accordance with the March 1997 joint declaration by Presidents Yeltsin and Clinton, the target for each party was to achieve a ceiling of 2,000–2,500 strategic nuclear weapons by December 31, 2007. Subsequently, as described above, President Putin proposed in November 2000 that this number be lowered even further: to 1,500 or less on each side. The U.S. administration countered the proposal with its own numbers. A bit earlier, we had given to the Americans—at the Okinawa G-8 summit [a meeting of the eight largest industrialized nations]—our proposals for START III implementation, which included measures to ensure transparency and adherence, encompass the full range of types of strategic nuclear arms, promote the irreversibility of deep reductions, and eliminate an entire class of sea-based ballistic missiles, among others. However, a disturbing trend in arms control is the tendency of some in Washington to abandon the process of negotiation in favor of unilateral steps, which are not subject to any of the types of mutually binding legal constraints, like on-site monitoring, that treaties would provide for.

In dragging out efforts to produce new START agreements, the United States will sometimes point to Russia's supposed superiority in the area of nonstrategic nuclear weapons. Here, too, not only is our country open to dialogue, but we have also taken concrete action. Russia has completely removed all tactical nuclear weapons from our surface ships and multipurpose submarines, as well as from our land-based navy aircraft. One-third of our naval tactical nuclear weapons have been eliminated. We are completing the destruction of all nuclear artillery munitions, nuclear warheads for tactical missiles, and nuclear mines. Half of our Zenith missile nuclear warheads and half of our nuclear bombs have been destroyed. . . .

The Economic Relationship Between the Two Countries

Russian-U.S. economic relations have taken off vigorously. Trade volume has increased, business cooperation has spread and become more diverse, consolidation of the treaty and legal bases for bilateral economic ties continues, and regional contact has intensified. Much of this increase is due to the successful creation of an effective institutional infrastructure that supports the needs of those who engage in cooperative business endeavors between our two countries today. Important steps have been taken toward easing several cold war–era restrictions on economic cooperation. The 1993 U.S. Friendship Act (Public Law 103-199) stipulated the reexamination of over seventy pieces of legislation that discriminated against Russia or former Soviet republics in one way or another. Russia received most-favored-nation status from the United States, which made a significant portion of our trade duty free. With the arrival of the [George W.] Bush administration, we need to create effective bilateral mechanisms to coordinate efforts for further expanding our trade and economic ties. On the whole, Russian-U.S. economic ties have proved to be "frost-resistant," both during periods of political tension and after the near global financial collapse of 1998. In 2000, the bilateral trade volume stood at approximately $10.2 billion, and Russia's trade surplus reached $5.8 billion.

Cooperation in the area of investment is expanding as well. The United States leads in investment in the Russian economy—more than 35 percent of all foreign direct investment comes from the United States. Most of this goes to the fuel and energy sector, where large-scale joint projects in oil field development are under way, particularly on Sakhalin [an island off Russia's Pacific coast]. Large projects are also being carried out in manufacturing, telecommunications, food processing, tourism and hotels, and financial services. There has been a shift in joint business and economic ventures, whereby the remaining obstacles are now of our own making; that is, political in nature and not related to business. Washington is nearly ready to acknowledge the full market status of our economy. When it does so, this will result in the final elimination of all remaining trade restrictions imposed on Russia.

It is unfortunate but true, however, that some in the United States continue to advocate economic measures as a means of political pressure against Russia. These kinds of connections were widely practiced during the cold war but are inappropriate and doomed to failure today. There are currently very real obstacles to more active business ties, in particular, obstacles standing in the way of large amounts of American investment. We know what these obstacles are and the reforms now under way represent an attempt to address, if not completely eliminate, them. . . .

Overcoming a Rocky Start to the Putin-Bush Era

It goes without saying that we cannot agree on everything. The fact that Russia and the United States each have their own national interests that are at odds with some of the approaches of the other side is perfectly natural and expected, and should not be harped on. For example, our countries may differ on how best to conduct relations with a particular country in the world. So, we resist when the United States tries to impose its perceptions of "good" or "bad" states. We are against the United States telling us whom we should have relations with and whom we should treat as outcasts, and we are against the most extreme of U.S. actions—the overthrow of a political regime in order to block our relations with a particular state. We conduct our cooperative efforts with third-party countries in strict adherence to existing standards of international law and all recognized international agreements, and we reject any claims by the United States to act as a court of arbitration in this regard. Nor will Russia accept Washington's blatant double standard. This is when a state with whom Moscow one day has been "advised" not to maintain mutually beneficial relations because of supposed "bad behavior," the next day joins the ranks of the United States' partners and its markets are suddenly flooded with American companies.

Some alarming tendencies in bilateral relations were apparent during the second half of the 1990s and at the beginning of the present decade. Certain forces in Washington, having wagered on global hegemony, were prepared to sacrifice the long-term benefits of cooperation with Russia in order to achieve this goal. To further this cause, they unabashedly made use of the U.S. presidential campaign, and the American media unfurled an anti-Russian campaign unprecedented in the post–cold war era for its scale and viciousness. As a result, it must be acknowledged that Russian-U.S. relations had a rocky start when the new Republican administration took power. Washington undertook a series of antagonistic steps toward Russia, including the unwarranted expulsion of a large group of Russian diplomats. The Russian side, following its principled line of protecting its national interests, responded accordingly. However, ongoing contacts between Presidents Vladimir Putin and George W. Bush conveyed Moscow's understanding that only mutually beneficial dialogue, as equals, and realistic interaction between Russia and the United States can effectively counter the new challenges and threats we face today. Over time, Washington displayed signs that it, too, was coming round to this realization. Moreover, the tragic events of September 11, 2001, have underscored the importance and urgency of our cooperation. . . .

On the whole, it is in Russia's interests for the United States to continue to play an active role in the international community's efforts to ensure a stable and orderly global society, and to facilitate development of a progressive world financial and economic system. This would give Russia and the United States expanded opportunities for interaction at the international level. Life itself dictates the need for pragmatic, constructive, and predictable relations between Moscow and Washington. This presupposes constructive use of opportunities provided by bilateral cooperation in areas that meet our national interests, firm defense of Russian views when cooperation is unrealistic for some reason, and not backsliding into a confrontational stance with the United States. This is the key in which the Russian leadership intends to work with the new U.S. administration.

CHRONOLOGY

1000–700 B.C.
The Cimmerians rule in Russia.

700–200 B.C.
The Scythians rule in Russia.

200 B.C.–A.D. 200
The Sarmatians rule in Russia.

200–370
The Goths rule in Russia.

370–453
The Huns rule in Russia.

453–558
The Bulgars, Utigurs, and Kutrigurs compete for dominance in Russia.

558–650
The Avars rule in Russia.

650
The Khazar state is founded.

Kievan Russia

862
According to the *Primary Chronicle*, the Varangians, led by Riurik, arrive in Kiev and quickly take power, marking the start of the Riurikid dynasty of Russian princes.

980–1015
Vladimir reigns as grand prince of Kiev.

988
Vladimir converts to Orthodox Christianity and forces the entire Kievan Rus state to do likewise.

997
The Republic of Novgorod gains the right to self-governance from the Kievan Rus.

1051
Metropolitan Hilarion is consecrated as the first head of the Russian Orthodox Church.

1072
Boris and Gleb are canonized as the first Russian Orthodox saints.

1136
The city-state of Novgorod gains complete independence from Kiev and begins challenging Kiev for social and economic supremacy of Russia.

1147
Muscovy (Moscow) is mentioned for the first time in the *Novgorodian Chronicle*.

1223
The first battle is fought between the Mongols of the "Golden Horde" and the Russians.

1237–1240
The Mongols overrun and conquer the Kievan Rus.

1240–1480
Russia experiences the "Mongol Yoke" (direct or indirect Mongol rule over Russia).

Muscovite Russia

1300s–1400s
The center of Russian culture gradually shifts from Novgorod to Moscow.

1310
Moscow replaces Kiev as the see (center of authority) of the Russian Orthodox Church.

1327–1341
Ivan Kalita (Ivan Moneybags) reigns as grand prince of Vladimir, the immediate precursor to the Muscovite state.

1367
The first stone kremlin (citadel) is built in Moscow.

1380
Dmitry Donskoi, grand prince of Vladimir, defeats a Mongol army at the Battle of Kulikovo.

1462–1505
Ivan III reigns as grand prince of Muscovy.

1463–1521
Muscovy conquers and annexes all other major states in northern and central Russia.

1480
Mongol rule in Russia ends after the Battle of Ugra.

1497
Ivan III issues a law code that limits peasant movement.

Czarist Russia

1533–1584
Ivan IV (Ivan the Terrible) reigns.

1547
Ivan IV adopts the title *czar.*

1551–1555
Ivan IV reforms legal, fiscal, and religious systems in Muscovy.

1558–1583
Russia fights the Livonian War against Sweden.

1564–1572
Ivan IV's *Oprichnina* terrorizes the Russian populace.

1580
Ivan IV enacts a law that bars peasants from changing landlords, thereby institutionalizing an early form of serfdom throughout Russia.

The Time of Troubles

1598
Fyodor I dies without an heir, ending the Riurikid dynasty.

1598–1605
Boris Godunov reigns as czar after being selected by a council of clergymen and boyars (nobles).

1609–1610
Poland invades Russia.

1612
The Poles are ousted from Russia.

1613
Mikhail I is elected czar, thereby establishing the Romanov dynasty.

The Romanov Dynasty

1649
Alexis I issues the *Ulozhenie,* a comprehensive law code that, among other things, reinforces serfdom.

1682
Peter I (Peter the Great) and his half brother Ivan V are proclaimed as co-czars, with Peter's half sister Sofia Miloslavsky acting as regent.

1689
Peter I assumes sole power.

1697–1698
Peter I travels to western Europe on his "Great Embassy"; not long after his return, Peter begins Westernizing reforms throughout Russian society.

1700–1721
Russia fights the Great Northern War against Sweden.

1700
The Russians are defeated soundly by the Swedes at the Battle of Narva.

1703

The City of St. Petersburg is founded at the mouth of the Neva River; many judicial and administrative agencies are transferred there from Moscow over the next two decades.

1709

Peter I leads the Russians to a rout of the Swedes at the Battle of Poltava.

1721

Peter I is proclaimed "emperor of all the Russias."

1722

The Table of Ranks is introduced.

1725

Peter I dies.

1762–1796

Catherine II (Catherine the Great) reigns.

1766

Catherine II publishes "The Great Instruction," which is intended to guide enlightened reform of Russian society.

1767–1768

Catherine II convenes a legislative assembly to write a new law code.

1773–1775

Emelyan Pugachev leads a rebellion of the Cossacks.

1801–1825

Alexander I reigns.

1812

Napoleon invades Russia; Moscow is destroyed by fire, but Napoleon is ultimately forced to retreat.

1825

The unsuccessful Decembrist revolt takes place.

1825–1855

Nikolai I reigns.

1835
The *Svod zakonov,* the first modern Russian law code, is enacted.

1842–1851
A railway line linking Moscow and St. Petersburg is constructed.

1853–1856
The Crimean War is fought against the Ottoman Empire, which was aided by Great Britain and France.

1855–1881
Alexander II reigns.

1861
Alexander II's Emancipation Manifesto ends serfdom in Russia.

1862–1874
Alexander II enacts sweeping reforms in the church, military, universities, and bureaucracy.

1881
Alexander II is assassinated.

1881–1894
Alexander III reigns, undoing many of Alexander II's reforms.

1891–1904
The Trans-Siberian Railway is constructed.

1894–1917
Nikolai II reigns.

1904–1905
The Russians are soundly defeated in the Russo-Japanese War.

1905
The abortive revolution of 1905 causes Nikolai II to issue the October Manifesto, in which he promises political and civil reform.

1906
The first popularly elected Russian legislature (duma) is formed.

1914–1917
Russia takes part in World War I.

The Soviet Union

1917
In February, socialist revolutionaries overthrow the czar and establish a provisional government; on March 2, Nikolai II abdicates, and the Romanov dynasty ends; in October, the Bolshevik wing of the Communist Party, led by Vladimir Lenin, seizes power.

1918–1921
The Bolsheviks consolidate their rule in the Russian civil war.

1921–1929
Soviet government attempts to implement the "New Economic Policy" (NEP).

1924
Lenin dies; Joseph Stalin begins accumulating power.

1930
The policy of land collectivization begins, contributing to massive famine in subsequent years.

1937–1938
Mass purges, arrests, and executions occur as part of Stalin's Great Terror.

1939–1945
World War II fought.

1939
A nonaggression pact is signed between Nazi Germany and the Soviet Union, and both invade Poland simultaneously in September, thus starting World War II.

1941
Germany launches a surprise invasion of the Soviet Union on June 22; German armies reach Leningrad and Moscow by early winter.

1942
The Soviet Union joins the Allies in May and gradually begins pushing the Germans back from Russian territory by the end of the year.

1945

The Red Army invades Germany in January and eventually advances as far as the Elbe River before stopping in April.

The Cold War

1946–1949

Diplomatic tension grows between the wartime allies; the North Atlantic Treaty Organization is established in 1949 to limit the expansion of Soviet influence in Europe.

1950–1953

The Soviet Union and the United States fight their first "proxy war" in Korea.

1953

Stalin dies and Nikita Khrushchev takes over as party secretary; the Soviet Union successfully tests its first atomic bomb.

1956

Khrushchev denounces Stalin's "excesses" at the Twentieth Party Congress, thus marking a period of relative liberalism in the Soviet Union. Khrushchev sends troops to Hungary in November to put down an insurrection.

1957

The Soviet Union launches *Sputnik,* the world's first artificial satellite.

1960

The Soviet Union shoots down a U.S. spy plane.

1962

The Cuban missile crisis erupts over the attempted placement of Soviet nuclear-tipped missiles in Cuba.

1964

Khrushchev is removed from power and replaced by Leonid Brezhnev.

1965–1978

Détente (a period of relaxed tensions) exists between the Soviet Union and the United States.

1968

Brezhnev sends troops to Czechoslovakia to suppress the Prague Spring democratization movement.

1972

The Strategic Arms Limitation Treaty is signed by the Soviet Union and the United States.

1979

The Soviet Union invades Afghanistan; the United States and most of its allies boycott the 1980 Olympics in Moscow in protest.

1982

Brezhnev dies and is replaced by Yury Andropov.

1984

Andropov dies and is replaced by Konstantin Chernenko.

1985

Chernenko dies and is replaced by Mikhail Gorbachev, who almost immediately announces plans for greater openness (glasnost) in Soviet society as well as an ambitious plan of economic restructuring (perestroika).

1986

A major accident occurs at the nuclear power plant in Chernobyl.

1988

The Communist Party's monopoly on power ends with reforms after the Nineteenth Party Congress.

1989

Soviet troops begin withdrawing from Afghanistan.

1990

Lithuania declares its independence from the Soviet Union, and Gorbachev's attempts to prevent this with military force fail; the Communist governments of several Soviet satellite states in eastern Europe fall as well.

1991

Boris Yeltsin is elected president of the Russian Federation in June; a failed military coup in August nearly deposes Gorbachev; six more republics break away from the Soviet Union in the aftermath of the coup; the Commonwealth of Independent States is formed on December 8; Gorbachev resigns on Christmas Day and the Soviet Union is dissolved on December 31.

Post-Soviet Russia

1992

Yeltsin assumes the presidency of the newly independent Russia.

1993

A dispute arises between Yeltsin and the Duma that culminates in Russian army troops storming the building that houses the Duma; the new Duma elected in December is composed heavily of former Communists and fervent nationalists led by Vladimir Zhirinovsky.

1994

A major currency crisis threatens the national economy in October; Russian troops invade Chechnya in December to suppress an independence movement.

1996

Yeltsin wins the first open presidential election in Russian history.

1999

In failing health and hounded by charges of widespread corruption, Yelstin announces that he will not seek another term as president and names Vladimir Putin as his successor, effective January 1, 2000.

2000

Putin wins the presidential election in May by a wide margin.

FOR FURTHER RESEARCH

General Histories

Robert Auty and Dmitry Obolensky, eds., *Companion to Russian Studies*. Vol. 1. *An Introduction to Russian History*. Cambridge, England: Cambridge University Press, 1976.

Isaiah Berlin, *Russian Thinkers*. New York: Viking, 1995.

Jerome Blum, *Lord and Peasant in Russia: From the Ninth to the Nineteenth Century*. Princeton, NJ: Princeton University Press, 1972.

Michael T. Florinsky, *Russia: A History and an Interpretation*. 2 vols. New York: Prentice-Hall, 1954.

Martin Gilbert, *Atlas of Russian History*. New York: Oxford University Press, 1993.

George Heard Hamilton, *The Art and Architecture of Russia*. New Haven, CT: Yale University Press, 1992.

V.O. Kluchevsky, *A History of Russia*. 5 vols. New York: E.P. Dutton, 1911–1931.

B.H. Sumner, *A Short History of Russia*. New York: Harcourt Brace Jovanovich, 1949.

Ancient and Medieval Russia

Charles J. Halperin, *Russia and the Golden Horde: The Mongol Impact on Medieval Russian History*. Bloomington: Indiana University Press, 1987.

Janet Martin, *Medieval Russia, 980–1584*. Cambridge, England: Cambridge University Press, 1995.

Alexander Presniakov, *The Formation of the Great Russian State: A Study of Russian History in the Thirteenth to Fifteenth Centuries*. Chicago: Quadrangle Books, 1970.

Czarist Russia

John T. Alexander, *Catherine the Great: Life and Legend.* Oxford, England: Oxford University Press, 1989.

Paul Avrich, *Russian Rebels, 1600–1800.* New York: Norton, 1976.

James Cracraft, ed., *Peter the Great Transforms Russia.* Lexington, KY: D.C. Heath, 1991.

Robert E. Jones, *The Emancipation of the Russian Nobility, 1762–1785.* Princeton, NJ: Princeton University Press, 1973.

Lionel Kochan and Richard Abraham, *The Making of Modern Russia.* New York: Viking, 1992.

W. Bruce Lincoln, *The Great Reforms: Autocracy, Bureaucracy, and the Politics of Change in Imperial Russia.* DeKalb: Northern Illinois University Press, 1990.

Isabel de Madariaga, *Catherine the Great: A Short History:* New Haven, CT: Yale University Press, 1990.

Sergei Platonov, *The Time of Troubles: A Historical Study of the Internal Crisis and Social Struggle in Sixteenth- and Seventeenth-Century Muscovy.* Lawrence: University of Kansas Press, 1970.

Twentieth-Century Russia

Abraham Ascher, *The Russian Revolution of 1905.* 2 vols. Stanford, CA: Stanford University Press, 1994.

Frederick C. Barghoorn and Thomas F. Remington, *Politics in the USSR: A Country Study.* Boston: Addison-Wesley, 1998.

Edward Hallett Carr, *The Bolshevic Revolution, 1917–1923.* 3 vols. New York: Norton, 1985.

Hélène Carrère d'Encausse, *The End of the Soviet Empire: The Triumph of the Nations.* New York: BasicBooks, 1993.

Robert Conquest, *The Great Terror.* Oxford, England: Oxford University Press, 1990.

John B. Dunlop, *The Rise of Russia and the Fall of the Soviet Empire.* Princeton, NJ: Princeton University Press, 1993.

Maurice Hindus, *Red Bread: Collectivization in a Russian Village.* Bloomington: Indiana University Press, 1988.

Martin McCauley, *The Khrushchev Era: 1953–1964.* New York: Longman, 1995.

Roy A. Medvedev, *Let History Judge.* New York: Columbia University Press, 1989.

Edvard Radzinsky, *The Last Tsar: The Life and Death of Nicholas II.* New York: Doubleday, 1992.

John Reed, *Ten Days That Shook the World.* New York: Penguin, 1977.

Hedrick Smith, *The New Russians.* New York: Avon Books, 1991.

Jonathan Steele, *Eternal Russia: Yeltsin, Gorbachev, and the Mirage of Democracy.* Cambridge, MA: Harvard University Press, 1995.

Boris Yeltsin, *Against the Grain: An Autobiography.* New York: Summit Books, 1990.

INDEX